A GEOLOGY
OF SCHOOL REFORM

SUNY Series, Restructuring and School Change
H. Dickson Corbett and Betty Lou Whitford, Editors

A GEOLOGY
OF SCHOOL REFORM

*The Successive Restructurings
of a School District*

Liane Brouillette

STATE UNIVERSITY OF NEW YORK PRESS

Published by
State University of New York Press, Albany

© 1996 State University of New York

For information, address State University of New York Press,
State University Plaza, Albany, NY 12246

Production by Christine M. Lynch
Marketing by Bernadette LaManna

Library of Congress Cataloging-in-Publication Data

Brouillette, Liane, 1947–
    A geology of school reform : the successive restructurings of a
school district / Liane Brouillette.
        p.   cm. — (SUNY series, restructuring and school change)
    Includes bibliographical references and index.
        ISBN 0-7914-2989-X (alk. paper). — ISBN 0-7914-2990-3 (pbk. :
alk. paper)
        1. School-based management—United States—Case studies.
    2. Educational change—United States—Case studies. 3. School
    districts—United States—Administration—Case studies. I. Title.
    II. Series.
    LB2806.35.B76 1996
    371.2′00973—dc20
                                                                95-33411
                                                                CIP

10 9 8 7 6 5 4 3 2 1

CONTENTS

LIST OF TABLES

ACKNOWLEDGMENTS

I would like to thank those without whose help this book could not have been written. Margaret D. LeCompte's continuing feedback was pivotal in helping distill a coherent picture of a school district's evolving culture from a daunting mountain of raw data. Richard J. Kraft offered invaluable insights into the politics of schooling in "Western State" and the differing philosophical underpinnings of the policies advanced by contending factions. I would like to extend my sincere appreciation to H. Dickson Corbett for his patient assistance throughout the editing process. To my husband, Jason, I would like to say "Thanks!" for his support through the multiple inconveniences associated with this project. Finally, I would like to express my heartfelt gratitude to the teachers, parents, administrators, and students of the "Cottonwood School District," whose decades-long search for ways to improve their local schools inspired this study.

PREFACE

Since the 1960s, a dizzying array of educational reforms have been introduced in school districts across the United States. Few are still with us, at least in their original form. This study focuses on how successive waves of reform interacted within a single school district. The suburban Cottonwood School District is followed from its beginnings in the early 1950s (when two rural schoolhouses made up the district) through the exuberant experimentation in the 1960s (when Cottonwood was one of the fastest growing districts in the United Stares); the back-to-basics reforms of the 1970s (when Cottonwood adopted a thorough-going system of criterion-referenced testing at all levels); the restructuring of the 1980s (when Cottonwood became a pioneer in the use of whole language and site-based decision making); and, finally, the severe budgetary restraints that were imposed on the district by state-level budget shortfalls in the early 1990s.

Fictional names have been used throughout this study, not only for individuals, but for places as well. Given the complexity of the project, the use of generic names—even for the "Western State" in which the Cottonwood School District is located—proved a useful way of keeping the focus on what was essential. The fictional names were selected to emphasize the meaning that places, issues, and events had for local residents. Thus, the city located in the most urbanized part of the Cottonwood district was called "Metroville." Metroville's newer and less urbanized neighbor was dubbed "Suburbia." "Foothills City" might seem an ironic choice as the name for the regional metropolis whose urban problems "Cottonwood" residents feared were spreading into their own school district, given the pastoral associations associated with the word "Foothills." However, as one respondent pointed out: "People talk now as if Foothills

City were always a violent sort of place. But, really, it's just the last ten years. Before that, if you broke down on the highway and someone stopped, you just assumed that they were stopping to help you."

We will examine the multiple misunderstandings that occurred, over a period of four decades, among individuals whose formative experiences with public schools—whether as students, teachers or administrators—were shaped by widely differing historical circumstances and philosophical perspectives. Interviews were carried out with, or written answers to questions submitted by, a stratified sample of individuals which included: two school board members; seven members of the school district's central administrative team; the principal; an assistant principal; and a counselor from each of the district's three comprehensive high schools; four district-level curriculum specialists; two district-level staff development specialists; nine building administrators at the K–9 level; seventy-one classroom teachers; seven paraprofessional/support personnel; and seven community members. Data for the study were also gathered from school district documents, newspapers, historical archives, government publications, journal articles, participant and non-participant observation.

In an effort to include a wide range of views, a reputational sampling method was used. During interviews, respondents were asked to describe opinion groupings within the district and to recommend individuals who might be able to offer alternative views. It soon became clear that each wave of reform had been seen differently by various professional and community groups. Since the major opinion groups in Cottonwood resembled those described by Kliebard (1987) in *The Struggle for the American Curriculum 1893-1958*, the terms "humanist," "social efficiency," "developmentalist," and "social meliorist" were used to describe them. (Please see tables 9.1 to 9.4 for further explanation.) The reader will note that the Cottonwood groupings do not correspond to those outlined by Kliebard in all respects. Nor do they do justice to the full diversity of opinion in Cottonwood. However, reference to such broad opinion groupings proved an invaluable tool for describing how power had shifted among competing factions during the 40 year history of the school district.

Consternation at being forced to cope with unwelcome social change was an important theme in parent interviews and public meetings, at times blotting out awareness of the good things that the Cottonwood School District was doing. Given that human beings take action on the basis of the meaning that specific events and issues have for them, understanding respondents' perceptions proved key to explaining their reactions. Since an important goal of this case study was to examine issues that affected similar school districts across the United States, lengthy discussion of purely local matters was foregone. Historical information was included only in so far as it was deemed necessary to illustrate the complexity of the school district's professional culture or to explain the stark economic and political realities with which Cottonwood decision makers had to deal. Each of the last four chapters in the book highlights how the Cottonwood School District dealt with a particular problem, exploring why a widely recommended innovation worked, or failed to work.

The reader will encounter teachers, parents, students, and school administrators speaking in their own voices about the issues and concerns closest to them. In this way, the debate on school reform is brought down to the human level, showing what it meant for teachers and administrators to be called upon to change their practices—again and again. Some took to experimentation gladly. Others reacted with cynicism or with a determined advocacy of the policies they favored. Eventually factions were formed. Over time, these factions became a stubborn roadblock on the path to far-reaching school reform. Only through finding ways around such barriers were Cottonwood teachers and administrators able to become more active shapers of their own future. It is my hope that sharing their experiences may prove helpful to educators who find themselves faced with similar choices.

CHAPTER 1

INTRODUCTION

Reacting to a state-level budget shortfall that would force school districts across Western State to make deep cuts in services and programs, Superintendent Dave Roberts set up a districtwide shared decision-making process to decide how the Cottonwood School District would deal with a projected shortfall of $10 million, out of a total budget of $91 million. The Cottonwood district had already been cutting back for several years and was very lean in terms of central-office staffing. New budget cuts of this magnitude would mean cutting jobs and eliminating popular programs. Although site-based decision making had been in use in the Cottonwood district for almost a decade, this time an unspoken question—which staff members might lose their jobs?—loomed behind each planning team's deliberations, creating strong emotional crosscurrents.

As the last of a series of fiery public budget meetings drew to a close, Superintendent Dave Roberts spoke to community members about the circumstances that had fixed everyone's attention on crisis management and prevented the Cottonwood district's site-based decision-making teams from playing the long-term planning role originally intended for them. Dr. Roberts made a public plea for wider community involvement in the shared decision-making process, adding:

> If there is anyone out there who is not already actively involved in their neighborhood school, please come onboard and help us out. Those of us who strongly believe in public education must regain the public's support and confidence. If we don't, we will face crises like this again and again.

Widely respected for its record of student achievement, its highly qualified teachers, and its record of keeping teachers informed about new research on teaching, the Cottonwood district has experienced striking successes as well as recurring frustrations since implementing site-based decision-making in the early 1980s. Serving a highly diverse suburban area that includes both affluent new developments and deteriorating low-income neighborhoods, the Cottonwood School District offers an intriguing example of how site-based decision making has worked in an environment characterized by challenges similar to those faced by large numbers of U.S. school districts.

FINDING OUT HOW IT ALL WORKS IN PRACTICE

The research literature has repeatedly pointed to discrepancies between formally adopted policies and the observable practices which actually become embedded in the regularities of the school culture. Sarason (1991) recalls what happened in the 1960s and 1970s when educational policymakers legislated wholesale introduction of the new math, the new biology, the new physics, the new social studies, while remaining "scandalously insensitive to what was involved in changing classroom regularities" (p. 90). Fullan and Miles note: "Schools are overloaded with problems—and, ironically, with solutions that don't work" (1992, p.745). Cuban (1990) describes the need, not for superficial first-order changes, but for deeper, second-order changes in the structures and cultures of schools.

Advocates of taking a more collaborative approach to school management hold forth the possibility of establishing true community standards, mutually acknowledged by parents, teachers, administrators, and community leaders, as the basis for interactions within schools. This does not mean merely moving many decisions about school improvement out of the central office and into the schools, but also implies changes in the roles of parents, students, and school personnel.

> Schools would be markedly different if their ongoing function was to ensure successful performance. . . . We would not put up long with a physician who sent our child home with an F for health, but no assistance in becoming healthy. (Goodlad 1984)

Here lies the rub. Most people agree, at least in a general way, about what constitutes good health. Agreement on what constitutes a "good" education is harder to come by. For a shared decision-making approach to be successful, there must be a reorientation not only in the way schools are operated but also in the way many members of the school community have habitually thought about schooling. As Barth (1991) has pointed out:

> Restructuring has suddenly become both a source of hope and a platitude in our profession. It's a big tent under which many people are saying and doing many things. It is a concept that means different things to different people and may, therefore, be in danger of becoming altogether meaningless. At the same time, restructuring has become a watchword for all of us who care deeply about good schools.

Restructuring has often been seen as a corrective to habits of mind common in bureaucratic environments, where private goals, particularly those related to an individual's positioning within the organization, too often take precedence over larger social goals. Site-based shared decision-making has been suggested as a way of counteracting such tendencies through evolving shared values and a strong sense of community at each school site. Fostering strong community goals is seen as a way to transform school environments where service to students and their families is too often deemed less important than taking care not to rock the bureaucratic boat. Shared decision-making has also been closely linked to teacher empowerment.

This book tells the story of one widely recognized experiment in putting these ideas into practice. Two years were spent gathering information from a stratified sample of over one hundred individuals in the Cottonwood School District, as well as from a wide array of written resources. An important focus of the study was how attitudes and procedures left behind by earlier reforms carried out in the district had affected acceptance of this newest restructuring effort. Another focus that evolved as the study progressed was the use of shared decision-making techniques to arrive at decisions about implementation of a new curriculum framework based on the whole language philosophy and an emphasis on the National Council of Teachers of Mathematics (NCTM) *Standards* in math.

COTTONWOOD SCHOOL DISTRICT

Serving a diverse population spread over an area of approximately sixty square miles, Cottonwood's thirty-five schools vary widely in student demographic characteristics—from ethnically diverse schools located near Foothills City, a large regional metropolis, to schools located in relatively homogeneous outer suburbs. Achieving effective communication across a suburban school district that includes all or part of five municipalities has presented a formidable challenge throughout Cottonwood's history. Indeed, in recent years the social and economic diversity of the district has become progressively more striking, with new developments designed around golf courses being built in the outer suburbs even while students living in the large trailer parks and deteriorating apartment complexes near Foothills City increasingly require breakfast and afterschool programs to provide adequate nutrition and physical safety.

In its forty-year history, Cottonwood has had only three superintendents, each with a distinctive philosophy and management style. Ed Larimer, whose tenure lasted from the early 1950s to the early 1970s, encouraged sturdy independence in both students and staff, coupled with traditional academic coursework and a strong emphasis on athletics. Bill Davis, reflecting the emphasis on accountability which dominated the 1970s, instituted a strongly centralized system of school governance and a skills-based curriculum reinforced by criterion-referenced tests. Dave Roberts, who came to the district in 1982, installed a more collaborative model of school governance and a more integrated, activity-based curriculum.

These shifts in emphasis in many ways typify the changes that school districts across the United States have undergone since World War II. However, the Cottonwood district is unusual in that shared decision-making, which is a relatively new idea elsewhere, has been in place in Cottonwood for almost a decade, long enough to have had a significant effect on the culture of individual schools. The curriculum framework that the district began implementing in the mid-1980s has been fashioned and refined through collaborative decision-making—a process that began when, soon after Dr. Roberts arrived, it became clear that many teachers had become dissatisfied with the test-driven curriculum then mandated by the district.

Finding the Right Lens

I have used Seymour Sarason's studies of school change as the lens through which to examine the data gathered. Sarason (1971) points out that possession of a mandate for change is often far from enough to insure achievement of one's intended purpose. The list of educational reforms which did not fulfill their initial promise, even though initiated with great fanfare and the best of intentions, is long. Many of these failures were tied to a failure on the part of reformers to take the complex social interactions of the school setting into consideration. The considerations which Sarason (pp. 58–60) has suggested must be taken into account by a successful theory of change include:

1. Explicit recognition that the setting is differentiated in a variety of ways (i.e., role, power, status) that make for groupings, each of which may see itself differently in relation to the purposes and traditions of the larger setting and, therefore, perceive intended change in different ways.
2. Since the introduction of an important change does not and cannot have the same significance for the different groupings comprising the setting, there will be groups that will feel obligated to obstruct, divert, or defeat the proposed change, making it necessary to have mechanisms in place to recognize and deal with this source of opposition.
3. As the history of the change process includes a series of decisions that increasingly involve or affect more and more groups in the setting, there must be balancing of and/or attention to the demands both of leadership and of representativeness in the decision-making group.
4. A comprehensive conception of the change process must tell one when something should be done and when certain outcomes are to be expected, at the same time furnishing a way of explaining why initial estimations made at the site concerning the time necessary to achieve intended change are usually a gross underestimation of the time actually required.

CONFLICTING CURRICULA DIFFER ON EDUCATION'S GOAL

Sarason's guidelines suggested what to look for, but left other problems unsolved. Explicit recognition of the variety of ways that the Cottonwood School District is differentiated, and the groupings that have resulted, required a way of adequately describing the differing ways various groups have viewed the purposes and traditions of the school district. Likewise, there was a need to characterize the differing import that important changes had for various groupings within the district. Since the history of the Cottonwood School District had been characterized by prolonged struggles between opposing factions, with conflicts within the district often reflecting struggles taking place at the national level, I made use of the terms that Herbert Kliebard (1987) used in his book *The Struggle for the American Curriculum 1893–1958* to describe competing reform movements: humanist, social efficiency, developmentalist, and social meliorist.

It should be emphasized, however, that, although Kliebard's terms did closely mirror the range of philosophical viewpoints voiced by Cottonwood respondents, there were inevitable differences between the controversies that arose in a single school district and the issues that have received attention at the national level. The manner in which the terms "humanist," "social efficiency," "developmentalist," and "social meliorist" are used in the following pages reflects the particular dynamics of the political/philosophical debate that took place within the Cottonwood School District. With this caveat, there follows a thumbnail sketch of each of these four viewpoints. Borrowing heavily from Kliebard, these brief descriptions indicate the historical roots and general objectives of each group.

Over the last century the role schools play in U.S. society has changed radically, as have positions taken by advocates of the humanist, social efficiency, developmentalist, and social meliorist curriculums. Of the four, the humanist curriculum has changed least. Humanists continue to emphasize study of the traditional liberal arts. Sarason describes the justification for such study: "The adjective *liberal* in liberal arts, historically at least, means liberation from narrowness and ignorance, and exposure to the best in human knowledge and accomplishment" (1990, 37). On a more mundane level, humanists tend to favor compulsory study of a core curriculum of academic subjects, although ideas about which subjects ought to be included have changed over time.

In 1893 Charles W. Eliot, chairman of the National Education Association's Committee of Ten and president of Harvard University, enunciated the humanist position that educators should not differentiate between "education for college" and "education for life." A liberal education was seen as that type of schooling which would be most suitable for a free human being, quite apart from any consideration of work or vocation. Educators were to be regarded as guardians of the finest elements of the Western heritage. Schools would be entrusted with using the teaching of this heritage to develop the reasoning power of students, thus enabling them to express their thoughts clearly, concisely, cogently.

There were, however, more and more educators who questioned these assumptions. Until the 1880s most academic schooling beyond the elementary level had been provided at private "academies" where entrance was limited to those who could afford the tuition (Bennett and LeCompte 1990). By the 1890s, publicly supported secondary schools were being established across the nation, and concerns about the social utility of teaching the traditional academic subjects were increasingly voiced. Officials designated to improve public schools and work out school laws increasingly challenged the humanist ideal. European, particularly German, ideas of vocational education were introduced in response to demands that education be made more efficient and "practical."

Businessmen elected to local school boards began to apply principles of "scientific management," originally developed in industry, to public schools. A social efficiency curriculum was developed that put a premium on acquisition of specific and observable skills. In an effort to make teaching more effective, skills to be learned were broken down into component parts. Over time, the component parts became increasingly decontextualized. Often they would be listed as behavioral objectives that teachers were required to check off as students mastered them. Methods borrowed from business were also used to systematize educational bureaucracies that had become increasingly large and chaotic. Uniform rules were created for codifying attendance, financial records, curricula, and time allocated for instruction (Butts 1978).

Social efficiency advocates also made a case for trimming the "deadwood" from the traditional curriculum. They argued that teaching of algebra and foreign languages to people who would not use the knowledge in their future jobs was an inexcusable waste. Their efforts were often focused on casting off what they considered to be wasteful and inert subjects and replacing them, for non-college-bound students, with courses that taught occupational skills students would need after they left school. Directly functional courses were advocated, with vocational subjects advanced as a prime example.

During the early years of this century, the main challenge to this businesslike approach to education grew out of the child-study movement, which was a product of the new status accorded to scientific inquiry. Child-study advocates, referred to by Kliebard as developmentalists, argued that the natural order of development in the child was the most significant and scientifically defensible basis for determining what should be taught. Developmentalists attempted to solve the curriculum riddle through gathering more accurate scientific data, focusing their attention on stages of child development and the nature of learning. They assumed that if they could devise a curriculum that was in harmony with the child's real interests, needs, and learning patterns, this curriculum would provide the means by which the natural powers within the child could be unharnessed.

Social meliorists took a more sociological view. In the late nineteenth century, at a time when Social Darwinism enjoyed great popularity, Lester Frank Ward argued strongly against the contention that survival of the fittest ought to be accepted as a natural law. He held that if moral progress is to be made, it must be the result of an *intellectual* direction of the forces of human nature into advantageous channels. Critical to further social progress was a properly constructed and fairly distributed system of education. Ward argued that social inequality was, fundamentally, a product of maldistribution of the social inheritance. The key to progress was the proper distribution of cultural capital through a vitalized system of education. Ward thus became the forerunner of the social meliorist curriculum which sees education as key to any meaningful movement toward a more just society.

Although, since the turn of the century, the social efficiency curriculum has had the strongest influence on United States public schools, the pendulum of public favor has swung back and forth. In the last century all of the philosophies outlined by Kliebard have played a part in influencing how Americans view the goals of schooling. Broadly speaking, the three Cottonwood superintendents have represented, respectively, a humanist, a social efficiency, and a developmentalist perspective (although none represented an ideal/typical instance of that philosophy, each having incorporated some elements of other viewpoints). Also, as in most public school districts, the policies favored by the superintendent have not been the only factor that has influenced what happened in classrooms. The struggle the present superintendent has faced in his attempt to alter various elements of the social efficiency curriculum put in place by his predecessor lies at the core of this study.

A GEOLOGY OF SCHOOL REFORM

The geological metaphor found in the title of this book was suggested in part by the spectacular topography of Western State, and in part by repeated references by respondents to earlier events. Historical circumstances they described were often key to understanding why various groups or individuals had reacted in particular ways to later events. Searching through archives and interview transcripts, to see how various groups had reacted to specific events, frequently resembled the work of a geologist, uncovering the characteristics an area had exhibited in earlier times by digging through layers of rock. Other times it seemed that, just as the force of gravity—which has always been in evidence all around us, drawing our planet's water into hollows on the earth's solid surface, forming oceans, lakes, and ponds—remained undiscovered till particular questions were asked, many of the social forces at work in Cottonwood could only be made visible by seeking out the causes behind broader patterns. Therefore, geological metaphors seemed the most effective way to describe many findings of this study.

A Brief Outline

Before delving into the historical strata that underlie current events in Cottonwood, we will turn our attention to the Cottonwood School District's present organizational topography. Chapter 2 outlines how the shared decision-making process was intended to operate within the site-based environment established by Dr. Dave Roberts. An understanding of the ideal type of governance structure the Cottonwood district was striving to set in place will be important to later discussions of those areas where success was attained, as well as of instances where school cultures evolved that departed in important ways from the envisioned ideal.

Chapter 3 will explore the historical bedrock upon which later events in the Cottonwood district were built. Ed Larimer, Cottonwood's first superintendent, administered a school district that was, for a number of years, one of the fastest-growing in the nation. His strong belief that the teacher stood at the center of the educational enterprise, along with the emphasis his administration put on using innovative methods to teach traditional academic subjects, played an important part shaping the culture of the Cottonwood School District. Larimer's tenure stretched from the early 1950s to the early 1970s. Many of the staff members whom he hired continue to have an important role in shaping Cottonwood's educational policies.

Chapter 4 traces the reforms implemented by Dr. Bill Davis, who headed the Cottonwood district from 1972 to 1982. A strong believer in Management by Objectives, as well as Mastery Learning, Dr. Davis transformed the loose-knit Cottonwood School District into an administratively unified whole which soon achieved national prominence for its emphasis on accountability and thorough-going use of criterion-referenced tests. Yet the use of criterion-referenced testing was relatively short-lived, running into widespread resistance from teachers who questioned both the value of teaching isolated skills and the validity of teaching the same lessons to all children at a given grade level, regardless of a particular child's developmental level.

Chapter 5 will describe the district-level organizational structure that evolved out of the shared decision-making process described in chapter 2. Strategic planning will be discussed, as well as how efforts to keep teachers informed about the newest research on teaching led to development of a new curriculum framework for the Cottonwood district. The new meaning given to the phrase "performance-based," which under Dr. Davis had referred to use of paper-and-pencil tests to measure basic skills, will be explained. During the Roberts tenure, "performance-based" came to mean the use of complex activities requiring higher-order thinking skills, both to teach and to assess student understanding of important concepts.

Chapter 6 will focus on how the Cottonwood district went about implementing its new curriculum framework in a site-based environment. The use of teacher/coaches to assist other teachers at their school with implementation will be described. Problems encountered during implementation will be discussed, along with changes that were made in the curriculum framework as a result of feedback from teachers. Among these changes was the use of mini-lessons to make sure that adequate instruction in spelling, phonics, and grammar was included within the whole language curriculum. The use of naturalistic assessment will be described, with a special focus on the struggle of curriculum coaches to help teachers understand the philosophy behind the new way of teaching.

Chapter 7 will trace the differing paths the Cottonwood district's three high schools have followed since implementation of site-based decision-making. The radically restructured Sagebrush High, built to closely follow the pattern laid out by Dr. Theodore Sizer and the Coalition of Essential Schools, will be contrasted with Suburban High, which proudly remained a "shopping mall" high school, and the more urban Metroville High, located in an area that was once considered "the suburbs" but is now coping with many social problems usually associated with the inner city. The impact of the individual leadership styles of the three principals will be discussed, along with resentments and jealousies that can be traced to construction of a new high school in the outer suburbs that siphoned off many middle-class students.

Chapter 8 will discuss the use of shared decision-making to address districtwide concerns, such as high school attendance areas and the budget cuts necessitated by a large state-level funding shortfall. Demographic changes in the more urbanized areas of the Cottonwood district are described, along with social tensions connected to the manner in which the regional media have reported crimes committed by members of minority groups. Also discussed are conflicts that arose between the ideal of participatory democracy inherent in shared decision-making and the reality of representative democracy as it was embodied in the local school board.

Chapter 9 will describe how the differing lenses through which various groups within the Cottonwood School District have viewed major issues have caused misunderstandings. In regard to some issues, a climate of distrust arose that made it difficult to build a consensus even behind changes that mutually distrustful groups both appeared to desire. When participants in the shared decision-making process were not able to put the best interests of the school community above personal concerns, planning meetings tended to turn aside from consensus building and to take on the characteristics of negotiating sessions. Also discussed are the effect the broader national debate about educational policy had on the attitudes of college-educated Cottonwood parents and the impact parent attitudes had on shared decision-making efforts within the Cottonwood School District.

CHAPTER 2

NOW . . . AND THEN:
A CHANGE IN PERSPECTIVE

To understand the factors that acted together to limit the success of the restructuring effort in Cottonwood, it is necessary to have some knowledge of the character of the restructuring effort as well as of the social and political context in which restructuring was carried out. This chapter will describe the form that site-based decision-making took in Cottonwood, focusing on the following questions: What was the goal of the site-based reform effort? How was restructuring carried out? What did the Cottonwood district's collaborative, decentralized approach to school governance look like in action? What sorts of problems were effectively addressed through the shared decision-making process?

Talking to school personnel who had begun their careers in different eras was, at times, reminiscent of strolling through one of the deep canyons that ran through parts of Western State. Just as the impress of past events could be read in the varied layers of rock exposed in canyon walls, the impact of past decisions or systems of school governance could be sensed in the differing ways in which people who had started their careers in different eras reacted to present innovations. For example, the staff members who proved most receptive to site-based decision-making were those who had either less than ten, or more than twenty, years of service in the Cottonwood district. This was because, during the 1950s and 1960s, Superintendent Ed Larimer had emphasized the centrality of the teacher to any concept of educational quality, making clear his expectation that staff members show themselves self-reliant, able to "make do." Curriculum innovation was encouraged. A teacher recalled the academic experimentation that characterized the Cottonwood district in the 1960s: "Talk about site-based management! Larimer did allow things to happen. The first years at Suburbia High were exciting, jumping years."

Toward the end of Superintendent Larimer's tenure, however, budget problems associated with rapid growth led to the school board's insistence that more emphasis be put on the business aspects of school administration. When Dr. Davis was hired as superintendent in the 1970s, there was an explicit desire among school board members to hire "someone who is a businessman." During Dr. Davis' tenure, central office control increased markedly, not only in financial matters but elsewhere. Curriculum decisions were centralized. Teachers who chose to join the appropriate committees had input in deciding on specific curriculum objectives or writing criterion-referenced tests (CRTs). But the curriculum worked out by these committees was then mandated, districtwide.

Dr. Roberts discussed the changes he had tried to bring about, noting that there had once been:

> a prevalent feeling in Cottonwood that before you can move ahead on the development of a new idea or plan, everybody above you in the organizational structure must be aware and give their approval. We now believe that as long as people who are impacted by the decision are represented in the process and stay within the parameters . . . it is not necessary for the superintendent to give approval of everything that happens within the learning services area or any other area of the district.

On a practical level, this change meant that building-level personnel could make decisions quickly and with enough flexibility to take advantage of fortuitous circumstances. Examples of innovative programs ranged from an elementary school in a low socioeconomic status (SES) neighborhood that now had a food sharing program that made regular deliveries of food to the school, to a suburban school that had reacted to parent concerns about honing their children's math skills by inviting parents to teach a popular workshop that showed parents how to use household projects to teach mathematical concepts. From a districtwide perspective, the new emphasis on site-based initiatives translated into increased feelings of local ownership, as well as a markedly greater diversity in the activities taking place in Cottonwood schools.

How Is the Site-Based Approach Different?

Basic to the switch to site-based decision-making was the belief that decisions made close to the problem were likely to be better. Bureaucratic lines of authority were de-emphasized and principals were encouraged to engage in on-site problem-solving. A concerted effort was made to break through hierarchical modes of thinking. When special needs arose, experienced principals were often put on special projects for a few weeks, or months, and charged with finding solutions. A veteran principal pointed out that the time he had spent coordinating the mainstreaming of severely retarded students had left him with a different perspective when he returned to his own school. Another administrator noted: "The whole idea of innovation and creative approaches is nurtured. That's one of the hallmarks of our school district."

What Is Meant by Shared decision-making?

The principle that the individuals directly affected by a decision had a right to have input into the decision-making process had been made a formal part of the Cottonwood School District's agreement with the teachers' union. Yet the right to have input was not taken to mean having the right to make the decision. The person who would be held accountable for a decision retained final responsibility for making it. "But," as a district-level administrator explained, "this [decision-making] must be done in a spirit of collaboration, after gathering input from those who will be affected. Then, when a decision is announced, the rationale behind it is explained."

How the Move to a Collaborative Approach Was Begun

When Dr. Bill Davis retired as superintendent of the Cottonwood School District in 1982, there were wide differences of opinion among staff members about the sort of management style the new superintendent should have. Dr. Davis had been a strong leader and the district had gained national recognition for educational excellence under his administration. Yet the amount of paperwork involved in Dr. Davis' management-by-objectives approach (discussed in chapter 4) had left some staff members feeling overwhelmed. They also questioned whether the classroom time required to keep up with the mandated criterion-referenced testing was well spent. Some of the more vocal teachers worried aloud that the isolated skills they were required to teach were quickly forgotten. Some parents were voicing questions at school board meetings as to whether the artistic and affective sides of education had been paid enough attention under the curriculum put in place by Dr. Davis.

The school board member who had headed the search committee charged with finding a new superintendent, emphasized the thoroughness of the search which eventually brought Dr. Roberts to Cottonwood. Search committee members met with principals, parents, and teachers to find out what they wanted in a new superintendent. Applications were examined with these priorities in mind. The top ten candidates were then interviewed by the board at a national conference. Subsequently, the top three candidates were invited to visit Cottonwood. After this, school board members visited the top three candidates in their home districts.

Dr. Dave Roberts had begun experimenting with collaborative decision-making a decade previously, in 1972. He had been assigned as principal to a difficult school and charged with the task of turning things around. To get a consensus of support behind that restructuring effort, he formed a committee of parents and teachers to set policy on budget and discipline. By asking, "How can we do this together?," he was able to focus attention on what needed to be done. The striking success of this approach convinced him that the best way to implement educational reforms was not to dictate solutions, but for the central office to search out ways to support schools in their efforts.

Superintendent Roberts pointed out that Cottonwood had always been a wonderful school district. As he saw it, in the 1970s, when many Cottonwood schools were operating on split sessions because of rapid suburban growth, there had been a need for a centralized approach. But, with the advent of the 1980s, there had been a growing awareness that centralized reforms attempted in the 1970s had not brought the intended results. A more participative management style was then needed to arrive at decisions all could support. In printed materials published by the district, Dr. Roberts explained:

> During the years prior to my arrival the district had received national recognition for the implementation of Outcome-Based Education and Computer-Managed Instruction. It was also very centralized. Most major decisions and plans for implementation

evolved directly from the central office administrators with little opportunity for input by those expected to implement the decision. Since my background reflected a participative approach to management, one of the things I began to do during my first year was to talk about decentralizing decisions that traditionally had been associated with the central office administration.

Dr. Roberts also emphasized long-range planning and staff development. Many staff members felt that a lack of systematic staff development had undercut the reforms attempted under Superintendent Davis' tenure. A long-time Cottonwood administrator expressed his view: "I think a lot of times we were asked to do things and did not have adequate training to follow through on it. To a large extent, that was one of the short-comings, that the training wasn't there."

Site-Based Decision-Making

Dr. Roberts put a strong emphasis on maintaining lines of communication and explaining just what he meant by various terms. This discussion of the change process will draw heavily upon Dr. Roberts' writings and observations, beginning with his rationale for choosing the term "site-based decision-making":

> The term that is widespread across this country to reflect the movement of site-based decision-making is site-based management. This term is a misnomer. Site-based management infers that teachers, community members and others are going to be involved in managing the schools. This is not the case with our site-based decision-making. The management of schools is an administrative function, and people should understand from the very beginning that this movement is not intended to move the managerial functions from building principals and other administrators to staff and/or members of the community.

Site-based decision-making was explicitly framed as a form of school district decentralization, not a taking of power from principals. At the same time it was made clear that the building-level administrator had the responsibility to implement shared decision-making among all constituencies: parents, teachers, administrators, students, noncertified school staff, and members of the local business community.

During the initial implementation process, Cottonwood followed the organizational model developed by the Institute for Development of Educational Activities (/I/D/E/A/) of Dayton, Ohio. Superintendent Roberts explained:

> In 1984 the district brought in /I/D/E/A/ to provide training for a selected number of schools that were interested in learning about "decentralization" as a vehicle for reforming education. /I/D/E/A/ called this training "a school improvement process" which quickly became the accepted term for shared decision-making in Cottonwood. /I/D/E/A/ did a magnificent job in providing teams of teachers, administrators, parents, and sometimes students, from seventeen schools the opportunity to explore the meaning of school improvement using a collaborative approach.

The Institute for Development of Educational Activities had been set up in 1965 by the Kettering Foundation to research ways to promote lasting educational change. /I/D/E/A/ now uses five-day workshops based upon experiential learning to facilitate the implementation of site-based management in individual schools. Through the workshops, facilitating teams (a parent, a teacher, and the principal) from individual schools learn what it means to bring a diverse group together and to begin moving toward school change. During the initial five-day workshop team-building exercises help these facilitating teams learn group-interaction skills they will later employ to bring together teams of eighteen to twenty-one people to begin planning for site-based improvement at individual schools.

Essential to the success of this effort is putting together a representative planning group. Each Cottonwood school was encouraged to put together a team which included representatives of all the major groups that had a stake in the school's performance. A school planning team might, therefore, include not only teachers, parents, and administrators, but also school secretaries and janitors, as well as community members without children in school (for example, city council members who could spearhead school/community partnerships or senior citizens concerned with seeing first hand how tax money was being spent). When picking students to serve on junior high and high school planning teams, an effort was made to pick students from all social groups, not just those normally expected to serve on student council.

For shared decision-making to be successful, school staff members who were not on the planning team had to feel that someone was adequately representing the needs of their group and could keep them informed about the policy changes the planning team might be contemplating. To achieve this level of meaningful representation, the nomination process had to be as broad-based as possible. An effective method of picking representatives was recommended by /I/D/E/A/ trainers. Members of various groups to be represented, such as second-grade teachers or members of the science department, were to write down the names of three people they would feel comfortable having represent them. The individuals whose names showed up most frequently were approached about making a year-long commitment to serve on the planning team. This method of selection often brought forward individuals who turned out to be excellent representatives, yet who might never have stepped forward on their own.

Such experience-based ideas from /I/D/E/A/ advisers proved invaluable in getting the school improvement process underway. Dr. Roberts recalled:

/I/D/E/A/ began training in 1984, and within the next two years the rest of our schools received introductory training in the development and implementation of school improvement planning. The school improvement process has been the foundation for site-based decision-making in Cottonwood. Every school has a school improvement planning team which conducts needs assessment, establishes priorities based on these findings, establishes design teams for the development of activities to accomplish the priorities and evaluates and repeats the cycle yearly. The school improvement planning process throughout the district has been the basis for the evolvement of many other forums where site-based decision-making occurs.

Deciding What Needed to Be Improved

Newly selected teams were encouraged to start the planning process by creating a vision of what a truly admirable school might look like. The first step was to find out about successful experiments being carried out elsewhere. At the beginning of the planning process the Cottonwood district gave each school $3,000 for speakers, materials, and other needs that might come up as individual school communities began to create shared visions of what they wanted their schools to become.

Teams were cautioned to avoid the pitfall of beginning the vision-building process by asking, "What's broke?" Trainers felt that it was all too easy for the vision-building process to be short-circuited if it started with a gripe session. Dwelling on present problems could create an atmosphere of hopelessness, or it could start a cycle of blame and defensiveness that could prevent the planning team from working together effectively. In such circumstances, problem-solving strategies could become a substitute for vision. When this happened, no overall "road map"—a plan including both a shared vision of what the school could become and an accurate assessment of where it was now—could be drawn up. With no shared vision, misunderstandings continually arise due to the differing visions for the school held by individual planning team members.

Organizational Issues

Once a shared vision was established, it became easier to set specific goals. The next step was prioritizing these goals and deciding which issues should be addressed first. A planning team member from a Cottonwood elementary school described how their school decided what issues to focus on each year:

> We create focuses through shared decision-making, through parent surveys, through teacher input, through what the administrators want. We have goals each year, and we're accountable to the district and the state department [of education]. Those become the focus and the design teams are generated from those. So we set goals and we meet those goals yearly.

The design teams were subcommittees led by members of the planning team who took responsibility for designing solutions to specific problems and reporting back to the planning team with specific proposals. Such design teams often included staff members who were not on the planning team but had a special interest in a particular problem.

In the early 1980s, when Dr. Roberts first arrived in Cottonwood, there weren't many districts around the country that were implementing shared decision-making. So, of necessity, many problems were solved by trial and error, with staff members working out over a period of years what responsibilities the schools would handle and which would stay with central office administrators. Of pivotal importance, throughout the years when implementation of site-based decision-making was taking place, was the Cottonwood school board's support for taking risks that had the potential to significantly benefit the education of Cottonwood children. Another important factor was the support of the teachers' union.

Dr. Roberts believed that fault-finding killed the feeling of trust necessary to collaborative problem-solving. In district training materials he quoted Churchill ("A mistake does not become a failure until you stop trying to correct it"), and argued that for staff members to feel comfortable being creative and trying new things they had to feel supported. Another precondition Dr. Roberts saw as vital to establishing trust was insuring a free flow of accurate information. By opening up the hiring and budget development processes, he overturned long-standing assumptions about who should be allowed access to key information.

As will be seen in the following chapters, opening up the flow of information challenged established habits of mind and management practices. Building principals and department heads at the district level who had been accustomed to keeping certain information private, as a way of enhancing personal power within the organization, resisted emulating the new pattern of openness. Changing such attitudes became an ongoing struggle. However, the emphasis the superintendent put on having the staff members he worked with read the relevant research literature, including that on organizational change, allowed those charged with implementation to fall back on the findings of nationally respected experts when acceptance of new norms took a frustratingly long time. Knowledge that others had encountered similar problems helped prevent discouragement and defensiveness.

Although change did come slower than had been initially projected, the enthusiasm of those principals who entered whole-heartedly into the shared decision-making process eventually aroused the interest of other principals. Over time, the retirement of several older principals, who had done little more than go through the motions of shared decision-making, changed the composition of the building administrators group. With collaborative behavior strongly supported at the district level, shared decision-making gradually became the district norm. However, a handful of relatively dictatorial principals, beloved of their parent communities despite their headstrong management style, were still in place a decade after shared decision-making had been implemented at the district level.

How Does Shared Decision-Making Work?:
The Cottonwood Model

When a building administrator has an issue or concern to resolve, utilizing the shared decision-making process, the first step must be clear identification of the issue. One way to make the area for shared decision-making specific is by putting it in question form. A question has the advantage of defining the boundaries of discussion more sharply than a stated topic. Later, if discussion starts to wander off on a tangent, the facilitator can remind the group that the focus question must be answered before they can move to other areas of interest.

Once the question to be answered has been identified, the administrator establishes the parameters for the shared decision-making process. Parameters might include whether the planning team's recommendations will be advisory or decision-making, or whether planning team members must include themselves in the follow-up evaluation. Other parameters might include an operational definition of what "consensus" will mean (85% agreement appeared to be the norm) or the amount of time the group has to complete the process.

These steps taken, the building administrator selects a qualified facilitator, making sure that the facilitator understands the task at hand. Only then is the shared decision-making group established.

Consensus Building

Next the group begins study and discussion of the problem that has been set before them. Basic to shared decision-making is the process of consensus building. This process involves considerably more than setting out alternatives and voting—an approach which can prove problematic when complex issues are involved. This is because the partisan positions taken in the debate leading up to a vote can often hide possible compromises from view. Also, when a group formally votes on an issue, it tends to become divided between those in favor and those against. A sizable minority may remain unreconciled to the decision and bend their efforts to passive resistance. The goal of the consensus-building process, on the other hand, is to reach a solution which every group member can support.

As mentioned earlier, the process begins with the posing of a focus question, for example: "What inservice activities are necessary to create staff awareness about site-based decision-making?" Once the problem has been defined, the group begins gathering information. Superintendent Roberts considered it impossible for a group to reach the best decision when the data base is insufficient. He strongly encouraged shared decision-making groups to read research literature. Articles describing possible alternatives were copied and read by all planning team members. When especially complex questions were being discussed, sometimes the facilitator would be a professor from the University of Western State, with which the Cottonwood district had forged strong links.

Once the facilitator feels that enough information has been gathered, options are discussed. Often the group participates in a brainstorming activity which allows as many alternatives as possible to surface. Afterward, suggested ideas are considered, one by one. Those that are clearly unworkable are discarded. Similar ideas may be combined. When possible solutions have been narrowed to two or three, arguments for and against each are listed. Group members may also suggest modifications to proposals under discussion in order to bring the group closer to consensus.

After considerable discussion, when it appears that many members of the group have agreed on a particular proposal, the facilitator will test for consensus. This gives those who are not convinced a chance to voice their doubts. The objections of each person are considered individually. Then the facilitator explores ways in which positions might be modified to allow consensus to be reached. If consensus is still not reached, the facilitator may call a break, allowing dissenters to meet with those who have more positive feelings. Or the facilitator may adjourn the meeting to another time. The facilitator might seek additional information by bringing in an outside expert or additional informational materials.

When consensus is reached, the process is not complete. An action plan must be developed. Then, the plan must be communicated to all stakeholders.

Pyramiding

Each person on a site-based decision-making team is assumed to be there not only in order to represent their own interests, but also in order to give voice to the concerns of others. Those they represent might be teachers in their department or grade level, parents, support staff, administrators, or students, but it is likely that they do not agree with their appointed representative on all points. The pyramiding process therefore calls upon team members to communicate with the stakeholders they represent in order to solicit reactions, input, and new ideas. Pyramiding is set up to ensure that: the shared decision-making team is not perceived by nonmembers to be a secretive group whispering behind closed doors; policy changes being considered do not come as a shock to the school community; and the views of those not on the shared decision-making team are considered.

Each member of a shared decision-making team has the responsibility of identifying three to five people to be part of their pyramiding group. Between meetings each team member has the responsibility to speak with this "pyramid group" to get their reactions concerning particular issues, topics, or concerns that are under discussion by the site-based planning team. By indirectly connecting many more people to the planning process, pyramiding provides a rich source of information. Team members are encouraged to include in their pyramiding groups those people who are known to be opposed to a particular idea or who have a reputation of resisting change. Including these people helps build trust in the process, while making it less likely that destructive rumors will undermine the best intentions of the group.

Through pyramiding those not directly involved with the planning effort are given reason to feel knowledgeable. Members of the school community are not taken by surprise when implementation of a new policy begins. Pyramiding also helps avoid implementation struggles. However good a job the shared decision-making team might have done in reaching consensus among themselves, if there has been little communication with those outside the group, they may well discover that other members of the school community refuse to support their decision, when they are announced.

Evaluation of Decisions Reached

The final step of the planning process is to determine: (1) how the success of the plan is going to be evaluated; (2) when this evaluation will take place; and (3) by whom it will be done. Planning the evaluation is considered the responsibility of those people who reached a consensus on the issue and should not simply be left up to the building principal.

SITE-BASED DECISION-MAKING IN ACTION

An example of how the site-based decision-making process proved its usefulness was the grade-level restructuring at Harding and Larimer elementary schools. These two schools are located within six blocks of one another. When the process began, Larimer Elementary was overcrowded and had mobile units on site. Just down the street Harding Elementary had many empty classrooms. Yet the emotion aroused in the parent communities over the subject of changing school attendance area boundaries had thus far stymied attempts to remedy the imbalance. Therefore, the district presented the dilemma to the school improvement teams of both buildings and asked for recommendations.

After several meetings, the two school improvement teams came to the board of education with the recommendation that the schools be merged, so that Harding housed kindergarten through second grade and Larimer housed third grade through sixth grade. The school improvement teams presented the board with examples of other districts that had successfully implemented similar solutions. Having worked closely with the district's support services, transportation, and food-service departments to work out potential difficulties, the planning teams were able to show that the proposed changes were within the Cottonwood district's vision and goals.

The board asked the planning teams to engage in pyramiding (sharing information with the other members of their school communities who would be affected). Six weeks later, the teams reported to the school board that there was support for the idea. The board scheduled a public hearing to present the school merger plan and get reactions from the two school communities. A widely publicized meeting was held, but no community members showed up. The school improvement teams had received support for the structural change and community members felt there was nothing left to discuss.

LEVELS OF SHARED DECISION-MAKING

The formal process described above was not the only form shared decision-making took. Dr. Roberts insisted it was a fallacy to believe that, when a school or a district embarked on shared decision-making, every decision had to be made by consensus. To illustrate this point, he suggested picturing decisions as occupying a place on a five-level continuum: A *level one* decision would be one in which an administrator developed a plan, then asked those involved for input. If the plan was changed as a result of their input, the degree of shared decision-making moved to *level two*. Shared decisions that fell at the *third, fourth, or fifth level* were those where the administrator brought a concept to those who might be impacted and solicited their participation in exploring alternatives, for example in developing a master schedule or budget.

In deciding what level of shared decision-making was appropriate, time was an important element. "Now" decisions typically allowed little chance for shared decision-making. Dr. Roberts cited a decision he had made years before, when he was a junior high principal in a suburban district where 80 percent of the students were transported by bus. As the buses were preparing to leave on the last day of school, his secretary ran outside and told him that a tornado had set down forty miles away. Overhead, the sky was black and the wind was picking up. However the school was not architecturally well set up to weather a tornado. Dr. Roberts held the buses and asked his secretary to call the weather bureau to determine how fast the tornado was moving. She quickly phoned and reported that the tornado was moving only twenty miles per hour. Since the tornado was still forty miles away, he waved the buses out of the parking lot. The tornado did set down in the district more than two and a half hours later, but by that time all the students were home.

Midway between such "now" decisions and the sort of long-range planning decisions where staff participation should be highest were decisions that dealt with immediate problems or high-impact situations. An example would be the choice of a department, or a grade-level, chairperson. Ultimately, the decision rested with the building principal. Yet an able administrator would not make such a decision without consulting the teachers involved, knowing that a unilateral decision could result in lack of support and participation by teachers who felt left out of the process.

High-participation decisions tended to be those dealing with future plans, with curriculum implementation, and with setting priorities for budgeting, staffing, or school improvement. In these areas it was imperative to have high staff involvement. Dr. Roberts noted that when long-range planning is done by a selected few, without an attempt to involve the rest of the staff or the community, the printed result of the planning process generally began gathering dust soon after the planning process was completed. He posited a direct correlation between the amount of participation in a decision and the reception that decision could be expected to meet when implemented.

Developing a Mission Statement

Vision building is the most important initial activity of a school planning team. Once a school made a commitment to a vision, a guideline had been established for developing the goals, objectives, and action plans needed to assure that the vision was attained. Vision statements Cottonwood school communities had developed included:

> A place where the staff and community enthusiastically work together so that students are encouraged to achieve their potentials as life-long learners.
>
> A student-centered community where individuals are valued and are encouraged to reach their full potential, to successfully experience life transitions, and to develop responsibility and a sense of self worth.
>
> A people-centered community that celebrates a passion for learning through challenge, growth, and success.
>
> A child-centered community that celebrates the joy of learning.

As a first step toward developing a school vision, each person on a new planning team was encouraged to write down no more than three sentences, describing their personal vision for education. Each individual was then given the opportunity to discuss their vision. Team members were also encouraged to voice any concerns they had, describing what they saw as the worst possible outcome of the shared decision-making process. Many people involved in the planning process revealed anxieties about whether site-based decision-making should even be implemented. Having an opportunity to express such concerns helped remove anxieties, fears, or doubts. The facilitator was responsible for making sure that each person was listened to with respect and supported as they shared their concerns.

After this, there was a group discussion of the best possible outcome of the school improvement process. Eventually, the school vision statement was derived from the best outcomes. But, before this was done, pyramiding took place so that the input and concerns of non–group members could be taken into account. A consensus building process was used to arrive at the final vision settlement, which all planning team members signed. As the vision building process drew to a close, the facilitator pointed out to the group that, by signing the collective statement, team members had shown their commitment to the vision they had developed.

DISTRICT SCHOOL IMPROVEMENT TEAM

The District School Improvement Team (DSIT) served as a link between the building-level groups and the district administration. The DSIT was composed of two parent representatives from each school, two senior citizens, and two other taxpayers without children in the schools. Secondary school students and representatives of the district's classified, certificated, and administrative personnel also served on the team. The DSIT reviewed individual school improvement plans, conducted studies in areas designated by the board of education, and provided a forum for districtwide communication. The president of the DSIT served as a nonvoting member of the elected board of education.

PUTTING THE NEW REFORMS IN PERSPECTIVE

The organizational description of shared decision-making given here is, of course, but one way of looking at the restructuring of the Cottonwood School District. For, although a school district inevitably appears to outsiders to be defined by its most distinctive characteristics, when seen close up that same district generally proves to be far from homogeneous. In the interest of clarity, I began by describing how shared decision-making might operate in a model Cottonwood school. However, the actual schools in the Cottonwood School District had characteristics that caused them to vary in unpredictable ways from the model described. Often these variations were rooted in the history of the Cottonwood School District. Indeed, the eventual adoption of site-based decision-making by the Cottonwood district was clearly influenced by earlier events.

Returning to the geological metaphor of chapter 1, it might be suggested that, just as the water that comes to the surface in freshwater springs is, in reality, rain that fell to earth and seeped beneath the surface somewhere else, attitudes favorable to site based decision-making in Cottonwood had their roots in habits of mind that once were widespread in the district. Many roadblocks to reform also sprang from seeds planted in the past. The next two chapters will provide a brief retrospective, reviewing policies implemented by former superintendents and demonstrating how these policies influenced subsequent events.

CHAPTER 3

BACK WHEN ALL THIS WAS FARMLAND: THE ADMINISTRATION OF ED LARIMER, 1953–1972

The three superintendents who have headed the Cottonwood district over the last forty years have represented what could be characterized—broadly speaking—as a humanist, a social-efficiency, and a developmentalist perspective. In this sense, the history of the Cottonwood district mirrors the evolution of thinking about the purpose of schooling in the United States as a whole. Still rural until after World War II, Cottonwood retained the straightforward emphasis on academics that more urbanized areas had abandoned earlier in the century in favor of a more complex social-efficiency curriculum that put more emphasis on vocational and other practical kinds of training. Cottonwood did not move to social-efficiency style of organization until 1972. During the late 1970s, detailed objectives spelled out what teachers were to teach in the classroom and a thorough-going system of criterion-referenced tests was used to see if these objectives had been reached. But, by 1982, enthusiasm for this system had waned and Cottonwood chose to follow the path outlined in chapter 2.

Each superintendent had a different vision of means and goals of schooling. For Ed Larimer, Cottonwood's first superintendent, educational excellence meant effective, innovative teaching of the core academic curriculum. In Larimer's view, the job of the school was to pass on to students the finest elements of the Western heritage. He thought curriculum should promote the reasoning power of students, enabling them to express their thoughts clearly and cogently. The goal of schooling was seen as enabling students to become competent, responsible citizens, able to make informed, meaningful choices.

Superintendent Larimer was a very religious man who did not hesitate to discuss moral or spiritual matters with parents and staff members. He and his original school board members assumed that the curriculum should have a strong focus on Western literature and traditions, so as to provide children with the opportunity to live imaginatively within the moral vision of the Western cultural tradition. Given this emphasis, they saw no reason why the same standard core curriculum should not be suitable for all students. College-bound students were encouraged to take academic electives such as foreign language during their high school years, while other students might sign up for vocational electives, but the core curriculum was the same for all.

Neither Larimer nor his original school board felt any need to debate what sort of education for Cottonwood students ought to have. Their ideas about what schooling ought to be had been formed during their own school years. Most had attended schools similar to Cottonwood's old Goose Pond School. Built just prior to World War I, Goose Pond was a K–12 school which, for most of its existence, had a graduating class of fewer than ten. Course selection was necessarily limited. For example, during the 1920–25 school years Goose Pond had offered seventeen courses (with sixteen of these required for graduation): English I, II, III, IV; Spanish; American History; World History; Civics; Ancient History; Economics; General Science; Physics; Chemistry; Geometry; Algebra; Solid Geometry; and Music.

Students who found these subjects uninteresting, or who met with little success in their studies, routinely left school and found jobs. During the forty years when Goose Pond School was the largest educational institution in the still rural Cottonwood area, high school graduation was not yet the accepted norm. Except during the Depression, there were plenty of farm and factory jobs available to young people who did not fit easily into the academic curriculum of the traditional high school. But at that time the Cottonwood School District was formed out of all or part of six small rural districts, and society was changing rapidly. In its early years, the Cottonwood district was relatively unaffected by social shifts taking place elsewhere. During most of Ed Larimer's tenure, residents of the relatively homogeneous Cottonwood district seldom disagreed with the superintendent's perception of the purpose and goals of public education. Public debate centered on financial issues.

GROWTH IN THE COTTONWOOD SCHOOL DISTRICT

A Cottonwood school teacher remembered what it had been like to attend the Goose Pond School in the 1950s. By then, the old K–12 school had been converted to an elementary school. Goose Pond was still a farming community. Everyone knew one another. Since there was no kindergarten, students started school in the first grade. They read from basal readers featuring characters like Dick, Jane, and Spot. Classes were traditional, very structured, with lots of direct teaching. Former students remembered loving fire drills because they got to slide down the fire escape tube from the second floor. As a special treat, on the last day of school before summer vacation, students were allowed to ride their horses to school.

Not until 1962 was there any formal curriculum supervision in the Cottonwood district. In that year an elementary principal, as well as and the district's only high school principal, were appointed curriculum coordinators and assistant superintendents for elementary and secondary education, respectively. A reading teacher became K–6 reading resource teacher. Another classroom teacher became the art resource teacher. The next year, two classroom teachers were made half-time mathematics consultants. A veteran teacher remembered, "There was a great deal of flexibility in terms of teaching and learning. You were given an outline of the curriculum, and you had a text. You were considered capable of finding resources and making decisions about what was to be taught."

All this was to change. By 1972, the Cottonwood School District would have grown from two small schoolhouses to twenty-two schools, including several of the largest elementary schools in Western State. The once-homogeneous community by then contained diverse opinions on both social and school matters. Many Cottonwood principals had been strongly influenced by the social-efficiency assumptions embedded in college courses they had taken in order to receive certification as school administrators. Like their colleagues nationwide, Cottonwood's principals did not question the assumption that children learned best when grouped with children of a similar ability level. A former Cottonwood student described the system of "tracking" that had been used in her junior high during the 1960s:

> Students were assigned to sections according to their grades and the recommendations of former teachers. There were seven or eight sections and students stayed with the same classmates all day. Getting to take a foreign language was tied to what

section you were in and was sort of an honor. The kids in 7-1, the highest section, got to take German. Kids in 7-2, the second highest section, got to take French. Kids in 7-3 got to take Spanish. That division seemed to be tied to how hard the teachers and administrators thought the languages were. I had a friend who was in section 7-8. I really felt sorry for her. Looking back on it, being ranked like that was sort of degrading.

Contrasting with such rigidity was the strong sense of community recalled by numerous informants. In the 1960s, many farm families still lived in the outlying areas of the Cottonwood district. A principal gave an example from Riverbend Junior High's first years: "When a foot and a half of snow fell the night before Riverbend's ninth grade football team was to play for the district championship on its home field, it was a natural thing to call a couple of parents. A couple of moms fit the family tractor with a blade and cleared the snow off the football field so that the noon sun could dry the playing surface. Riverbend went on to win the afternoon game and the district championship." This sort of parental involvement, coupled with a flexible "make do" attitude on the part of staff members, was remembered with considerable nostalgia by many who had worked in Cottonwood during the 1950s and 1960s.

Superintendent Ed Larimer

In 1953 the newly formed Cottonwood School District was comprised of only 238 students and 11 teachers. Ed Larimer, the first superintendent, had degrees in history, geology and school administration. He came to the district from a nearby town, where he had been a school principal. A longtime teacher remembered Superintendent Larimer as "a very kind man, congenial, very conservative, very dedicated." But, although Larimer was respectful of teachers as professional people capable of making sound decisions on the classroom level, he retained tight control over spending and was very sensitive to how community members perceived the school district. An administrator recalled: "Ed Larimer pretty much ran everything. When I started teaching, I used to work for the district as a painter in the summer. I even had to order the paint through Ed. He'd tell you where to order the paint and how much you could get. The district was that small and Ed did everything."

Many long-time Cottonwood staff members trace the strong community feeling which still exists among district personnel to Ed

Larimer's tenure, noting that the superintendent's life seemed to revolve around the school district. The superintendent went to army surplus stores to get tools as cheaply as possible for the shop in The Annex just north of old Metroville Elementary School. In order to save $200, Ed Larimer would travel to Detroit to pick up each new school bus. He and his son would sleep on the bus as they drove it back. The former auxiliary services director remembered Larimer as "the most honest, hard-working man I've ever seen. There were years when the district, which might have had 5,000 or 6,000 students, would get another 1,000 the next year. Just imagine what it was like, trying to absorb a 15–20% increase over the prior year!"

The "make do" attitude of the superintendent was well suited to the nature of the Metroville community at the time. When a hot lunch program was started in the 1950s, a cook transported food from the central kitchen in a "yellow jalopy." Superintendent Larimer could often be seen with his sleeves rolled up, pre-rinsing heavy army trays in an old washing machine and carrying them across the room to the dish machine. The superintendent believed in keeping in close touch with what was happening in the schools. In the early days, he made a point of going to each school on payday and walking into each classroom to personally hand the pay envelop to each teacher. A teacher recalled, "He really delighted in that." A veteran principal remembered wondering, as a new teacher, if he might lose his job when Ed Larimer walked into his classroom to hand him his check and one of his third-grade pupils called out, "Hey, mister! What are you doing in our room?" However, the Cottonwood district was rapidly growing beyond the point where even a superintendent as dedicated as Ed Larimer could be known by every student or visit monthly with every teacher.

By 1957 there were an estimated 10,350 people living in the city of Metroville. In order to meet the educational needs of the young people living within its sixty-two square miles, between 1954 and 1978 the Cottonwood district passed nine bond elections, totaling over $96,000,000. Throughout most of its first thirty years the Cottonwood district was faced with a population growth rate that was nearly twice the national average. An administrator who worked under Superintendent Larimer for nineteen years, remembers the challenge of absorbing such phenomenal growth. "Ed Larimer operated the district like he was spending his own money, somehow making ends meet during a period when the district was getting as many as 1,300 additional students every year."

Many long-time staff members insisted "there was a real closeness among teachers" during the years of rapid growth. When Suburbia High was opened in 1965, with sophomores only, its students were bused to Metroville Junior/Senior High for all activities. Superintendent Larimer, who was very interested in athletics, often stopped by the practice field. Suburbia's football coach remembered how Ed Larimer loved to hold the football for players as they practiced kicking extra points. One year the superintendent went to an army surplus store and bought huge mittens for the football team to wear on the sidelines in cold weather. "You could get six hands in each one!," the coach recalled.

Part of the track coach's job was to make sure that burnt coal cinders were properly distributed over the track in the spring. He used a handmade wooden drag, which he pulled behind an old Buick, in order to level the surface. Pointing out the egalitarian atmosphere that had prevailed among the staff, a principal described how one day, when he was talking with Ed Larimer in the superintendent's office, the head mechanic from the bus garage had called to inquire about where he could find a certain kind of wrench. Larimer called a halt in their meeting, went home, got his own wrench and brought it over to the bus garage so that the mechanics could get the bus fixed. A veteran teacher recalled the atmosphere in a somewhat different way:

> Paternal. Run by a bunch of "good ol' boys." Low key, but with an unpredictable quality. Larimer was an old farmer who expected his staff to be self-reliant. I'd say his attitude was Emersonian, in an unself-conscious way. Larimer never called a snow day. We'd have a twenty-inch snowstorm and some teachers might suggest that a snow day might be a good idea. He'd just advise them to buy snow tires.

Superintendent Larimer had made it known that he expected teachers to always dress, when they went out in public, as if they expected to see a student. School district rumor had it that Ed Larimer wore a tie even while mowing his lawn. During the district's early years, male teachers were required to wear a coat and tie. Female teachers wore skirts. During the 1960s the teaching staff became steadily more assertive. However, women teachers continued to wear dresses to school until, late in Larimer's tenure, there was a "revolt." A large number of women teachers wore pantsuits on the same day, forcing acceptance of such attire by the Cottonwood district.

Despite such cultural conflicts, Ed Larimer remained support-ive of teacher creativity within the classroom. A teacher who had joined the district just as its second high school opened remembered the early days at Suburbia High as "a heady time," when innovation was encouraged. A science teacher described how, at the junior high levels, discussions about the effect of scientific laws had come up during home economics classes:

> At the junior high I taught Home Ec. for four years. It relates perfectly. The very same things you do in the lab you do in the kitchen. There's a safety issue. There's an organizational issue. There's a procedural issue. It was the same type of teaching, just a different area. . . . It was an exciting time, doing some dif-ferent things.

Nor was innovation limited to discussion of how to efficiently turn the small amount of water in a popcorn kernel to steam, or the opti-mum mixture of air bubbles and ice crystals to create the "creami-est" ice cream.

A university professor who had supervised student teachers in the Cottonwood district since the 1960s described his early experi-ences at Metroville High:

> That first semester, the cooperating teacher's students were reading Greek tragedies. I think it's typical of Cottonwood that they have highly educated teachers who like teaching at the K–12 level and have consciously chosen to stay there. They had a very strong commitment to language arts and a strong English curriculum coordinator. They were not afraid to hire English teachers who were forward-looking and inno-vative.

Metroville Becomes "Western State's Newest City"

Back in 1953, Superintendent Larimer could not have foreseen the manner in which an unprecedented out-migration from the nation's established urban areas would transform his small rural dis-trict. A brief review of historical statistics gives an idea of the dimen-sions of the social change of which the postwar migration to the suburbs was a part. Back in 1820, 71.8 percent of Americans were farmers. By 1990, when the use of modern mechanized farming methods meant that far fewer people were needed to raise the same

amount of food, farmers comprised only 2.4 percent of the population (Johnson 1992).

The search for a more comfortable life played a part in the huge
population shifts which occurred in the decades following World
War II:

> In 1940, more than a fifth of the population still lived on farms,
> less than a third of the farms had electric lights and only a
> tenth had a flush toilet. Among all Americans, 56 percent were
> renters. More than half of the households didn't have a refrig-
> erator, and 58 percent lacked central heating. Nearly half the
> labor force worked at grueling farm, factory, mining or con-
> struction jobs. Home life was demanding. The famous study
> by sociologists Robert and Helen Lynd of "Middleton" (Muncie,
> Ind.) in the 1920s found that wives in working-class families
> (about 70 percent of the total) were typically up by 6 a.m. to
> start cooking; 40 percent rose by 5 a.m.
>
> Postwar suburbanization represented a huge leap in living
> standards for most Americans. It is not simply that they had
> better housing or that more Americans became homeowners—
> about 64 percent, up from 44 percent before the war. The qual-
> ity of everyday life was superior. (Samuelson 1992)

The excitement which accompanied the building a new community
is evident in stories told by those who remembered moving into the
new suburban developments built in the Cottonwood area in the
1950s.

In December of 1952 a prominent developer announced that
he would build "Western State's newest city" on a stretch of land
seven miles north of Foothills City. The area was then mostly open
prairie, with a few scattered farms and gentle valleys. His construction company broke ground for the first 5,000 homes in the spring of
1953. The development that eventually grew into the city of Metroville, which was planned from the start to be a complete city with an
eventual population of 20,000. The new "Miracle City" would consist of moderately priced brick homes on 1,500 acres, with planned
areas for schools, churches, and recreation. On 28 April 1953, the
first three model homes officially opened. Several thousand people
attended the open house. The new Metroville homes sold for $8,000
to $11,000. A family could move into a two-bedroom brick home
with a $650 down payment and FHA payments of $57 per month, or
they could move into a three-bedroom home with a down payment

of $1,250 and monthly payments of $67 per month.

Many people who could not otherwise have afforded to buy a home were enabled to do so by the GI Bill of Rights, which allowed them to get into a home with no money down. Over 300 homes were sold in a matter of weeks. To cut costs, homes were built in assembly-line style with one contractor pouring the concrete pads on which the houses were built, another doing the framing, another putting in plumbing, and so forth. Construction workers moved steadily from house to house, constructing whole neighborhoods of sturdy brick veneer residences in a manner that maximized efficiency and minimized costs.

The Metroville Community Association was formed in April 1954. Each city block selected a representative to sit on the Metroville Board, which addressed such issues as recreation, streets, and lighting. The increased number of people in Metroville brought a great need for additional school buildings in the area. In 1954 residents approved a bond issue to build Metroville's first school. Businessmen and local residents donated the materials and labor for construction of a temporary frame building call The Annex. Until The Annex was completed at Thanksgiving in 1954, the school district rented space in the fire hall for a few elementary classes and a central office. Superintendent Larimer hired the district's first secretary in September 1954, while the superintendent's office was still in the fire hall. When Metroville Elementary was opened in the fall of 1954, Superintendent Larimer's office was moved there.

By the end of 1955 there were an estimated 5,500 people and over 1,200 homes in Metroville. City council meetings were held in the home of the city clerk until a used military Quonset hut could be erected to serve as a temporary city hall and headquarters for the fire and police departments. The original fire and police departments in Metroville were both volunteer organizations. Metroville merchants donated $1,385, with which the Metroville Volunteer Fire Department purchased a used La France fire truck and equipment. In a short time, the Metroville Fire Department became known as one of the best volunteer fire departments in the state, with tremendous esprit de corps among the firemen.

During this same period, the school district built its first high school. In the early 1950s the Cottonwood School District had paid tuition for its students to attend whatever high school was most convenient. Although the new junior/senior high school was still under construction, in the 1955–56 school year a temporary building was put up between the construction site and Metroville Elementary. High school students attended classes in the temporary building, where three teachers taught grades seven through eleven. Graduates of Goose Pond and Metroville elementary schools were now able to stay together through their high school years.

A teacher who moved to the new junior/senior high school the year it opened remembered: "There was quite a lot of open country between Foothills City and Metroville back then, mostly irrigated crops. They raised a lot of hay." A Metroville student who graduated in 1961 pictured the open fields that then surrounded the school: "Over where the Interstate is now there was a two-lane road, with a stop sign where they have the interchange now." The former basketball coach recalled winter practices in the Metroville Elementary School cafeteria. One student stood up on the stage, holding up a wastebasket as a goal. When a new hot lunch program, under the National School Lunch Program, was started at Metroville Elementary in 1956, the food was cooked in army surplus kettles. High school students scrambled down the hill to eat lunch in the elementary school lunchroom. Lunch counts were high, with as many as 800 children eating.

Superintendent Larimer brought in Ben Gibb, a former college classmate, to act as principal of the new school. An elementary school principal remembers "Larimer had high expectations of the people he hired. Although he was very autocratic, he was very loyal. He literally chose administrators himself, but if you were a good administrator he'd support you." At the new junior/senior high school, which had a student population of 370, Ben Gibb set up very strict dress codes. Girls were required to wear skirts and boys had to have their shirt tail tucked in at all times.

Despite the spectacular growth which took place in the Metroville area during the 1950s, few social tensions surfaced within the school district. The modest one-story homes built in Metroville during the 1950s were bought by working-class people whose values did not conflict with those of the farm families who lived around them. A resident who moved into one of the higher-priced developments that were built in later years, further from Foothills City, characterized the Cottonwood school board in the early 1960s as "a bunch of old farmers who rubber-stamped everything the superintendent did." Other residents remembered those early years as a time of remarkable esprit and harmony. In any case, it was unanimously agreed that the building of a new, higher-priced housing development, further from Foothills City, introduced a new kind of social tension into the Cottonwood School District. Going back to the geological metaphor, a new layer was about to be added to the demographic makeup of the area; a layer that would resist mixing in with the population that was already in place.

Suburbia Subdivision Emerges

North of Metroville there was still plenty of open farmland. The rural character of this part of the district began to change in the spring of 1959, when a group of local development companies finalized plans for a large subdivision beyond Metroville. Development plans called for a total community, designed to center around a regional shopping complex. Because the developers were also the sole land owners, they were able to control the layout of streets, the location and design of commercial and industrial areas, as well as the planning of recreational areas and the location of schools. Ground was broken in June 1959. By 1960 there were approximately 500 residents in the new Suburbia subdivision. Between 1960 and 1962, Suburbia grew rapidly and received national recognition, including numerous design awards.

The city of Metroville saw Suburbia subdivision as a desirable annexation and began the necessary legal process to bring it within its boundaries. However subdivision residents had other ideas. Suburbia's more expensive houses had led higher-income families, with different goals for their children, to move there. By that time Metroville had an established working-class/lower-middle-class character—from which Suburbia residents were determined to separate themselves. Suburbia citizen groups and service clubs opposed annexation by the city of Metroville, beginning a long legal battle. In 1969 the Western State Supreme Court ruled that Suburbia could not be annexed by Metroville. Suburbia then went ahead with plans to incorporate, officially becoming a city on 18 April 1969.

The Suburbia Mall opened in 1968, serving the consumer needs of both the local community and the surrounding region. The Suburbia Mall generated sales taxes revenues that, at their peak, provided approximately 67 percent of Suburbia's public revenues. To insure citizen involvement, the mayor and the city council started a program of town hall meetings, the first of which was held 19 May 1969. Eventually these were replaced by city council meetings and study sessions, but this initial attempt at citywide shared decision-making indicates the expansive mood of Suburbia's first years.

Crime was not a serious problem. The fifteen men hired to form the nucleus of the new police department patrolled the streets of Suburbia in two cars loaned to them by the Garfield County Sheriff's Department. The continuing close relationship between the city of Suburbia and the development company that had built both the Suburbia subdivision and the Suburbia Mall was demonstrated by the donation, by Suburbia Development Company, of the site for a new municipal building. By the time Suburbia's new municipal building was dedicated on 19 July 1970, the new city's population had grown to 26,000.

Unable to build permanent buildings fast enough, the district bought or leased homes and turned them into "cottage schools," with the intention of converting them into homes again once permanent school buildings were built. The cottages had four classrooms in each, two upstairs and two downstairs. There were no adult restrooms for teachers. A principal explained: "In the fall of 1960 they started with two cottage schools, each with about 25 kids per class, but by Christmas they had added about 95 children. So they added a third building during Christmas vacation." A teacher who had worked in the cottage schools explained that, "with so many new children arriving, the way the schools coped was to keep adding students to a class till it got to thirty-six or so, then take about ten kids and start a combination class, such as a third/forth grade split. Before long, there would be enough new students for a whole third grade and a whole fourth grade. Things changed all the time, which gave working in the district a feeling of adventure."

Teachers in the cottages got their only break at recess. There was no teacher's lounge, no place for teachers to be by themselves. One teacher recalls going out to his car, turning on the radio, and smoking a pipe during recesses—until a neighbor made a comment to the principal, who then reminded the teacher that Superintendent Larimer did not approve of smoking. From then on the teacher had to go for a drive to smoke his pipe. Hot lunches were all cooked at Goose Pond Elementary, the food put in hot containers, taken to the cottages, and served in the basement. Students took trays through the line, then went back to the classroom to eat.

By the fall of 1964 some 800 students, mostly first- and second-graders, were attending eleven cottage schools. Three new school buildings, with a total capacity of 1,200 students, were planned for construction in 1965 but it was anticipated that the district might receive 2,000 new children in that time. In 1960 Garfield County had been the fifth fastest-growing county in the United States—and most of that growth was in the Cottonwood School District. The Suburbia Development Company was finishing seven homes per day. Between

1950 and 1970, the population of Garfield County increased by 400 percent. Around 1970, three of the four largest elementary schools in Western State were in the Cottonwood district. During the 1970s, the population grew at a 34 percent annual rate. School district finances were stretched almost to the breaking point. There was no kindergarten because there was no space for it.

Superintendent Larimer explained that, in terms of tax dollars, it took 2.5 houses to support one child in school for a school year. Yet the families moving into the Cottonwood district averaged 2.9 elementary school children per house. Until the Suburbia Mall was built, there was little commercial property to tax. So the assessed valuation behind each child was small. State law said a school district could not be in debt more than 10 percent of the assessed valuation of the district. If need were proved, that could be expanded to 15 percent. Cottonwood was at 15 percent almost all the time, often building more than one school per year. In its first year, one elementary school averaged forty-five new students per month. A yearly cut off point in April was instituted, after which schools would not enroll any more new students.

During the period of Cottonwood's greatest growth, split sessions were unavoidable at all grade levels. The first students arrived at Suburbia High at 7:00 a.m. and students continued arriving till 1:00 p.m. The first students left the school at 11:00 a.m. and students continued leaving every hour, the last not leaving school till 5 p.m. Political pressures became an ever-growing concern as the district was forced to go to the voters again and again with bond issues. Accustomed to farmers and working-class people who shared his own rural roots, Ed Larimer found it ever more difficult to convince the growing population of suburbanites in Cottonwood that their children's schools were being efficiently run.

POLITICAL TENSIONS GROWING OUT OF THE METROVILLE/SUBURBIA RIVALRY

By the time Ed Larimer retired in 1972, the composition of both the district and the school board had changed dramatically. The farmland was fast disappearing beneath ever-expanding housing developments. The businessmen who now dominated the school board showed considerable impatience with the school district's frequent need to borrow money at the end of the school year. An individual who had been privy to the negotiations reported that school board members, meeting to discuss the school district's needs after Larimer retired, had unanimously agreed on one thing: The next superintendent would be "a businessman."

The new breed of school board member tended to see the school district as just another kind of business—one which could surely be managed better than the current superintendent was doing it. Looked at through such a lens, the outgoing superintendent's accomplishments were taken for granted, while the weaknesses of the Larimer era stood out painfully. On the national level, a reaction to the free-wheeling spirit of the 1960s "back to basics" movement was taking hold in the Cottonwood School District, the change of thinking was made more noticeable by the self-confident ascendancy of the business community after Suburbia Mall opened in 1968. Tensions between largely working-class Metroville and middle-class Suburbia were growing. Exemplified by the intense rivalry between the two high schools, these tensions had begun to cause morale problems among school district staff. A veteran teacher recalled:

> Suburbia was the "academic school." Folks at Metroville were miffed at that. If anything appeared in Foothills City newspapers about education that was good, it mentioned Suburbia. If it was something bad, it mentioned Metroville. Teachers were very aware of that. The secretary in the counseling office at Metroville High would "go crazy" about how Metroville was ignored or mistreated.

Such tensions added to the pressure to install a stronger, more centralized district administration that would have the power to minimize rivalries between competing school communities. Yet to adequately understand the depth of the rivalry between the cities of Metroville and Suburbia—a rivalry which would create substantial administrative and financial difficulties for the Cottonwood School District—some familiarity with local "pocketbook issues," especially the two municipalities' continuing battle over water rights, is necessary.

Like schooling, water is something most people tend to take for granted. You turn on the faucet and the water just gushes out. Yet developers, who are in the business of buying and selling land, are acutely aware of how the availability of water affects the value of land. In 1961, open farmland in the Cottonwood School District was hard to sell for $300 an acre until city water and sewer lines were made available. Then the price of that same land rose to $3,500 an acre overnight. However, as cities sought to buy more water to serve their ever-growing populations, the price of water rose sharply. Driven by ever-increasing demand, the price of a share of the irrigation water in the Garfield Ditch rose from about $500 in 1961 to $115,000 (and up) in 1990.

The original homes built in Metroville had all been serviced by a single well. As more homes were built, the utilities system grew. In 1963 Metroville voters approved the purchase of the Garfield Utilities Company, providing their city with its own water and sewer system. Problems soon arose, though, because approximately 60 percent of the 30,000 Metroville Utilities System customers lived outside the Metroville city limits. These customers, many of them Suburbia residents, had to contract with Metroville Utilities because Suburbia had made no provisions for contracting with another company. But, since they were not Metroville voters, Suburbia residents had no official representation in the administration of the system.

In 1959, when Suburbia was first developed, the subdivision had not owned the water treatment system on which it depended, nor even the pipes that serviced its citizens. By 1977, the city council had decided that it was in Suburbia's interests to develop its own water system. Approximately sixty meetings were held to discuss and explain the system to citizens prior to holding a special election on 12 July 1977. By a margin of 3,003 to 1,500, the citizens of Suburbia voted to issue general obligation bonds in the amount of $31 million to acquire a joint municipal water and sewer system.

Between 1977 and 1979 the city of Suburbia acquired the water lines located in Suburbia from Metroville. A plan was established to construct a new waste-water facility. The water treatment plant was completed in 1980 and the final severance of Suburbia's water lines from the Metroville Water System took place. However, cost overruns on the water project placed a severe financial burden on Suburbia, resulting in the termination of many city employees in order to cut costs. The final cost of the water system turned out to be considerably greater than the $31 million approved in the election of 1977. Among the reasons were general inflation, a much higher cost for purchasing the lines from Metroville than had been originally estimated, and legal fees for the many lawsuits filed against the city in regard to the water project.

The capital charge added to pay for the water system made water bills in Suburbia much higher than in the surrounding areas. Citizens angered by these costs filed petitions to demand the recall of the mayor and four of the city councilmen. After protest hearings resulting in a great deal of media coverage, the city clerk deemed four of the five recall petitions sufficient. An election was held in June 1983, but none of the demanded recalls were successful. However, the effects of this highly publicized recall election were long-lasting. Suburbia's water problems—and the attention that regional media coverage had focused on the inability of the financially strapped city to invest either in municipal services or in its commercial center—caused subsequent growth to shift to adjacent suburban areas.

This, in turn, caused yet another change in the balance of power within the school district. For, during this time, Metroville had engaged in an aggressive annexation program that allowed it to eventually out-flank and surround Suburbia on three sides. Returning to the geological metaphor, ascendency of the particular group who took over control of the school board after the Larimer years was short-lived, their influence becoming but one of the richly layered influences that have formed the culture of the Cottonwood School District.

Retrospective on the Larimer Years

The two superintendents who succeeded Ed Larimer adopted strikingly different approaches toward setting coherent educational priorities and allocating resources fairly despite the tension and sus-picion that blocked meaningful cooperation between Metroville and Suburbia, the two largest municipalities within the Cottonwood district. Under Superintendent Bill Davis, the district moved in the 1970s to a strongly centralized system, in which all schools taught the same curriculum in the same way. Faced with divisive political forces, Dr. Davis adopted a policy of strict even-handedness. Both administrative and curriculum decisions were tied to specific objec-tives. During the Davis tenure, Cottonwood's administrative phi-losophy swung to the opposite pole from Ed Larimer's willingness to let teachers make their own instructional decisions. Criterion-refer-enced tests were adopted to assure teacher accountability. Not all staff members were enthusiastic. Much as they came to prize the professionalism and national prominence that Bill Davis brought to the Cottonwood district, many teachers yearned to combine these attainments with the easy-going acceptance of human individual-ity characteristic of Ed Larimer:

> Not only are teachers professional people, but they are indi-viduals. We would not care to have our children led and

directed by a stereotyped image of perfection—"by the book." Each teacher has his own method of teaching and operates within that context most effectively. (Excerpt from the *Cottonwood Newsletter*)

When it came time to choose a successor to Dr. Davis, there were Cottonwood staff members who still remembered fondly Larimer's insistence on the importance of teachers:

> People are often misled by "high-sounding cymbals" of news articles or other publicity media claiming some unique "super programs" which are represented as solving all problems and placing that educational system on a high pedestal of attainment.
>
> The basis of any successful educational system, however, is measured by the quality of its teaching personnel. Well-prepared, innovative, personable and dedicated teachers are the key to all successful instruction. Physical facilities such as fine buildings and optimum tools of learning are of importance, to be sure, but these physical provisions fade into insignificance in the light of the human factor of individual teacher dedication and excellence. (Excerpt from the *Cottonwood Newsletter*)

Fittingly, it was through the people he hired, who continued to form the core of Cottonwood's talented professional staff, that Ed Larimer's legacy lived on. A teacher with over twenty years of service in the district recalled: "Larimer just had a feel for people, which is probably no worse than any other way of hiring, and better than many." A community member whose children had graduated from the Cottonwood schools remembered: "What's been distinctive about this district has been the high quality of the staff, and Larimer started that. My children, who went through school under Larimer, got a good foundation."

Looked at from a geological perspective, it was Ed Larimer who laid down the foundation on which later innovations would be built. It was the people he hired who would do much of the building. Years later, despite stark demographic changes, old Metroville High continued to offer a quality education to an increasingly at-risk population. This was made possible by the persistence and dedication of teachers orginally hired by Ed Larimer. Likewise, it was the cohesiveness among these teachers that allowed schools in the Metro High feeder system to develop a wide array of in-school services to support the learning of children whose needs for health care, proper nutrition, and counseling were not met in their home environment.

Yet, outside the school district, community consensus about the means and goals of schooling which had made formalized means of enforcing accountability unnecessary during much of the Larimer tenure, had begun to fray. The businessmen who controlled the school board in the early 1970s did not share Larimer's view that teaching children "by the book" was self-evidently undesirable. Nor were they convinced that giving high school students "a good foundation" meant offering a wide choice of courses in subjects like history, writing, and literature. By the early 1970s Cottonwood had become a deeply divided district, where the definition of "a good foundation" was up for grabs.

CHAPTER 4

MANAGEMENT AND LEARNING BY OBJECTIVES: THE ADMINISTRATION OF BILL DAVIS, 1972–1982

By 1972, the Cottonwood School District had grown from two small schoolhouses to twenty-two schools, among which were several of the largest elementary schools in Western State. This phenomenal growth had created a school district of such a size that it seemed to demand a less personal, more systematic management style. The membership of the school board had also changed. No longer did rural board members have the strongest voice. Businessmen had come to dominate the school board.

SUPERINTENDENT BILL DAVIS

Bill Davis, who became superintendent of Cottonwood School District in 1972, was a recognized leader in school management. A principal described him as "wonderful, truly an educator, with a focus on teaching kids." Immediately prior to coming to Cottonwood, Davis had served as a professor of educational administration. Previously, he had served as superintendent of three different school districts.

A researcher writing about educational administration interviewed Dr. Davis about his goals for the Cottonwood district:

In 1972, Bill Davis was a man with an idea. "If education is to retain any credibility with the general public," he believed, "we must define clearly what students should know in terms of instructional objectives, and we must make those objectives public and measurable." Armed with that conviction, Davis left the University in search of a school district where he could translate his beliefs into action. . . . He knew that a match between superintendent, board, and district was crucial for the superintendent to have a real impact on the direction of the schools, and felt such a match was more possible in a suburban district. Davis found what he was looking for in Garfield County's Cottonwood School District.

MANAGEMENT BY OBJECTIVE

In 1972 the Cottonwood School District was gearing up to write instructional objectives in response to a Western State school accountability law that had been adopted in 1971. A profile of the district published by a Cottonwood Regional Educational Laboratory pointed out that the fast-growing district faced common problems: There was no clear statement of organizational mission. The district's goals were extremely broad. There were no long-range and few short-range goals. Although, in response to the accountability law, up to 100 instructional objectives had already been written in each subject for each grade level, few of them were terminal objectives. Student assessment was not tied to the objectives, but was tied instead to standardized tests that compared local performance to national norms.

Working with the Board of Education, Dr. Davis set up two major objectives:

1. Apply the principles of management-by-objectives (MBO) to the district's organizational structure.
2. Implement objectives-based mastery learning in the instructional program.

Dr. Davis reorganized the central administration by dividing responsibilities among three divisions: curriculum and instruction, management services, and auxiliary services. Implementation of the new objectives was to start with the management and leadership issues, with the intent of working back to instruction. Key to the MBO approach was the clear definition of organizational goals. According to MBO theory, the more clearly goals are known, the more likely they are to be achieved; moreover, change was assumed to increase when it could be measured against clearly defined goals. In 1973 the board of education adopted districtwide educational goals, translating the district's historically vague goals into measurable and observable terms. Teams of teachers and administrators spent the next two years clarifying course objectives in terms of basic skills and developing pilot-test sets of criterion-referenced tests.

Superintendent Davis had come to Cottonwood with a management agreement (unusual at the time), which clearly defined his responsibilities. He pledged to implement a management-by-objectives system within three years. The school board pledged to limit its activities to legislative and judicial policy matters. Davis was also given authority over the contracts and salaries of all administrators—a kind of authority which, he pointed out, "builds loyalty in a hurry." He immediately began implementation of management procedures meant to make people at all levels of the district structure very accountable. Assistant superintendents wrote objectives for themselves that were in line with the objectives set down in the superintendent's management agreement. Each principal also wrote down objectives that matched those of Superintendent Davis. Assistant principals had written goals which met those of their principal. Teachers were expected to report to parents on how the district's objectives were being met in their individual classrooms.

By 1976 all administrators were writing their own management agreements, which spelled out the administrator's specific tasks relating to school system goals. Under the plan, each principal reported to a central office supervisor who continuously monitored the principal's work. On the agreement, in a column opposite each task, was a standard against which Dr. Davis could measure whether the objective was met. One principal's 1981 management agreement, for example, contained the following key task: "to ensure that progress is made in implementing the school system's instructional objectives." To measure whether that was accomplished, the principal set his standard: students would increase test scores by a specific percentage.

Superintendent Davis quickly catapulted the fast-growing district into national visibility. His vision of educational excellence was informed both by theoretical conceptions of how school districts should be organized and by his own earlier experience as a superintendent. Whereas, during Larimer's last years, media coverage of the Cottonwood district had emphasized the challenges presented by steep population growth and the inevitable delay between the arrival of new students and the arrival of tax income from the new residential areas, Superintendent Davis' frequent speaking engagements brought attention of a different and more welcome kind. Both the Cottonwood school board and their constituents enjoyed the positive regard that came to the district as it came to be recognized as a front runner in the national movement toward greater accountability in school district management.

"It's very difficult for those in the central office to know what's going on in individual buildings," the Cottonwood Director of Organizational Development declared, in a remark quoted in a professional journal. "Likewise principals don't know central office administrators' problems. Through the monitoring system, the 'firing line' almost disappears. We're a team." A principal commented: "The [management agreement] form might look inhuman, but it's one of the best things that's happened here." Dr. Davis wanted administrators "to have vision and be professionally tops." He thus offered opportunities for training and professional growth which local administrators would not otherwise have had. Personnel were sent to conventions. Consultants were brought in. An administrator recalled: "There was a feeling of being an administrative team, with the focus always on student learning, teaching kids."

The board of education was part of the planning and implementation of the management system. Board members attended many workshops and study sessions, both at home and in various parts of the country, to assure a comprehensive understanding of the new administrative process as well as the immediate and long-range impact of implementation. Policies and directives of the board thus reflected a high level of commitment to the ultimate installation and operation of management-by-objectives. Community awareness of the changes in the management of the school district was fostered by the District Accountability Advisory Committee.

Each school in the district had an elected Parent Advisory Committee (PAC) which worked with the school on matters of policy and school-community relations. A state-required District Accountability Advisory Committee (DAAC) advised the school board regarding district goals and quality of programs. The DAAC consisted of two representatives elected from each of the PACs, along with four high school students and several central administrators. Members of the DAAC attended in-district workshops similar to those presented to the board of education so as to assure understanding of the new management process. The board asked members of the DAAC to receive information from, and provide feedback to, their constituents on six major areas:

1. Assessment of the needs of the district
2. Appraisal of goals
3. Appraisal of goal-oriented student achievement
4. Appraisal of co-curricular concerns
5. Appraisal of district policies and practices
6. Appraisal of resource needs

Implementation of the management system was expected to take place in defined stages over a period of years, beginning first with the superintendent and his cabinet (assistant superintendents), then moving to central office directors, then to principals, and finally to teachers and classified employees. The plan called for no application of performance-based compensation (merit pay) until all groups were comfortable with the overall process. The superintendent established a separate division within the central office to spearhead the MBO implementation. Named the division of management services, it brought together personnel with expertise in systems planning, evaluation and organizational development. As each division, department or school in the district became competent with a given aspect of the system, the management division shifted from the role of initiator to a role of support and maintenance.

Resource allocation was tied to MBO through the building-level master plans that were developed each year by the principal and staff in each building. Individual, departmental, and building objectives were set for the coming year in the areas of student achievement, student citizenship, organizational health, and resource management. Such objectives became "predictions" of expected performance. Just as the entire staff had been involved in developing the building master plan, all staff members were expected to be committed to it. After all schools in the district had completed their master plans, tentative goals were set by the board. Resources were allocated on the basis of these priorities.

"We tell the principals, 'If you want your resource allocations, we're going to have to see your master plan'," Dr. Davis explained to a visiting researcher. "And I'm convinced that if I had to do it all over again, I'd start with the building master plan. If people are really involved in goal setting, their achievement can be just out of this world."

STAFF COMMITTEES ORGANIZED ON LINKING PIN PRINCIPLE

The teacher input used in creating each building's master plan was solicited through the Faculty Advisory Committee (FAC) at each school. The FAC was elected by the teachers and consisted of one member for every ten teachers. The FACs—which ranged from two or three members to as many as fourteen, depending on the size of the school—worked with the principal and met regularly once or twice a month to perform a liaison function with the rest of the staff. The FAC and the principal planned the agenda for the staff meetings, which were held at least monthly.

District-level direction of curriculum was thorough and systematic. Whereas under the previous administration there had been separate assistant superintendents in charge of curriculum for the elementary and secondary levels, curriculum was now integrated on a K–12 basis. Subject area specialists were appointed to coordinate curriculum in specific areas. In order to insure articulation, each of these coordinators had K–12 responsibilities. Each of ten subject areas—art, language arts, mathematics, music, physical education, reading, science, social science, special education, and vocational education—had a Standing Subject Area Committee (SSAC) which included one representative from every school, as well as representatives from the central curriculum department and citizen representatives from the DAAC.

These standing committees provided "program and instructional objective construction, objective validation, basic text adoption, program review and/or modification, curriculum scope and sequence recommendations, and improvement of teaching strategies." They also acted as the liaison between individual buildings and the central office. Standing committees met once a month, after school, and generated instructional objectives for the district. These objectives were then sent out to the teaching staff for validation. Seventy percent of the teaching staff had to validate each objective or the objective was not acceptable. The District Curriculum Coordinating Team (DCCT), made up of one representative from each SSAC as well as central office representatives, reviewed and made recommendations on districtwide curriculum planning, new developments, revision, and improvement.

Structurally, the communication and decision-making organization which evolved under Superintendent Davis was based on a linking pin principle (Likert 1967) where committee membership often consisted of representatives from other committees and thus provided a basis for the systematic linking of information and decisions at different levels of the system. A Suburbia High social studies teacher described the greater feeling of openness which resulted when Dr. Davis began to encourage teachers and administrators to meet together. Opening up the process also created avenues for the superintendent to get needed information about how teachers "on the front line" were affected by the reforms that were being put in place.

THEMES USED IN SETTING OBJECTIVES

Superintendent Davis believed strongly in the personnel selection and management system developed by Selection Research, Inc. (SRI). A key part of this system was the setting of objectives based on one or more of twelve "themes" that were thought to characterize first-rate, scientific management. Sample themes for school administrators were:

"Relator"—a manager who both desired to and did have strategies to build relationships with the staff. Such a person expressed feelings and thoughts openly and encouraged others to do likewise.

"Delegator"—extended responsibility to associates, knowing each teacher's strengths and interests and delegated appropriately so that each teacher grew professionally and was successful.

"Ambiguity tolerance"—a characteristic which was present when the manager displayed a tendency to suspend judgment until as much evidence as possible was available, a quality assumed to restrain impulsive decision-making.

Other themes included "catalyzer," "arranger," and "group enhancer." These themes were used in two ways: (1) as the basis for highly structured interviews given all teachers and administrators before they were hired and; (2) in setting up the management agreements all principals were required to sign. In the hiring process Dr. Davis used a 72-question interview that he believed was very useful in identifying successful teachers and administrators. The goal of the interview was to show how highly developed the various "themes" were in each interviewee. "I felt when the teacher shortage ended that we needed something better than a calculated guess as to who would make a superior teacher," Davis was quoted as saying (*City Observer*, 26 August 1976).

Themes for teachers differed from those for administrators. The list for teachers included such themes as "empathy," defined as "the apprehension of the state of mind of another person," and "investment," defined as "the teacher's capacity to receive satisfaction from the growth of students." Both the teacher and the administrator lists included the theme "mission" but it was defined differently. For teachers it was "a deep-lying belief that students can grow and attain self-actualization," whereas for administrators it was "one's personal commitment in terms of making an affirmative impact upon the lives of others." However, each principal was required to promise: "In order to gather information from the faculty about my performance as a principal. . . . I will design or select and administer an opinionnaire to all . . . certificated staff members." Findings from this survey were to be reported both to his staff and to the superior assigned as his "monitor." A personal "growth plan" would be developed from the results.

On 26 September 1976 the *City Observer* carried an article describing Superintendent Davis' application of Management-by-Objectives, grounded in the list of themes applicable to administrators, to himself. He had just signed a management agreement which committed him, among other things, to improve by 10 percent his "ambiguity tolerance" in dealing with subordinates. He would be allowed a leeway of plus or minus 2 percent on the 10 percent improvement objective. Later in the year his subordinates would tell Davis, via his scores on anonymous questionnaires, whether he had passed or flunked. How did he know that he needed to improve in these respects? That's what they had told him on similar questionnaires the year before.

The same *Observer* article noted that in 1975 Cottonwood had been one of a dozen school districts in the nation picked by the U.S. Office of Education as leaders in performance-based management systems. In 1976 the district was one of sixteen school systems in the nation whose reading programs had been selected for nationwide dissemination by the federal agency. In 1978 Cottonwood's Management-by-Objectives approach was singled out for special recognition. An independent research firm had studied over 200 school districts in the United States and Canada and selected Cottonwood as having one of the three top working models of organizational development.

Predictable Learner Mastery

A curriculum master plan was first developed in 1975 to provide direction for present and future "learner mastery" programs. Under the direction of Dr. Davis the district moved toward a Predictable Learner Mastery System which was based on the idea that a majority of students can "master" the subject matter covered in any given class. In 1976 the district implemented its own program criterion-referenced tests aimed at measuring more precisely the degree of students' achievements in relation to the district's instructional objectives. Each year the district used these tests to measure how well students were mastering the district's instructional objectives. Ten educational objectives, which established specific goals for learning, were defined as district priorities for 1978–82. The goal was to have 80 percent of the students master 80 percent of the objectives.

When Dr. Davis started the mastery learning program, he did not have a detailed plan formulated. His idea was to define the constellation of things needed to support the learning process. As instructional programs were refined, the district turned to mastery learning techniques as a means to increase student achievement levels. Only in 1980 were all elements of the objectives-based approach and the use of mastery learning adopted as district policy, by action of the board of education. Predictable Learner Mastery (PLM) was defined as "the process of supplementing regular group instruction with diagnostic procedures and prescriptive methods and materials in such a way as to bring most pupils to a predicted standard of success, and which emphasizes altering and providing the time different individuals need for attaining the predicted standard."

The Cottonwood program incorporated both locally developed processes and generally accepted elements of mastery learning (Bloom 1981). A former curriculum specialist recalled:

We "Benjamin Bloomed" everything. I don't know whether you remember that era when objectives were the thing. We were all trained in writing objectives. In fact, I've had a number of courses from various universities on instructional objectives, goal setting, that sort of thing. So the district ended up, in every discipline, with an entire objective-based curriculum. Teachers wrote it. We wrote in that 86% of teachers had to support an objective or it was revised or deleted. That became our curriculum.

One effect of the introduction of mastery learning was to call into question the long-standing assumption that "tracking" students was a natural reaction to their inherent differences in ability. In a phone interview in the spring of 1992, Dr. Davis explained that he had long felt strongly that "tracking was simply a matter of convenience for teachers and that ending tracking could improve education for all kids without hurting the brighter kids."

The institution of the PLM system and the continued monitoring of performance at all levels in the district were successful in raising student achievement scores. Gains in student reading and mathematics achievement scores on district tests were significant and consistent between 1975 and 1982. As gains occurred, the district increased its expectations of students and refined staff performance standards upwards to reflect these expectations. Very high test results were produced by the PLM system, resulting in increased recognition for the district, both nationally and internationally. A principal recalled: "There was a pride people felt to be working with Cottonwood, a feeling that we were graduating kids with a higher-quality education than they could have gotten nearly anywhere else."

ACHIEVEMENT, GROWTH, AND CHANGE

Meanwhile, population growth within the Cottonwood School District had continued at a high rate. The table below summarizes the growth that occurred, just in the city of Metroville, during the early 1970s:

Year	Metroville Population
1970	13,326
1971	15,000
1972	18,500
1973	23,000
1974	26,500
1975	29,000

By the fall of 1980 the Cottonwood district had thirty schools, nearly 19,000 students, over 2,000 employees, and a general fund budget of $37.8 million. A bond issue for $29 million had been passed in 1974 for construction of two junior high schools and five elementaries; as well as the remodeling of Suburbia High and two junior high schools. In 1976 the central district administrative offices were moved into a new administration center.

Vocational training also received much greater emphasis during the Davis administration. Trade and industrial programs had been begun at Suburbia and Metroville high schools, with four trades offered: auto mechanics, drafting, carpentry, and electronics. When the new Voc-Tech Center opened in 1974, auto body, welding, commercial art, printing, and industrial cooperative education were added to the vocational curriculum. In 1975, both for ease of administration and to counteract a growing tendency to pigeonhole Metro High as "the vocational school," the district's vocational center became a separate school. Masonry and house-wiring were added to the curriculum. By 1980 the Voc-Tech Center's eleven programs served some 750 students daily.

Despite Dr. Davis' emphasis on building formalized, hierarchical relationships between teachers and administrators, cultural remnants of the district's rural past survived. The informal, jocular attitude still prevalent among many staff members was exemplified by an incident that took place the day a new junior high opened. Tied to the door leading to the main office, munching on a bale of hay, was the goat that was to become the school's unofficial mascot—with a note which said "Happy first day! Good Luck!" No one knew who had delivered the goat to school. Only years later was it revealed that one of the counselors, whose husband was attending veterinary school, had come up with this innovative idea for livening up the first day of school.

The Legacy of Dr. Davis

Superintendent Davis is remembered for his directness, for letting everyone know very clearly where they stood. Davis also tended to keep staffers, from the assistant superintendent level on down, somewhat at a distance. When he met with large numbers of employees, there was little interaction. Many were intimidated by his presence. If someone did tell a joke in the back row and there were momentary chuckles, the superintendent would seem nonplussed. Yet some administrators recalled Dr. Davis telling great jokes and stories after meetings, when everyone was relaxed. Davis also became famous for his "coffee calls." When he heard about something within the district about which he had questions, he would call the employee concerned and say "I'll meet you at the Sears Coffee Shop." They would then meet and discuss the situation, one on one.

Long-time district employees agreed that Superintendent Davis tended to keep the staff "working at a high frustration level," believing that the challenge presented by a large workload increased productivity. Several administrators insisted that, although demands put on staff members had been great, those had been productive years. Aggressive curriculum mapping was done. Teachers were asked to map out the school day in fifteen-minute increments. The objective was to see what teachers were really doing, a technique which a former principal remembered as having initiated some interesting dialogues among the teaching staff.

Superintendent Davis' multifaceted approach to school improvement—encompassing management-by-objectives, intensive in-service training, and a comprehensive program of mastery learning—paid off in a dramatic improvement of student scores. In 1976 only 48 percent of students in grades three through eight had been able to demonstrate mastery of the district's minimum learning objectives for mathematics; 49 percent mastered the reading objectives. By 1982, 75 percent of the students demonstrated mastery of the minimum learning objectives. Gains were also demonstrated on national standardized tests. Feeling that his goals for the Cottonwood School District had been met, Dr. Davis decided to retire. His staff took a collection and bought him a handsome new saddle and tack as a going-away present.

OTHER VIEWS OF THE DAVIS ERA

The social-efficiency point of view, which provided the basis for the restructuring done during the Davis era, had the goal of decreasing risk and increasing certainty by specifying minutely described goals for both administration and teaching. In chapter 1, two unintended outcomes known to plague bureaucratic organizations were mentioned: (1) goal displacement, which happens when attention to formalized, impersonal procedures (such as checking off basic skills tested) become more important than accomplishment of the overall purpose (giving students a good education); (2) conflict between the pressure on the employee to follow procedures (such as giving criterion-referenced tests) and the client's (students' and parents') demand for personal, individualized attention. To what extent were these problems in evidence in Cottonwood during the Davis superintendency?

Respondents who were knowledgeable about conditions in the Cottonwood district under Dr. Davis differed sharply in their views. A university professor who had worked with many Cottonwood teachers offered his perception of the overall impact of management-by-objectives and criterion-referenced tests:

> The regimentation of the back to the basics movement just stopped all the exciting stuff Cottonwood had been doing. There were uniform teaching strategies, objectives like something Madeline Hunter would have done, close supervision of teachers. But it's something that happened all over the nation.

On the other hand, a number of veteran Cottonwood administrators looked back at the Davis era with fondness. They remembered the feeling of camaraderie among the administrative staff, the feeling of being in control, of having their fingers on the pulse of their schools. A principal recalled the curriculum writing process:

> It was a great time. I absolutely loved what I was doing. I enjoyed the discussions of what curriculum should be, how it should be developed. It was very exciting and we got a lot of opportunities for personal growth. They did not hesitate to bring in the top names in the country as consultants and so you became . . . friends, and really enjoyed the process. I thought it was part of something that was really valuable.

Yet these veteran administrators also admitted that teacher perceptions of the restructuring efforts undertaken by Superintendent Bill Davis tended to differ from their own. Elimination of criterion-referenced testing was described by several respondents as a teacher victory. An administrator described the chain of events:

> While we were implementing various phases of the curriculum, there were uprisings coming from various faculties because, at the same time we were introducing these curriculum changes we were also introducing the teaching-learning model. It was *the* staff development model. We would go into

the schools, sometimes not at their request, sometimes at the request of the principal but not of the teachers, and they would be subjected to a series of courses of instruction on Madeline Hunter or what have you.

So there was sort of a groundswell of resistance. They became more and more critical of the objectives-based curriculum. There were "too many objectives." Then, when we got to criterion referenced testing, where the kids were accountable—and the teachers—it really became a threat and a challenge. So those people who did not agree with the philosophy in the first place became quite vocal, and eventually this resistance was pretty well organized. They did not want to do this any longer. About that time Bill decided to retire.

A member of the Western State Language Arts Society took a different view, recalling the atmosphere when the criterion-referenced tests had first been adopted:

In the mid-70s people became fearful; everyone was counting things. The accountability movement was characterized by that word in the middle, "count." One could not write an objective where student behavior was not immediately observable. Words like "appreciate" and "understand" could not be used in writing objectives. Now there were several English teachers in Cottonwood who fought that movement. The Western State Language Arts Society fought it and several Cottonwood teachers were in the forefront. They lost, in the state and in their district.

An administrator admitted that Dr. Davis had believed in strong centralized leadership, foregoing consultation with staff members who might have reservations:

Bill was a strong leader who believed that if you had 50% of the people with you, go for it. Now, with the consensus model, I think it's closer to 85 or 87%, if you're lucky enough to have that point reached for consensus. But his philosophy was that if you had half the people behind you, do it! So that's how we operated, from central administration out. We would go out and meet with the various faculties, share the direction the district was going, enlist their support, hire them to do the work of writing the curriculum and stuff.

A professor who had supervised student teachers in Cotton-wood during both the Larimer and the Davis administrations recalled the effect the test-driven curriculum implemented by Dr. Davis had on teachers:

> In Cottonwood it was absolutely destructive. They had some wonderful things going on. They were anticipating the writing process, even though the writing process was not widely published at that time. Their curriculum specialist would send copies of articles to the teachers. Not only were the teachers being encouraged to do things, but they were seeing the original research. So they were clamoring for this sort of research. They knew about it before a lot of scholars knew about it. You can imagine, with that sort of thing going on, and then teachers suddenly being told "You must conform!" when they were told earlier "You must be different, and we love you for it!"

Student attitudes toward the criterion-referenced tests can only be known indirectly, through recollections of teachers and of local citizens who attended the Cottonwood schools during the 1970s. "The kids enjoyed the criterion-referenced tests about as much as I enjoy doing my income tax," an elementary teacher shrugged. "Let's just say it didn't do wonders for their attitudes toward school." A beginning teacher who had been student in the district during the Davis era described her own experience:

> I'd read out loud without an problem, but with little comprehension. I read without taking it in. School was fun. I enjoyed it. I had an excellent memory so I excelled in school. I was an all "A" student. But I never really liked to write or to read until after I'd become a second-grade teacher and encountered whole language through the district curriculum specialist. Now I love it. I don't remember any authors' names from elementary school. Everything was basals. Now I use literature with my students and emphasize the authors. I tell them they are authors.

Another teacher, who had been on the committee involved in writing the criterion-referenced tests, expressed skepticism about how meaningful the test results were:

> Of course, those of us on the committee always set objectives that we knew we could easily meet. We wrote questions for

the criterion-referenced tests that we knew our students would be able to answer. If you knew where the teachers writing the tests were coming from, you knew that having an impressive percentage of students pass the tests was pretty much a given. That was a rather different version of "predictable learner mastery" than the district was selling to the public, but we felt that our jobs might be at stake.

An observer who had been away from the district for a number of years and had returned when the Davis era was well under way speculated about the overall impact of the Davis-era reforms:

> What I saw was that there was a different population in the schools. At first I attributed that to curriculum. Kids were lethargic. They didn't volunteer much. They were sometimes unwilling participants in the educational enterprise. Teaching seemed a lot less fun. It may have been changing student profile.
>
> What I do know now is that the student profile in the district is vastly different than in 1968. What was upper middle class, upwardly mobile, now is a very mixed community.

A veteran secondary teacher shared the view that the impact of criterion-referenced testing ought not to be over emphasized, asserting that the test-driven curriculum had less effect at the high school level:

> All I remember about Davis was the CRTs: criterion-referenced tests. He favored outcome-based education, which seems to be resurfacing. Of course that collapsed during his tenure. It was unmanageable. The assessment scheme was well articulated, but people didn't give a blink. Teachers just set the stuff aside and never got to it.
>
> The whole thing had been initiated from the top, with no shared-ness. Confusion resulted. It was dropped during Davis' tenure. Of course I have no way of knowing for sure, but I had the feeling that it might have contributed to his leaving . . . or his retirement.

The view of a longtime Cottonwood community activist, whose children had attended the Cottonwood schools during the Davis tenure, was somewhat harsher:

The Cottonwood District was used by Dr. Davis as a guinea pig to try out his ideas. Then he went on to greener pastures, selling what he had developed here—something we could hardly wait to get rid of.

A former curriculum specialist during the Davis era gave an insider's view of why criterion-referenced testing was abandoned:

I have a feeling that a lot of teachers started out trying to do it [the criterion-referenced tests] appropriately, found it very difficult, got frustrated, and said "Oh, to hell with it!" you know. The process was never fully implemented. I think as long as a group of people have resistance to an idea or an activity they're going to find a way to subvert it, and I think that is exactly what happened here. They just didn't follow through. . . . There were three years, maybe, where the process was effective and people were into it to a greater degree. But then, at about the end of three years, it was central ad's decision not to pursue it any further and to shift to a school-based plan.

COTTONWOOD IN THE 1970s

One factor in switching to a school-based plan may have been the increased demographic diversity of the Cottonwood district. During the 1970s, more expensive homes were being built in outlying areas even as, near Foothills City, a less privileged population was moving in. The changed demographics in the most urbanized parts of the district were exemplified by the fast growth of the city of Buffalo Mesa.

The City of Buffalo Mesa: Dealing with a More Diverse Population

The municipality of Buffalo Mesa is located on a low, rocky outcropping. Buffalo Mesa also has an unusual population profile: approximately one-third of the residents are senior citizens, one-fourth are young adults, one-fourth are young families. Only one-sixth are middle-age families. Most of the housing units within this 1.775 square mile area are mobile homes and apartments. As an incorporated town, Buffalo Mesa is older than either Metroville or Suburbia. In 1940 a group of local citizens, who had joined together to find a way to obtain a better water supply, incorporated the town. A mayor was elected and a new well was dug. In 1949 an army surplus building, 20 by 50 feet, was purchased for $745. After several weeks of volunteer labor, and the use of donated materials, Buffalo Mesa held the first meeting in its new town hall on 7 February 1950.

During the 1950s more people moved into the area, but at a far slower rate than was happening in Metroville. A second well was dug. By 1957 the population had reached 512. There were 77 mobile homes in town. The town's first annexation was 280 acres of land called the "Monticello Heights." During the next few years more wells were dug, more land annexed, and more mobile homes moved in. By 1970 the population of Buffalo Mesa had grown to 1,502. Large mobile home parks were being established, but there were not yet enough local residents to warrant building a separate school. However, growth showed a sharp upward trend. In 1972, the population of Buffalo Mesa reached 4,500. By 1974 the estimated population was 12,000. Representatives of the Cottonwood School District began talking with the Buffalo Mesa Council about the construction of an elementary school.

Buffalo Mesa Elementary was built at a time when it was widely believed that the mobile home parks it served would be temporary. The owners of the land upon which the mobile home parks sat had indicated that they intended to eventually convert the area to an industrial park. Therefore, the original open space school built on this site was designed so that it could be converted to other uses if the school's clientele should move away. In fact, the mobile home parks have stayed and a new, more conventional, school was built after a fire devastated the original building. Yet the student turnover rate at the Buffalo Mesa school continued to be greater than elsewhere in the district, creating unique challenges for the school staff.

At Buffalo Mesa Elementary, the Davis-era ideal of adopting a uniform curriculum which could be implemented in all schools proved to be out of reach. Many Buffalo Mesa students arrived at school with very different life experiences than Suburbia students. Site-based curriculum policies were instituted as a matter of necessity. A staff member pointed out that many Buffalo Mesa kindergarteners came to school with verbal skills that lagged two years behind the language skills of kindergartners in the outer suburbs, explaining:

> They're developmentally delayed, and it is impossible for us
> to catch them up. By fifth grade they're still sometimes two

years behind in performance. We accept that as normal here. Two years below grade level is sort of the standard before you even make a referral to special ed. And yet we staff over a hundred children out of a population of 604 kids [into special education]. So that's a really high percentage, if you're familiar with elementary staffing patterns.

The effect of such a disparities among schools on the district as a whole becomes clear when it is remembered that, under the Predictable Learner Mastery system put in place by Dr. Davis, it was assumed that—if basic skills are carefully broken down into small enough pieces—all children will be able to learn all skills taught at each grade level. For teachers to disregard the district's minutely detailed objectives for each student at grade level—either on a whole-school basis, as at Buffalo Mesa, or on an individual basis, as a large number of Cottonwood's secondary-level teachers were rumored to do—undermined the integrity of the Predictable Learner Mastery approach. Such experiences caused ever greater numbers of Cottonwood personnel to openly question the social efficiency philosophy underlying the test-driven curriculum advocated by Dr. Davis.

Do We Emphasize Liberty! Equality! Fraternity!

Although the values conflict which arose in Cottonwood has thus far been described in terms of the "social-efficiency," "humanist," "developmental," and "social meliorist" philosophies, during interviews those Cottonwood personnel who had been participants in the debate used less scholarly terms to describe the underlying issues. To be true to their spontaneous description of the values conflict, it is necessary to adopt terms that more closely reflect those used by Cottonwood personnel. What conceptual framework underlay their discussion of issues such as "having the freedom to adjust your teaching to the needs of your students," "having some assurance that students in all our schools get an equally good education," or "having a voice in the decisions that directly impact you"?

People who had been on different sides in the Davis-era curriculum debate, appeared to be informally expressing one or another of the ideals embodied in the motto of the French Revolution: "Liberty! Equality! Fraternity!" So often have these three ideals been mentioned together that their incommensurability, the natural tension which exists among them, is readily ignored. Yet, although few Americans would argue against any of these ideals in the abstract, our society is far from reaching a consensus on what to do, on a practical level, about the conflicts that routinely arise when one of these ideals is pursued to the exclusion of the others. Our law courts and our schools continually struggle with such questions as:

> What limits must be put upon the liberty of individuals in order to insure that the rights of other individuals are not infringed upon?
>
> How do we simultaneously honor the fact of human difference and guarantee equality of opportunity?
>
> How do we foster individual excellence and expertise within a democratic environment where individuals of average talents will necessarily predominate?

As in the larger society, the compromises that are worked out within school districts often contain inconsistencies. For example, the Larimer era in Cottonwood had been one of considerable individual liberty. But the emphasis on having freedom to build on the individual strengths of teachers and students existed in a constant state of tension with contrasting elements, such as the academic tracking of students, which were little questioned in the United States at that time. Thus, although Superintendent Larimer emphasized allowing each student to reach his or her full potential, district resources were more often spent on adding new and exciting (advanced) courses than on investigating ways to lift the achievement of students who were performing below grade level. In the world view of the Larimer era, it was the student's responsibility to come in for extra help, if needed.

Bill Davis, in contrast, emphasized equality of outcomes, at least at the elementary level.[1] Dr. Davis cited Bloom's argument that all children can learn; that children vary only in how long it takes them to learn. Curriculum committees were directed to break down the curriculum to be taught into basic skills and behavioral objectives that each teacher could use with every student. Under Davis' system of Predictable Learner Mastery, children were considered to be the raw material of the educational system. Schools were held responsible for producing roughly equal outcomes through using scientific teaching methods to process this human raw material. Yet the assumption that the educational system could "process" all students in such as way as to bring them up to a certain academic standard was, in its turn, called into question as the student population of Cottonwood became more diverse.

When the Davis-era reforms did not produce the results promised, disgruntled advocates of greater academic freedom asked: If the benefits to the low-achieving student were not what had been promised, did that not add urgency to the argument that the objectives-driven curriculum unnecessarily limited academic liberty, emphasizing conformity and eventually leading to mediocrity? How do you teach a child who is thoroughly bored by the material and has long since stopped listening? Given the questionable results, why should the time-consuming and energy-intensive system of criterion-referenced testing be continued? To this, some of those who took such questions seriously (and assumed that a return to academic tracking is not an acceptable alternative), added further questions:

- Was there a third choice that did not lead to either meritocracy or mediocrity?
- Could a system be devised which treated individuals equally, yet did not treat them as mere interchangeable units?
- Could such a system be structured so that many voices were heard, yet the discussion was channeled toward consensus and not allowed to degenerate into a mere battle of words or of wills?

In attempting to provide answers to such questions, Cottonwood's next superintendent, Dave Roberts, put in place a system of shared decision-making that emphasized the third element of the famous motto: Fraternity. Aware of the discontent of teachers and parents who missed the *esprit*—the sense of shared achievement—that had marked the district's early years, Dr. Roberts sought to foster a renewed sense of community. He cultivated a feeling of mutual confidence: a sense of trust that parents, teachers, administrators—as well as the pupils themselves—were deeply committed to creating the best possible learning environment. Within such a collaborative environment, "liberty" could be subtly redefined. No longer "freedom from constraint," liberty was then understood to mean a shared freedom, which implicitly carried with it the responsibility to make use of one's individual liberty in such a way that one's actions benefited others, not just oneself.

Differences in roles were recognized. Voice, not formal equality, was mandated through consensus-building. Yet the goal of the decision-making process was agreement upon on a course of action that would be in the best interests of all. The road to such collaboration was not a smooth one, however. Since Cottonwood was one of the first school districts in the nation to adopt such an approach districtwide, there were few models to follow. Despite the intuitive attractiveness of the ideal of "fraternity" (or "community"), it is only recently that serious attempts have been made to build this ideal into hierarchical administrative systems. However, elements of this "community-based" philosophy can be seen, at least in rhetorical form, in both the developmental and the social-meliorist philosophies described by Kliebard.

The developmentalist curriculum approaches the spirit of "fraternity" through its conception of the school as a community of learners. An assumption is made that, if the child's capacity for feeling and imagination are fostered, a sense of wonder and discovery will be brought into school lessons, causing the child to see learning as meaningful and valuable, instead of meaningless and tedious. As will be discussed in chapter 5, the new curriculum framework that the Cottonwood district developed under Dr. Roberts incorporated many elements of the developmental curriculum. Shared decision-making, which attempted to nurture a sense of partnership and mutual support between home and school, was also intimately connected to the ideal of the learning community.

The social-meliorist curriculum, with its strong emphasis on using the schools as tools for social intervention, was also in evidence during the Roberts tenure, but to a lesser extent. Social-meliorist concerns were addressed primarily through opening preschool and afterschool programs in elementary schools that served low-income neighborhoods through instituting school-based social service programs. Often these programs were dependent on "soft money" from outside sources, with no guarantee that these funds would not dry up when the priorities of other governmental agencies changed. The Cottonwood school board, which continued to be dominated by members of the business community, remained unconvinced of the efficacy of such programs and showed little inclination to put district money into them. Indeed, this proved to be one of the few points on which the board proved impervious to arguments offered by the charismatic Dr. Roberts.

The intransigence of the Cottonwood school board on this point reflected a widespread uncertainty among those who held political power in the local area concerning how the schools could best serve Cottonwood's increasingly diverse population. By the time Dr. Roberts took over, Cottonwood had come to serve a significantly less homogeneous student population than it had during the Larimer era. These changes were accelerated when, just as Superintendent Davis retired, the regional economy went from "boom" to "bust." The economic downturn deeply affected the budgetary outlook for school districts across Western State, while also triggering dramatic demographic changes in the Cottonwood School District.

WESTERN STATE COPES WITH ECONOMIC CHALLENGES

Through the 1950s, 1960s, and 1970s, the local economy was booming, seemingly with no end in sight. However the energy industry, upon which much of this prosperity was based, ran into hard times in the early 1980s. Immigration into Western State slowed abruptly, plummeting from 41,000 in 1983 to 7,000 in 1984. Construction and a wide range of service industries were hard hit. Western State remained in the grip of an economic recession through most of the 1980s.

The 1990 census showed nearly 18 percent of Western State children under the age of five to be living in poverty, compared with 13.6 percent in 1980. Median household income, when adjusted for inflation, fell slightly, from $30,262 in 1980 to $30,140 in 1990 as some of Western State's higher-paying jobs went elsewhere. Broader social changes also affected the public schools. For the first time, the 1990 census showed that a majority—63.2 percent—of Western State women with pre-school-aged children were in the labor force. This figure contrasted sharply with 1980, when only 46.4 percent of women with children under six were working. Western State's farm population dropped 23.7 percent between 1980 and 1990, with 14,034 people moving off of farms, while the percentage of Western State residents living in cities grew to 82.4 percent.

At the same time, Western State experienced strong job growth in key segments of the economy, for example among technicians and related support occupations, as well as in the managerial fields. The technician group grew by nearly 41 percent over the decade, while the number of executives and managers grew by 37.4 percent. On the other hand, the number of highly skilled blue-collar workers dipped 11.4 percent over the ten years, with a loss of 20,600 jobs in the precision production, craft and repair occupations. Construction employment also dropped by 11.4 percent during the 1980s. The pressure put on government resources by the recession could be seen in the fact that, although the number of private wage and salary workers grew by nearly 22 percent over the decade, growth in the number of government workers rose by a more modest 9.2 percent.

Information collected in 1978 showed that the Cottonwood district at that time described its community as 10% upper middle class, 40% middle class, 40% working class (blue collar), and 10% working class (semi and unskilled). The reduction in the number of highly skilled blue-collar jobs had a devastating economic effect on working-class families in the older part of Metroville. In the early 1980s large numbers of single-family houses were sold at bargain prices when their owners were forced to move elsewhere in search of work. Many of these houses were eventually turned into rental properties. Managers of apartment complexes, who found themselves unable to fill their buildings with working-class tenants, became more willing to rent to families on public assistance, relying on government rent guarantees. This meant that, by the late 1980s, those Metroville elementary schools located closest to Foothills City found themselves serving a markedly different student population from the homogeneous working-class population they had served during the 1970s.

Weak Local Economy Creates Ripple Effect

Like all tax-supported institutions, public school districts benefit when the economy is healthy. When the economy is booming, the amount the state collects in income tax goes up; sales tax revenues go up; school districts also receive more income through property taxes because a booming economy causes property values to rise. Conversely, when economic times are hard, the amount of tax support available to public institutions goes down. Thus, just as local economic growth had been important in helping Cottonwood to expand and build more schools, the economic downturn Western State experienced during the 1980s forced the school district to cut back in its expenditures.

In the four years between 1985 and 1989 the local recession caused property values in nearby Foothills City to drop an average of 10 percent. Property taxes collected for the support of schools fell. Suburbs and districts such as Cottonwood suffered a similar fate. Nor were the schools the only tax-supported entity to suffer. We have discussed how important possessing sufficient water is to a municipality's ability to provide essential services. A healthy local economy is also of key importance, as is attested to by this document published by the Suburbia Urban Renewal Authority:

Suburbia, a planned suburban community, was incorporated in 1969. The downtown area including the Suburbia Mall and a variety of business, commercial, office and high density residential enterprises was established in the 1960s and the 1970s. This regional mixed-use commercial center served consumer needs of the local community and a regional trade area generating sales taxes that, at their peak, provided approximately 67 percent of Suburbia's public revenues. Due to a variety of factors, including financial, commercial, and changes in consumer purchasing habits, Suburbia's downtown area began to decline in the early 1980's. Since 1986, Suburbia experienced annual decreases in sales tax and property tax revenues accompanied by deteriorating conditions in both public and private facilities.

"It's like a ghost town up there!," a community member commented in the spring of 1992, referring to the Suburbia Mall. "For the merchants it's been real hard times." Two of the mall's four anchor department stores had closed. The problems faced by Suburbia Mall were similar to those faced by several other suburban shopping malls in the metropolitan area. Upon opening, they had been considered prototypical showcases. But they had since lost business to newer, trendier malls. Most had watched key anchor stores pull up stakes and leave during the 1980s. A spokesman for a large suburban mall said the situation had become "quite a headache since our large department store moved out. Sales have declined significantly, and the future is very uncertain. It really hurt. You know what they say: 'When a major anchor leaves, a shopping mall goes dark'."

Some experts insisted that the real problem was that the metropolitan area was now "overstored," that it had been inundated with retail outlets, strip centers, shopping malls, and specialty shopping areas over the last twenty years. National statistics collected by the International Council of Shopping Centers showed that Western State enjoyed more shopping space per customer than most states, with 26.2 square feet per person, compared with a national average of 18.2 feet per person. The metropolitan retailing picture "is maxed out," an expert asserted. This had become a special problem in the Cottonwood area since, during the era of intense competition between Metroville and Suburbia, Metroville had built two shopping malls of its own, one very close to the Suburbia Mall.

"These older malls must find a raison d'être," insisted a Foothills City retailing analyst. "In a way, those generational malls are like computers and video games. If they haven't upgraded, they've become obsolete."

In 1987 the Suburbia Mall had been purchased from its original owner by Suburbia Mall Associates, an out-of-state partnership with plans to renovate the mall. A renovation plan had been developed which included the four anchor stores. But, within eighteen months, two of these anchor stores had vacated Suburbia Mall. Loss of two major anchors added to the regional economic recession, and the proliferation of shopping centers within Suburbia's regional trade area added momentum to Suburbia's downward economic slide.

SCHOOLS STRUGGLE WITH PROBLEMS NOT OF THEIR MAKING

Demographic changes and economic challenges were among the numerous external factors that influenced the Cottonwood district's shift from a highly centralized system of school governance to a shared decision-making model. Several community respondents commented that they found it "ironic" that the school district had made a significant move in the direction of consensus-building just as the population it served was becoming more diverse. Social stresses associated with the economic downturn had made reaching consensus on major issues more difficult. Many Cottonwood staff members, on the other hand, perceived the move to shared decision-making in terms cause-and-effect. As one teacher noted, "Some process had to be found to bring people into a better understanding of one another's views."

In retrospect, management-by-objectives appeared to have worked best in a relatively stable environment where detailed directives about how to carry out certain school functions were not rendered out-of-date within weeks, as a result of new budgetary restrictions handed down from the state legislature, intense political agitation by parent groups, or gang-related incidents that had to be responded to. As the social environment in which the school district was embedded became more volatile, more flexible management practices became increasingly necessary. However, along with increased flexibility came a different relationship between staff members at the school district headquarters and those out in the schools.

Bill Davis had defined success in terms of test scores and the budgetary bottom line. His management-by-objectives approach was set up to allow him to keep his finger on the pulse of the district. Subordinates were put in a defensive posture, knowing that the superintendent could, at any moment, look up the goals a particular principal or district-level manager had set and quiz that person on the progress being made. The objectives-based curriculum, enforced by criterion-referenced tests, allowed elementary school principals to do much the same thing with teachers. A hard-nosed manager, Davis felt that he got more out of his staff if he kept them working at a high frustration level. The school board saw him an effective manager.

Over time, however, the frustration of many teachers—and the resentment of parents who felt deprived, through Davis' centralized approach, of influence over what happened at their neighborhood schools—gradually shaded over into opposition. Although only the boldest teachers openly verbalized their feelings, passive resistance to "the system" became widespread. Yet it would be inaccurate to give the impression that this resistance led to a complete reversal of the Davis-era reforms. Bill Davis' emphasis on setting long-term goals stands as his legacy within the Cottonwood district. Under his successor, goal-setting has been done in a more collaborative manner, yet the practice of setting specific goals and evaluating the progress made in meeting them has remained a strong tradition in the Cottonwood School District. Although accountability has been redefined, so that stakeholders have a greater role in setting goals at both the building and district levels, emphasis on accountability remains strong.

Metaphorically, the transformation of an earlier version of accountability to a later one in the Cottonwood district might be said to have some similarity to the geological processes that, over time, transformed the dense vegetation of a prehistoric swamp into the rich petroleum deposits which lay deep beneath the open prairies of Western State. In each case, a social or ecological system that once had flourished had withered in the face of social or climatic change. The winds of change covered the site with new layers of topsoil, upon which new kinds of flora and fauna grew. A cursory glance might easily convince one that the last remnants of what had gone before had long since been crushed out of existence by the pressure of subsequent events. Yet, when passing through Cottonwood, the alert eye catches sight of small, creaking metal pumps, spaced at odd intervals, which bring to the surface stored energy resources not apparent to the casual observer. In curriculum meetings, one can hear teachers talking about how they went about transforming the old behavioral objectives into broader measures of student learning.

NOTE

1. The emphasis that Davis put on vocational education at the high school level served, in practice, to create two very different educational tracks for high school students.

CHAPTER 5

NEW KINDS OF ACCOUNTABILITY: NEGOTIATING THE PROCESS OF REFORM

In the opinion of many of the teachers who were interviewed for this study, the social efficiency orientation of Superintendent Davis had, in fact, been strikingly "inefficient." Based on too narrow a view of human nature, they felt that the test-driven curriculum installed by Dr. Davis had removed the elements of creativity and excitement from teaching, making the school experience boring for both students and teachers. As one principal asserted:

> We'd gone from an administration that was pretty respectful of teachers [under Superintendent Larimer] to the system set up by Davis, who was pretty much a behaviorist and tried to make everything teacher-proof, all these goals and objectives, with no chance for teachers to make their own decisions.

This chapter explores how the change in administrative philosophy, from a highly centralized structure to a site-based organization utilizing shared decision-making, led to a rethinking of curriculum.

ESTABLISHING DIVISIONS OF RESPONSIBILITY: LONG-TERM GOALS

Although the school board was well satisfied with the accomplishments of the retiring superintendent, especially the prominence he had brought the district on the national level, the school board decided to hire as the new superintendent Dr. Dave Roberts, whose leadership style seemed likely to establish a more conciliatory atmosphere. In accordance with the school board's desire to ease tensions and improve communication, Dr. Roberts gave first priority to setting up a system of collaborative decision-making. Through site-based decision-making, building-level personnel were given much more flexibility in responding to the needs of the communities they served. Some decisions were still made at the central office level, with the understanding that a change of direction in any of the areas listed would only be done after collaboratively working with those impacted. These included:

1. Budget development/allocation
2. Curriculum framework/graduation requirements
3. Data processing
4. Food services
5. Maintenance/construction
6. Negotiating contracts
7. Personnel screening
8. Printing
9. Purchasing
10. School boundaries
11. Transportation

Major areas of decision making at the building level included:

1. Budget implementation
2. Hiring
3. Curriculum selection/implementation
4. Staff development

The district took responsibility for establishing a curriculum framework which consisted of significant learnings, general in scope, which allowed the flexibility for individual schools to implement curriculum based on the needs of the population they served. The district also monitored coordination and articulation of the curriculum among the elementary, junior high, and high school levels. Individual schools were allowed to select a textbook from several approved by the district standing committee on reading. The standing committee included teachers from each school who met on a monthly basis to collaboratively determine what options should be available to individual schools.

When an individual school decided that it had found a better way of doing something currently handled by the central office, areas of authority could be adjusted. For example, one of the high schools decided that it could save money, and expand student participation in the lunch program, by having its lunch program catered by McDonald's. The school brought the proposal to the board of education. The board approved. The petitioning school then took on a new responsibility, one that had traditionally been handled by the central office.

There were also four areas in which schools were required to give teachers an opportunity to participate in decision-making. These were eventually identified through the negotiated master agreement with the teacher's union and included:

1. Budget
2. Planning time
3. Curriculum implementation
4. Hiring

Strategic Planning

Strategic planning was used to develop clear, agreed upon, districtwide goals. The consensus-building process used to develop these goals was similar to that described earlier, in reference to planning committees at the individual schools, except for the involvement of personnel from across the district. The strategic plan served as a guide for distributing district resources. Dr. Roberts noted that, in examining an organization's declared values, it was critical that each perceived value be put to the test: Was the organization moving beyond rhetoric in achieving that value? He suggested analyzing the value against the following four criteria:

1. Does it permeate the organization?
   Using the value "success for all students" as an example, does this radiate throughout the organization? If a school district has a high drop-out rate or certain groups of students consistently score below others on standardized tests, 'success for all students" may be a perceived value but, in reality, it is not happening.

2. Does the value drive decisions?
   If "success for all students" is important, are resources allocated with that thought in mind? Using the example of students performing below grade level, do the school district, school and individual teacher consistently look for ways to improve achievement among those students most in danger of dropping out?

3. Is there a strong reaction when the value is violated?
   Is there unrest within the community when a report shows dis-
   turbingly high numbers of students from certain neighborhoods
   dropping out of school? Do changes occur in order to address this
   problem, or does business continue as usual?

4. Is the value something that you won't give up?
   An example is the district that has implemented site-based decision making over a number of years and begins searching for a
   new superintendent. If the school board is willing to consider candidates who haven't displayed the necessary skills for success
   with shared decision making, that would mean that the value of
   shared decision-making had not really permeated the organization. On the other hand, if the job description clearly stated that
   the superintendent must show evidence of working collaboratively, be proficient in conflict resolution and in delegating
   responsibility, that would be a strong indication that the value of
   shared decision making had permeated the organization and the
   school district was not willing to give it up.

After values are identified, the core team develops a brief, clear
mission statement. Good mission statements are expected to address
three fundamental questions:

1. What is the purpose of the school district?
2. For whom does the school district perform its function?
3. How does the school district go about performing the function?

Once the values and mission statement have been agreed upon,
the next step is setting goals. In Western State some goals had been
set by the state. Each school district was required to come up with a
plan to improve: (1) student achievement, (2) graduation rates, and
(3) student attendance. These were automatic goal areas and provided a starting point for developing measurable outcomes. Other
goal areas were arrived at by studying the values that were identified
for the district. Examples of such values included: success for all
students; community partnerships, an orderly and safe environment,
efficient use of resources, shared decision-making, and self-actualization. The core team then reached consensus on a priority listing of
the goals.

After the goal areas had been prioritized, work began on establishing measurable outcomes for each goal. These outcomes

included both five-year goals and one-year goals. For example, if a goal is to increase the graduation rate, the five-year goal was: "By 1995 the dropout rate will be reduced 50 percent through design and implementation of innovative ways to deliver instruction, pre-K through 12." A one-year goal might be: "By June 1991, each high school will have developed a school profile identifying the characteristics of students who have dropped out of school during the past two years." Once goal areas and measurable outcomes were identified, the strategic planning core team assessed whether the expectations for the organization over the next year, and next five years, were likely to prove so overwhelming that they resulted in frustration and/or confusion on the part of individual schools/administrative units.

Establishing a New Curriculum Framework

Controversy over curriculum lay at the root of much of the discord among staff members. Both the Elementary Curriculum Review (1985) and High School Study (1984–85) indicated strong teacher dissatisfaction with the old objective-based curriculum. Teachers complained that it presented learning as a set of segmented skills, emphasized memorization of facts rather than application of knowledge, and focused on content to the exclusion of process. A second-grade teacher explained why she, as a teacher, had distrusted the Davis-era curriculum:

> When I started [teaching], there were still criterion-based tests that you would give to the kids. All sorts of little skills that were tested for, unrelated to anything else. Of course, you'd have no idea if the kids would remember that skill in the third grade or know how to relate the skills to anything.

The district decided in 1987 to develop a curriculum framework which would take advantage of new research on learning, encouraging students to apply skills in context while also outlining the knowledge, behaviors, skills, and attitudes which were to be acquired during each student's K–12 experience. Instead of mandating which skills were to be learned in each grade, the new curriculum framework would be based on a continuum. Children at different developmental stages might be at different places on the continuum, even though they were in the same classroom. The teacher's responsibility would be to individualize instruction so as to help all students gain a deeper and fuller understanding of the subject matter.

Development of the curriculum framework was led by Liz Moore, the new assistant superintendent of curriculum and instruction brought in by Dr. Roberts. A highly successful high school principal before coming to Cottonwood, Moore was convinced of the importance of taking a student-centered approach. Many of her discussions (and struggles) with longtime Cottonwood administrators centered on differing interpretations of what was meant by educational equity. During the Davis era, equity had been equated with standardization: it was assumed that giving all students an equal education meant making sure all students got exactly the same thing. As Moore pointed out in an interview, "That's the most inequitable! Too often the one thing that is given to everybody suits the talents of some students well—but does not serve other students well at all."

As Cottonwood curriculum specialists developed new curriculum guidelines, they drew on "whole language" research, as well as materials published by the National Council of Teachers of Mathematics and Project 2061 in science. As in the adoption of shared decision-making, an attempt was made to respect individual needs and goals. Discussions included different ways of looking at the needs of varied school communities and of diverse populations of students. Nationally recognized speakers were brought in. Programs were put in place to keep teachers informed about the newest research on teaching. The central importance of motivation was recognized; considerable effort went into making sure that adventure, surprise, and the thrill of discovery were not banished from the schools.

The staff members who developed the curriculum framework assumed that the subject matter taught to the youngest children should be the most actively involving, taking advantage of the intensely curious nature of children as well as their keen interest in demonstrating competence in their interactions, both with other people and with their physical environment. At the secondary school level, the goal was to preserve this experiential basis for learning, integrating hands-on learning into such traditional academic subjects as language arts, science, and social science. The questions and answers listed below were taken from the Cottonwood School District's guidebook for curriculum coaches, which clarified specific terms and procedures used by the district:

How is the Curriculum Framework different from the objective-based curriculum?

The Curriculum Framework presents a holistic view of learning that applies skills in context. It views learning as a process and acknowledges that effective instruction requires the use of a variety of instructional strategies and resources. Thinking skills and processes are built into the curriculum in a balanced approach with content.

Are there any similarities between the Curriculum Framework and the objective-based curriculum or are we starting over—again?

A large number of the objectives are embedded in the continua of the Curriculum Framework. The language arts and math objectives have been correlated with the Curriculum Framework.

What are the component parts of the Curriculum Framework?

The Curriculum Framework is based upon broad outcomes which have been developed for each content area. Significant learnings, learning continua, proficiencies, and assessment tasks are identified, based upon the outcomes.

What are outcomes?

Outcomes are broad statements describing the knowledge, behavior, skills and attitudes achieved throughout a student's K–12 experience in a field of study.

What are significant learnings?

Significant learnings are the key or essential learnings that contribute to the achievement of an outcome. They are developed by analyzing an outcome and breaking it into its component parts. Significant learnings span grade levels.

What are learning continua?

Learning continua specify the content, knowledge, skills, or processes to be taught for a given significant learning. They reflect both what is developmentally appropriate for the learner and what is necessary to be taught to develop the important concepts or applications of the content, knowledge, skills or attitudes. The learning continua guide articulation from level to level.

What are proficiencies?

Proficiencies are the most important *measurable* key student learnings identified for a given grade or level. They describe the part of the significant learning to be addressed at a given grade or level for the purpose of district assessment. When proficiencies in a content area are sequenced, they provide the scope and sequence of the curriculum.

A Different Way of Thinking about Curriculum

Advances in research on learning have called into question the assumptions upon which criterion-referenced testing was based. Researchers have found that students can learn to give correct answers on tests without acquiring a meaningful understanding of the subject matter. Naive conceptions about the workings of the universe (such as the assumption that the earth is closer to the sun in the summer than in the winter) have been found to persist in students of normal abilities, despite exposure to both well-written text and direct teaching that contradicted this view. Clearly, the minds of even very young students are not a "blank slate." By the time they have entered school, children have evolved naive assumptions about the workings of the world that must be reimagined if they are to develop conceptions about the way the world works that are in keeping with the findings of science.

Arthur W. Combs (1972) pointed out that focusing on behavioral objectives of the kind used in the Cottonwood district during the Davis era is a symptomatic approach to behavior change that can be useful in imparting specific skills; but, behavioral objectives may not lend themselves to attaining more general education goals. Public schools must do far more than produce students with specific cognitive skills. Education must produce humane individuals, capable both of successfully applying the skills they have learned and relating to others in a responsible and cooperative manner. Research has emphasized the importance of the social scaffolding that supports the learning of a young, inexperienced child. Children can be profoundly influenced by the environment in which learning takes place. Structuring the curriculum so that learning is fun and interesting draws children into the learning process, setting them up for success; whereas constant testing on isolated skills can produce performance anxiety and the alienation of the child from the learning process.

John Allen Paulos has become a best-selling author by pointing out to his "intelligent and literate, but largely innumerate" adult audience how little they know about mathematics, despite years of studying it in school. He explained the destructive effect bad teaching could have:

> Imagine that 90 percent of every course in English up until college was devoted to grammar and the diagramming of sentences. Would graduates have any feeling for literature? Or consider a conservatory which devoted 90 percent of its efforts to the practicing of the scales. Would its graduates develop an appreciation or understanding of music? The answer, of course, is no, but that, given proper allowance for hyperbole, is what frequently happens in our mathematics classes. Mathematics is identified with a rote recitation of facts and a blind carrying out of procedures. Decades later this robotic mode of behavior kicks in whenever a mathematical topic arises. Countless people feel that if the answer or at least a recipe for finding it doesn't come to them immediately, they'll never get it. The idea of thinking about a problem or discussing it a bit with someone else seems novel to them. (Paulos 1991, 52)

When all their school subjects have been taught in the same narrow, skills-based way, the problem becomes that much worse. Students can graduate from school with little feeling for literature, thinking that history and science consist of the same rote recitation of facts and blind carrying out of procedures that Paulos insists have convinced people that they will never understand math.

New Meaning Given to the Words "Performance-Based"

Dr. Davis had referred to management-by-objectives as a "performance-based management model." By that he meant a system in which administrators at each level within the district drew up their own set of objectives, based on the objectives Dr. Davis had set for himself as superintendent. Specific tasks were spelled out, relating to the school district's goals. For each task a standard was defined. This standard would later be used to measure whether that task had been accomplished. Each principal reported to a central office administrator who continuously monitored the principal's work. When used to refer to student learning, the phrase "performance-based" had a similar meaning. Criterion-referenced tests were used to ascertain whether students had learned the facts and skills required in each subject at each grade level.

During the Roberts era, the phrase "performance-based" took on a quite different meaning. In the new math curriculum framework, paper-and-pencil tests were kept to a minimum during the early grades. Students were asked to perform problem-solving activities in order to show that they could not only perform specific mathematical operations, but also knew how to use math concepts to address the sort of problems that they were likely to meet in the world outside school. "Performance-based" became the commonly used phrase for getting away from reliance on paper-and-pencil tests and the teaching of isolated skills—the very things that had been at the heart of the test-driven curriculum set up by Superintendent Davis.

Whole Language Philosophy

The whole language approach to teaching reading and writing involved a broadly defined curriculum that combined ideas gained from research in language acquisition, linguistics, cognition, child development, reading, writing, and other related fields over the last several decades. The name "whole language" relates to the principal that children learn oral language quickly and instinctively, without having it broken up into isolated or abstract bits and pieces, as is commonly done in grammar books and basal readers. In class this means that students are encouraged to read literature appropriate for their age and interests and to write daily, usually on self-selected topics. Writing instruction focuses on writing as a process of formulating ideas, communicating them with words, and revising work as necessary for clarity and effectiveness (Education Commission of the States 1991).

THE IMPACT OF EXTERNAL ECONOMIC FACTORS

The energy boom of the 1970s brought tremendous economic expansion to Western State. In 1969 Foothills City had only three downtown buildings of more than twenty stories. By the late 1970s Foothills City had as much office space under construction as already existed. When the boom ended, however, the local economy ran out of steam. Construction dried up in the mid-1980s. For several years Foothills City had one of the highest office vacancy rates of any urban area in the United States. School districts were hard hit because of their dependence upon property taxes. In the four years preceding a 1989 bond election, Foothills City property values had dropped approximately 10 percent. The suburban Cottonwood School District received far less property tax revenue than expected. Between 1986 and 1988, a total $4 million in expenditures had to be eliminated from the Cottonwood budget. Again in 1988–89, $2.4 million was cut from the Cottonwood budget.

Shared decision-making did help make budget cutting more equitable. When the district was forced to cut $4 million, the principals suggested that they be allowed to decide how the last $1.6 million would be cut. The school board agreed, saying only that principals had to cut .9 percent of their budget and that they had to use shared decision-making processes to do it. A board member later recalled that, although budget-cutting measures were often divisive, agreeing on these cuts at the school level made them more acceptable to individual school communities. One school decided that, in order to save money, each child should bring a ream of paper to school. An irate parent called a board member, who said: "Call the principal." The principal said: "Call the parent planning committee head," who in turn said "Where were you when we had the meeting to decide on this?" The parent quieted down.

NEGOTIATING THE PROCESS OF REFORM

Even after a decade, large differences remain in the extent of shared decision-making undertaken in individual buildings. As a principal pointed out, in describing teacher attitudes:

> It's a struggle. There's a camp that says "Oh, my word! Don't take all this structure away! I want it all laid out by the steps, by the numbers, by the grade level." Then there's the others who applaud what Roberts has done and say "At last, we don't have all this overlay to deal with! Let's go back to the district just giving us an outline and trusting our intelligence, creativity and imagination to make things fly."

The difficulties inherent in moving away from a social-efficiency style of organization were magnified by the fact that ingrained habits proved difficult to overcome. Staff members who expressed dissatisfaction with the top-down administrative hierarchy put in place by Dr. Davis often found themselves unable to imagine effective, nonauthoritarian ways of handling specific problems. Staff members found themselves on terra incognita, trying to implement reforms for which there existed, at that time, no working model.

In Cottonwood the initial movement toward site-based decision-making took place in an environment which had for a decade been shaped by a centralized, authoritarian administration. Any use of centralized authority, including one aimed at decentralizing power, was colored by that history. Accustomed to carrying out directives coming from above, experienced administrators at times dutifully set up formal structures aimed at encouraging a sharing of power—while preserving attitudes which largely invalidated the processes they had set up.

Predictably, there were building principals who were less than enthusiastic about the proposed changes. As one principal explained, "We were just starting to get to a place which smelled really good to many of us, where we really felt we had our fingers on the pulse of the school."

Curriculum Change

In implementing the new curriculum framework a number of principals opted for a cautious, "go slow" approach. Given the site-based environment that had been established, this forced the administrative team set up by Dr. Roberts to address a number of challenging questions:

1. Just how prescriptive should the curriculum be in a site-based district?
2. How much variation ought to be allowed among schools?
3. If a consensus was reached at the district level that curriculum change was desirable, how should that change be brought about?
4. When a particular curriculum change was tied to a new research-based understanding of the learning process, how were teachers whose current method of teaching was grounded in an earlier model of cognition to be brought onboard?
5. How could implementation be effectively carried out during a period of cost cutting and budgetary restraint?

In keeping with the philosophy of site-based decision-making, teachers were encouraged to use a variety of techniques and resources to meet student needs, with due allowance made for the fact that students have a variety of learning styles and teachers have different instructional strengths. The thorny question of how much latitude individual teachers and schools would have in choosing their curricular approach was addressed in the following carefully worded paragraph:

> The C&I (Curriculum and Instruction) Services Department provides information, inservices, and resources based upon educational research. Research conducted in the 1980s indicates that student achievement is higher when: content is taught in a meaningful context rather than isolation; pupils are given the opportunity to apply what they have learned; and content areas are integrated. Since whole language, math problem solving and the integration of social studies, science and health are consistent with the research, we encourage their use. However, it is the prerogative of each teacher, under the supervision of the building principal, to identify the most appropriate instructional techniques for a given group of students.

The district's Curriculum and Instruction Services Department (hereafter referred to as C&I) took responsibility for researching new approaches to teaching, developing the new curriculum framework and planning in-service training and support for teachers. Those schools most eager to explore new options became the pilot schools for the evolving experiential curriculum. Initial implementation took place primarily at the elementary level. Language arts was addressed first, since this was the subject area where resistance to the old test-driven curriculum had been sharpest.

Experienced teachers who were enthusiastic about the experiential approach were recruited to act as part-time curriculum coaches at each pilot school. These coaches attended classes on the new curriculum framework taught by district curriculum specialists. Afterward, the coaches offered similar classes to the teachers at their own schools, modeling the techniques they had learned. Coaches also served as on-site resource persons. A sixth grade teacher who had served as language arts coach for her school described her experience:

> I had a student teacher in the fall, so during the time that she was able to take over my classroom, I served as a resource person and went to all of the grade levels, and asked who would be interested in having me come in, and how I could best help them. Then, I set up meetings with them during their planning times and we looked at the curriculum framework. I said, "Where are you having the most difficulty, or what would you

like to see? What isn't going well?" We picked out a specific area and planned. I would plan a lesson based on that particular outcome, go in and present the lesson, and then usually I did a follow-up lesson. I did at least two lessons with them, and then I debriefed with them again during the planning time to give them ideas on how they could follow up, or other things they could use, or how it went when I wasn't in the room, you know. I really think that was really effective.

Last year we hired substitutes and I had a lot of teachers come observe me doing lessons in my classroom, and I had all different grade levels come and observe. Then a sub covered my class immediately after that, so I could go and debrief with them. And that was also very effective, because they were all brainstorming how they could change it, and use it for their grade level, or how different it was to see different level kids. That was also pretty effective.

Originally, the plan had been to provide extensive on-site support to teacher-coaches through the district C&I department. However, significant budget shortfalls at the state level reduced the funding available for such support. To keep reduction cuts as far from the classroom as possible, the Cottonwood district was forced to make large reductions in the C&I staff. The classes and advice provided by teacher-coaches at each pilot school thus became the primary means the new curriculum framework was introduced to teachers.

Building-level coaches sorely missed the regular visits from district curriculum specialists that had been available before the state budget crisis. In many schools an accommodation had been reached whereby the literacy resource teacher also acted as language-arts curriculum coach. This was made possibly because the duties of the literacy resource position had been changed from operating a remedial pull-out program to working collaboratively with regular classroom teachers. A literacy resource teacher described her duties during the Davis era: "They wanted pull out, and there wasn't administrative support for anything different. 'Pull out the low kids.' That is what they wanted. So, the teachers were doing criterion referenced tests, but I wasn't involved in it at all."

Now that had changed. The new curriculum framework emphasized the integration of all students within the classroom setting whenever possible. Literacy resource and Chapter 1 teachers, now emphasized in-class support. A literacy resource teacher described her present role:

Sometimes I would teach all three (reading) groups, and the teacher would observe . . . because they didn't have training, you know. I would try to sell the district classes that were being offered about adapting a basal reader. They could still use the basals as long as they would not depend on the teachers' guide to tell them what to do with it, because the basals weren't structured so that (the students) could utilize skills once they taught them a skill. So, they would have to look at the story, and see what skill they could pull from it, then teach that, and then give them a chance to practice by reading a story where they would need that skill. I mean, that's still fine. It doesn't matter what material you use to teach as long as it is natural language.

The coaching function assigned to the literacy resource teachers filled part of the gap left by cuts in the district C&I department. But, since many pilot schools felt a need for both a primary- and an intermediate-level curriculum coach, there were not enough literacy resource teachers to fill all the language-arts coaching positions. In those schools which did not qualify for federal Chapter 1 funds, the second language arts coach was a regular classroom teacher. Also, all but one of the math coaches were regular classroom teachers.[1] Classroom teacher/coaches reported feeling torn between helping colleagues and focusing on the needs of their own students.

Redefining "Excellence," "Accountability," "Collaboration"

To comprehend the extent of the shift in thinking that Cottonwood personnel were being asked to make, one has to understand the extent to which expectations had changed. The three superintendents who had headed the Cottonwood district over the last forty years had each assigned a different meaning to three key concepts: excellence, accountability, and collaboration. Superintendent Larimer had seen the effective teaching of a heavily academic curriculum as central to educational excellence. During the Larimer era, when the student population was growing much faster than the Cottonwood district's tax base, accountability had been seen in terms of the efficient use of scarce resources. Collaboration was understood in terms of staff cooperation in meeting the needs of students.

Bill Davis, the second superintendent, had put a new emphasis on the tangible outcomes of the educational process. Davis saw himself as the school district's chief executive officer (CEO). Like a CEO in the business sector, he defined excellence in terms of product (in the form of test scores) rather than process (methods of teaching). Accountability was defined as making sure that 80 percent of the students in each classroom mastered 80 percent of the district-mandated objectives in each subject area, with mastery measured by criterion-referenced tests. Standards for evaluating staff performance were arrived at through the objective-setting process. Collaboration was seen in terms of staff membership on committees set up to develop curriculum and/or evaluation procedures.

Dave Roberts, the third superintendent, insisted that any definition of educational excellence had to include independent thinking and problem-solving on the part of both students and staff. Accountability was seen in terms of insuring that students knew how to use the skills they were being taught. Criterion-referenced tests were abandoned in favor of complex activities that required a range of higher-order thinking skills. Collaboration took the form of shared decision making at both the building and the district levels. Nationally known experts were brought in to advise staff members about how to create an intellectually challenging environment for students.

Such broad policy changes did not, of course, take place without opposition. What seemed like "success" to individuals who held one understanding of "excellence," "accountability," and "collaboration" seemed more like "failure" to individuals who had a different understanding. However, the length of each superintendent's tenure—a decade or more meant that even those staff members who did not favor a given policy had time to study its strengths and weaknesses. Low staff turnover allowed change to be negotiated in such a way that elements which proved useful in the reforms implemented during one era could be incorporated into the next round of restructuring. Thus each "layer" of reform interacted in observable ways with the restructuring efforts that came before and after.

NOTE

1. The one exception was a school which had opted to do without a literacy resource teacher for one year in order to release a teacher to work as a full-time math coach.

CHAPTER 6

IMPLEMENTING THE
NEW CURRICULUM FRAMEWORK:
THE DYNAMICS OF CHANGE

This chapter discusses implementation of the new curriculum framework in the Cottonwood School District. Comments made by Cottonwood personnel fell into eight general areas: the new curriculum framework; special challenges in the areas of math, spelling and grammar; application of social implementation strategies; articulation between grade levels; assessment techniques; assistance requested from the district's department of curriculum and instruction; teacher understanding of the philosophy behind the curriculum framework; parent reactions; practical problems/suggestions. In many of these areas, differing answers tended to be given by building level personnel at differing stages of the implementation process.

In all but a handful of schools, piloting of the math portion of the curriculum framework had begun just months before the present study was undertaken. Thus, there were substantial differences in the problems encountered by language-arts and math coaches, even in the same schools. These differences were made more pronounced by the fact that the math coaches were classroom teachers, while many of the language arts coaches were literacy resource teachers (referred to in earlier years in Cottonwood as reading specialists).

TEACHER PERCEPTIONS OF CHANGE

Language arts coaches whose schools had been piloting the curriculum framework for several years generally reported that the lan-

guage-arts curriculum framework was well established in their buildings. Teachers in the early grades repeatedly commented on the far-
reaching ramifications of changing the language-arts emphasis from
"learning to decode words" to "learning to communicate through the
written word." Under the new curriculum framework the read-
ing/writing connection was stressed and students were asked to take
a more active role in the learning process. This contrasted strongly
with the approach that had been taken in the era of criterion-referenced tests, when it had been enough to simply find the "right"
answer.

As the literature-based curriculum had taken hold, textbooks
had become less important. Interactions between teachers and students had intensified. Several teachers commented that they now
found themselves more reluctant to bring in a substitute to take
over their class. Whereas it had once been enough to say, "Start on
page 23," writing plans for use by substitute teachers had become
much more time-consuming. This caused special problems for building-level teacher/coaches, who felt torn between wanting to be with
their own classes and wanting to help colleagues who had asked
them to model the new teaching methods in their classrooms.

Some teachers admitted to feeling anxious about whether or
not they were implementing the new curriculum in the correct manner. They expressed a certain nostalgia for the security of the test-
driven curriculum which demanded only that 80 percent of students
achieve a score of 80 percent on a criterion-referenced test. Other
teachers insisted that they would not want to go back to a curriculum which did not allow children to demonstrate what they had
learned in a concrete manner that was in keeping with their stage of
development. These teachers argued forcefully that they had seen a
significant difference in the quality of learning going on in their
classrooms since moving to a whole language curriculum. The following comments are typical of those made by the teachers involved
in piloting the new curriculum framework:

> All they were doing (when criterion-referenced tests were used)
> was mindlessly parroting back what we told them to. It's as if
> we were telling them that understanding was unimportant.

> You need to meet children where they are, then help them to
> move to where they must go. But you can only do that through
> two-way communication, not by talking at them and expecting
> them to memorize what you say.

In the old days the teacher that was admired kept a quiet class-room. The children were expected to be passive. We kept them passive by feeding them all those abstractions. Who could get enthusiastic in a class set up like that?

REACTIONS TO THE CURRICULUM FRAMEWORK

The most significant variable affecting teacher reactions to the curriculum framework was the length of time since beginning the implementation process. A few respondents were still trying to find time to read the curriculum framework document for the first time. At other schools, staff members showed considerable familiarity with both the language arts and the math curriculum frameworks. A coach at one of the schools which had been most receptive to the new curriculum reported: "We've been doing language arts for five years and math for . . . this will be the third year."

Experienced coaches pointed out that a teacher's understanding of the new approach to teaching changed over time. A math coach succinctly expressed the progression she had passed through:

> It's hard, I think, when people first start, to understand that it's a philosophical way of teaching, that it's not a collection of activities and that if you teach it as a collection of activities, you're still not teaching to the whole child. So if you look at this as "whole language" and "whole math" it's beyond a col-lection of activities. Many people don't understand because that philosophical step has been skipped. I mean, I think I'm just starting to learn, myself, the implications of that. If you just end up doing these cute little activities and [say] "Oh, this is great!" but you don't make the connection for the kids, then it's just a cute little activity.

A parallel change in the way students approach their work was reported by a math coach in a school where both curriculum frame-works have been in place for some time:

> It's all so interconnected that you can't just separate it out. What I found is if they start being better problem solvers in their reading and writing, that applies in mathematics and they look at things differently in mathematics. But they have to have a way to talk about it. You're talking about a whole dif-

ferent language that the kids have to use. They can't just say "the alligator mouth" any more. They need to know that it's the greater than/less than symbol . . . because it doesn't make . . . it's not appropriate any more. You know. And to say you go next door and knock on your neighbor's door and ask to borrow something isn't appropriate any more. You have to give kids those skills and those tools.

In schools just beginning to use the new curriculum, mention of the curriculum framework document tended to elicit comments about how overwhelming it was to be handed this large book. Yet, there was a good deal of enthusiasm for the curriculum framework on the part of those teachers who had been able to study it with others, in building-level classes. Teachers particularly liked the use of broadly described significant learnings, and the way these were placed on a developmental continuum. Comments included:

> I like the continuum because it helps you to know that you're on target. The significant learnings help to make sure you cover everything from grade to grade.

> It encompasses so much more that it makes you aware of other things you have to teach.

> A process approach makes a difference over a year's time. The kids become problem-solvers. They organize their thinking and their information when they write. They are able to look at problems that are social issues.

Teachers in the implementing schools were especially gratified by the slight rise in standardized (CTBS or Comprehensive Tests of Basic Skills) scores that had accompanied implementation of the curriculum framework. Few had foreseen such a result. Many were cautious about putting too much emphasis on the increased scores, lest the scores, rather than encouragement of a more integrated learning experience for students, be taken as the primary justification for the new curriculum. However, an experienced coach at one of the original pilot schools enthusiastically described how interactive learning had improved the test-taking skills of her class. She listed factors she saw as affecting this carryover:

> I find more kids using logic to decide on answers on the CTBS test. Last year they doubled their scores in one year. I had gone

to a hands-on approach. We had conversations on math concepts. I taught strategies for logic and problem-solving, making sense of something that was too complex on first reading. But they were a special group of kids. This year's group is not as focused. The leadership chemistry in the class is different. If the class leaders value showing off and being "cool," not as much learning takes place.

There were areas, however, where the cutbacks in the district C&I office had clearly taken a toll. Work on fleshing out the curriculum framework had been stalled. Despite widespread enthusiasm, there were complaints about the rudimentary nature of many suggested activities. Teachers requested more activities, with more interest and variety. Some teachers had made improvements on their own. For example, one language-arts coach described a creative solution she had discovered when she realized that, for many students, literature logs meant simply retelling the plot, which they found tedious:

> I took a survey and the reason why they [students] hated them [lit logs] was: (1) they'd been doing them for years; (2) they said they didn't know what to say. So there's a strategy called "coding lit journals" that I got out of *The Journal of English*. I just rewrote it to fit elementary kids. What it is, it's taking the thinking skills and demonstrating how you can make a choice of the kinds of comments you can make in a lit log, by metacognitively knowing what kinds of comments you can do. For example, you can compare and contrast . . .
> I use labels, labels, labels. They cut the sticker. They label their comment and they write, so that the teacher, and they themselves know that they're going to do a comparison entry here. Then there's another one that's called "evaluation" and there's a little scale, the triangles . . . what evaluation is, is you make a judgment—goodness, badness, prettiness, ugliness—on something that happened in the book. They have these choices. There's seven different ways they can make a comment. You teach each one of those comments and give them a label that they can use to let the teacher know what they're trying to do. But they, themselves, can choose what thinking process they're going to use for that chapter.

Problems with Math, Spelling, and Grammar

Some teachers expressed doubts about the background students were receiving in math, spelling, and grammar in the primary grades. Intermediate level and junior high teachers worried that students who had come up under the new curriculum framework did not know math facts, or proper spelling and grammar, when entering grades where teachers could once have been assumed that students would have mastered these things. A junior high coach observed: "We're getting kids now in junior high with no grammar skills, no spelling skills. They can write creatively and freely, but they can't spell. They don't know word usage or the technical parts of language."

Elementary-level curriculum coaches argued that this was a temporary problem. An elementary coach explained that teachers who were just beginning to work with the curriculum framework tended "to pick up first on the more superficial aspects, like the use of manipulatives in math, and the use of literature instead of basals in reading." Deciding to give the hands-on approach a try, teachers often swung from one extreme to the other, forgetting to teach math facts and spelling. Although these teachers had changed superficial aspects of their teaching, they had missed the more important point of the new curriculum, which was teaching children to make connections. Yet coaches feared to be too critical of such initial attempts, lest the teacher give up on the curriculum framework entirely. A coach described her experiences:

> The term "mini-lesson," as it's sometimes described and defined, makes some teachers think that if you can't do it in five or ten minutes, then you shouldn't do it at all. There's a lot of negative connotation with terminology. See, to me, the word "mini" . . . that could be 45 minutes if you're going to practice the "isolated" skill you're teaching. . . . If you expect to see it somewhere down the road, in their writing or in their reading, some things can't be done [in five or ten minutes]. For example, a think-aloud strategy, or a retelling strategy, or cued retelling, those things are not mini-lessons. They're a framework, and those frameworks need to be explained a tad more, and modeled by the teacher; and then they need to be given opportunity to practice with a small group, a large group. It's a release of responsibility type thing. You don't just throw them to the wolves and expect them to learn it.

Several coaches mentioned that they were trying to correct such mistaken impressions and to help teachers put the emphasis not on "mini" but on "lesson." In the meantime, however, the initial impression that many of the upper-grade teachers had received of the new curriculum had been unfavorable. A fifth-grade teacher who was currently teaching a class which had, in earlier grades, been the first in that school to be taught using the new math curriculum framework, noted:

> This group of kids has been going through the transition, so their reaction may be due to this. They seem to enjoy using the manipulatives, but they don't transfer what they learn there to paper. They have a lot of trouble with regular math. When they came into fifth grade, they didn't know their multiplication facts, which is something I had not encountered before. One-third of the class still does not know their multiplication and division facts. They seem to see the manipulatives as something to play with and have a hard time moving into applications.

The use of manipulatives in math also caused classroom-management problems for teachers unaccustomed to their use. Unlike science teachers, math teachers were not accustomed to dealing with the procedural side of getting physical objects out and putting them away. Part of the problem appeared to be that physical arrangements to make efficient use of these learning tools were often lacking. Manipulatives could not be easily put away. Students who were unaccustomed to using manipulatives, or who did not recognize them as serious learning tools, experimented to see what they can get away with. There were complaints about junior high students throwing manipulatives.

Math coaches suggested that the Cottonwood School District put out a list of practical suggestions to help those teachers who were presently hesitant to use manipulatives. Putting out and picking up the manipulatives could be made a part of the lesson, so that an elementary teacher would not need to always teach math right before or after recess or lunch. Such an approach would also lessen the resentment of teachers who presently felt that they had to pick up the manipulatives themselves, a task which cut into their scarce planning time.

APPLICATION TO SOCIAL STUDIES AND SCIENCE

The difference is not just in reading and math. There's also the difference between teaching geography as the memorized capitals of all the states and using geography as a way of teaching responsibility for the earth—what one receives from the earth and what one does with it. There's a whole other layer of meaning.

Because of budget cuts, the curriculum specialist assigned to developing the science and math curriculum frameworks had only a half-time position and often had to divert her energies to other projects. However, despite the lack of formal coaching, some teachers were determinedly forging ahead, experimenting with new ways of teaching social studies and science. A teacher noted how this new way of teaching had allowed him to approach ethical questions in a natural manner:

> It used to be we'd just stand there and tell the kids, "You should be grateful for all that you have." With all the changes in social attitudes now, though, you just can't handle it that way. Instead, I let the ethical undercurrent emerge out of the facts. "Let's list everything that people in our class had to eat yesterday. . . . Where did these things come from? . . . How was it transported? . . . How many people worked to give us what we ate yesterday?" This way a sense of community, of each area of the world having something to offer the rest, arises naturally.

IMPLEMENTATION

Implementation had taken place in two phases. During the initial phase, district curriculum specialists were readily available to visit the pilot schools. A language-arts coach described this phase, as well as her regret that district curriculum specialists were no longer available to visit buildings:

> Well, what we used to have were specialists. A curriculum specialist would provide the feedback to teachers, or the modeling for teachers. Generally about once a month they would be in the building for a day, and you would sign up if you wanted them to come into your class, either to observe or to do a lesson, and I really think that provided a lot of support. It showed that the administration was behind this, and that this was expected to be implemented in our buildings. But it was also a

lot of support for teachers, and I can't do that, teaching full-time in my classroom, and then taking every planning time to go and work in somebody else's room. I just can't do that.

Because of budget cuts resulting from state budget shortfalls, the number of curriculum specialists had been cut back sharply. The teacher/coaches became the key to curriculum framework implementation.

Time demands on teacher/coaches were an ongoing theme of the interviews. Math coaches reported feeling especially hard-pressed. Unlike the literacy resource teachers, who often acted as language arts coaches, the math coaches had to take the time they spent helping other teachers out of the time they would have otherwise spent with their own classes. A typical remark was "I feel like I'm working two jobs. I feel like my classroom gets gypped." Most felt that they needed release time. One coach suggested that the situation might be alleviated if teachers were able to always have a particular substitute teacher to help out when they were otherwise engaged:

> If we could have the same sub, who came in all the time, to provide some consistency for our students and for us, it would make it so we were more at ease about the children [when we visit a peer's classroom]. Requesting the sub and then getting someone else there leaves you ill at ease when you have to do these things that you really want to do for your peers.

Math coaches also were troubled about another kind of time crunch, the need to have "more time to thoroughly look over the materials, and work with other people at other schools, before we tried to implement them at our building level." There was uncertainty as to whether the district would be able to commit the resources necessary to implement the math curriculum framework effectively. One school had spent building funds to release a teacher to work as a math coach and seemed very satisfied with the result. One principal made a point of saying that if the district wanted the math curriculum framework to be implemented effectively, it would have to furnish funds for release time: "Our staff needs support. Our coaches need support. It's difficult to ask a classroom teacher to do all the coaching duties. It's difficult to get pulled out of class, both time-wise and energy-wise."

One literacy resource teacher suggested that the district provide in-services to train literacy resource teachers to teach students (and teachers) how to write about math, since the new curriculum often required written explanations of solutions, proofs, and methods used. This would take some of the burden off of math coaches.

A language-arts coach spoke at length of the difference between the situation the math coaches now faced and that which had prevailed when the language arts curriculum was first introduced.

> When we changed from basal, total basal focus, to more literature-based, that change would never have happened without the resource teachers, without the reading teachers, without the Chapter One teachers to be there for support. That's the kind of change where we went from skill based instruction to incorporating skills into a broader spectrum. We are asking people to make that same change in math instruction, but there is no support. There are no people to come out, there is no building person to go into your classroom for six weeks, or for a quarter to provide the kind of support that people are definitely going to need to change. I have seen incredible changes over the last seven years in the district, but it has taken seven years for some people to feel comfortable, to say, "Okay, now I am willing to try this stuff."

Disadvantages of the gradual manner of implementation, which had meant that pilot schools had begun implementation several years before other schools, were also pointed out. A language-arts coach, math coach and their building principal discussed problems they foresaw resulting from the wide difference in experience among participants at district-level meetings:

> *Math coach:* I think, too, that there are people at so many different levels, and . . . I kind of shudder to think what the math coaches meetings will be like next year when there are more people on-line, so you have people up here (gestures, holding hand at head level), talking about things these people (gestures, holding hand at table level) aren't going to be doing for five years. I mean, there's just no way they can because they have to go through the same process we've been through.
>
> *Language arts coach:* And then, boy, you go back and you feel like you're not doing your job, because you go back just feeling overwhelmed, because I run into that with new schools in the language arts, too. They feel like "Wow! This is just such an overwhelming job."

Math coach: "We can never do it!" You know, it's very defeating, I think, for those people.

Interviewer: To see the people who are way ahead of them?

Language arts coach: Yes, because it's so different from what they are used to. You go from a skills-generated curriculum to what this is, it's so different. We were talking about that not too long ago. Where we've been, if we went back six or seven years, and looked at the increments . . . it's like you don't notice it so much until you step back and look from 1985 to 1992. There's an amazing difference in this building. It's just incredible what goes on that's different than it used to be! I think in any one year you wouldn't have noticed it so much. . . . We didn't have anybody that was ten yards ahead of us like some of the schools that are coming on-line now. So they hear us talk and they see what we're doing, and I think that they really do get overwhelmed and feel like "We've got to catch up! We've got to rush!" Then that's the *worst* thing they can do.

Math coach: Yes.

Language arts coach: If you try to do too much at once, it'll really cause burnout.

Principal: Well, it's going to fall apart, too.

Language arts coach: Teachers can't change two or three curriculums in one year. It's unrealistic to think that you can do that. We, fortunately, had a *good* handle on language arts when we started with math.

All respondents agreed that the training of teacher/coaches in each building had been essential to the progress that had been made. Even when district curriculum specialists had been more readily available, the advantage of having an "in-house expert" lay in that person's availability and intimate knowledge of what was going on in that school. Questions could be asked and information shared informally in the halls. Also, there was greater accountability. As a coach pointed out, it was much easier to pin people down and find out what they are actually doing when the coach was there in the building:

You can't hand people a notebook, and say "Here you go! Here is the curriculum!" and expect them to use it. I mean I had to have people dig it out lots of times. I'd talk to teachers and they'd say: "Well, just come in and do whatever you would like to do."

I said "No, I am not coming in to do a dog and pony show. I am here to help you implement this curriculum. What part do you need help with?"

They'd say: "Oh well, I don't care."

"Yes, you do, let's look at it, let's go through, step by step, and see what you have done, what you haven't done."

So, once you pin them down . . . I mean, they had the notebook for a year. So, I just really think that it helps to have a presence there . . . it really helps to see something modeled, or to get feedback on your own instruction.

ARTICULATION PROBLEMS POINT TO A
WEAKNESS IN SHARED DECISION-MAKING

Articulation between the elementary, junior high, and high school levels remained problematic. Junior high teachers complained that many of the activities suggested in the curriculum framework had already been presented to their students, back in elementary school. When they were asked to repeat an activity they thought they had "outgrown," junior high students often reacted with sarcasm and complaints. Curriculum specialists had recommended that junior high teachers exercise their creativity in adapting suggested activities to explore more complex problems with older students. However, junior high teachers who were just beginning curriculum framework implementation often lacked experience using manipulatives, and therefore found it difficult to creatively alter suggested activities to suit the needs of older students. Elementary coaches agreed that more complete resource books, with a larger selection of activities for use at each grade level, would be useful. But all agreed that such materials were unlikely to be forthcoming until money could be freed up to fund the project.

Not all articulation problems between junior high and elementary levels were the result of budget problems, though. Sixth-grade teachers complained that they had often heard from former students that they had "wasted" their first months in seventh grade, reviewing topics they had already covered in depth. Some sixth-grade teachers perceived the debate over manipulatives as useful, in that it brought attention to long-standing communication problems. They saw the manipulatives as offering an opening for overcoming the long-standing indifference secondary teachers had shown to opening meaningful channels of communication with elementary-level teachers.

Curriculum coaches suggested that encouraging sixth-grade teachers to spend a day at a junior high, and seventh-grade teachers to spend a day at an elementary school, could start a useful dialogue, opening the eyes of each to the challenges the other set of teachers faced. Seeing what their students had experienced the year before would enable seventh-grade teachers to provide more continuity. Knowing what junior high teachers expected, would enable sixth-grade teachers to better prepare their students for the transition. Such grassroots cooperation was what shared decision-making was supposed to lead to. However, junior high teachers remained resistant and elementary teachers found it difficult to take the lead, on their own, and organize such exchanges.

Old habits died hard. Nor were problems with articulation limited to lack of communication between elementary and junior high teachers. Intermediate-level teachers in the elementary schools often pointed out that children had often already done incomplete versions of recommended activities for their present grade level in an earlier grade. Indeed, the articulation problem had in some schools led to open resentment. During interviews, several teachers stated a desire that the district go back to dictating which activities could be used in which grade. Despite the existence of shared decision-making mechanisms in all schools, some buildings clearly had avoided confronting the grade-to-grade articulation issue. Apparently, this pattern of avoidance was rooted in the friction discussion of such issues tended to cause among teachers.

Indeed, a frequently mentioned complaint about shared decision-making was the tendency of staff members to simply avoid discussion of difficult issues. Although the Cottonwood School District stressed the importance of engaging in frank and open discussions, many teachers admitted that they had no wish to "open a can of worms." They pointed out that, when a highly emotional issue was put on the table at a staff meeting, multiple meetings were usually needed to resolve it—and these meetings were often of a tense, emotionally wearing nature. Therefore, teachers who brought up topics likely to require significant amounts of time and energy often found themselves the target of critical sidelong glances from colleagues. The subtle pressures thus created discouraged teachers from bringing up possibly contentious issues.

ASSESSMENT

Student self-assessment, which emphasized teaching students to look at their own work to see their progress, was a major focus of the new curriculum framework. A coach pointed out that assessment "teaches a kid what's important. Now that we're assessing problem-solving, writing and communicating, they're realizing that it's important." One teacher mentioned that her class had a much more positive attitude toward naturalistic assessment than toward standardized tests: "They were thrilled when they found out they were going to write for a writing assessment, not be asked to analyze pieces of sentences."

A teacher, with a great deal of experience using the curriculum framework, described how self-assessment helped her students:

It really helped me to refocus on self-assessment, which I have always tried to do. But this [curriculum framework] just gave me some real specific ideas, which were real helpful when we had student-led [parent] conferences, because they had assessed themselves and were real pleased with their growth. I guess, that is the good thing about it: they are just amazed at how far they have come this year.

Another teacher described the dialogue that went on around the "book fairs" held by Cottonwood elementary schools in the spring. Handmade books published by students were exhibited. Usually an afternoon was set aside for students to browse and talk to other student authors. At least one evening was set aside to give parents a chance to visit:

I talk to kids about "Why did you decide to publish this piece?" They say, well, it was their best, they liked the topic. So it takes them awhile to begin realizing that it becomes your best, maybe, because you worked the hardest on it or because you used a skill that you weren't able to use before.

Both teachers and coaches felt that teachers needed additional practice in using rubrics to describe student progress. A number of teachers recalled being perplexed, for example, about what sort of student performance should be scored as a "3" on the rubric and what should be a "4." Teachers expressed a need to get used to using new assessment tools throughout the year, to have available "lots of samples of assessments that we can try out and practice." But a former reading teacher who was now a teacher/coach in language arts was enthusiastic about the flexibility and usefulness of the rubrics, once they were understood:

> We did a project using rubric assessment in math in the fall, and it is just so nice to have a spectrum that isn't labeled first grade, second month, and to get children to focus on all of the different things that they should be looking at, not just how many books they put down on their list that they have read, or how many pages are in their story.

Coaches stressed the importance of helping teachers to understand how assessment could tell them a great deal about a student. Several coaches felt that, if teachers understood how alternative assessment could inform their teaching, then they would be less resentful of the extra time needed. Clearly, the time required for individualized testing was a concern for teachers. A typical question was: "What do I do with the other twenty-eight kids?" Some teachers suggested offering districtwide training for parent volunteers to prepare them to give nonacademic mini-lessons, or do enrichment activities with the rest of the class, while the teacher was doing assessment. (Teachers felt they did not have time to train parent volunteers effectively.)

A few teachers also expressed concern over the strong emphasis the new district math assessments (based on the NCTM *Standards*) put on writing skills. These teachers felt that students who had little trouble with computation often did have trouble expressing themselves about math. A sixth-grade teacher pointed out that she had several high-functioning, but nonverbal, students. She said she understood the value of getting students to discuss their thinking processes and not "just grind out answers." But she felt it was too bad that all assessments had a written product, since the nonverbal students lost out somewhat on their chance to "shine."

Several teachers questioned the district's continuing emphasis on the CTBS, which had been mandated by the school board. One coach felt especially strongly:

> You can't measure anything with a one shot CTBS test given once a year in January, usually, with no tracking whatsoever of the kids that you're giving it to. At the junior high closest to Foothills City, their turnover there is so tremendous, because of the trailer parks and apartments and everything, that the student body they start with is not the same student body that

they end up with. They have a 65–70 percent turnover in their student body. They keep generally the same number of kids, but it's that high a turnover in one year. So what are you measuring? Unless you have a pretest on a particular kid and a posttest on a particular kid, you're not measuring anything.

There were also teachers who thought the balance between district assessment and the use of the CTBS was beneficial. They argued that, since their students would eventually have to know how to take a CTBS-like test, "they might as well get used to it." Some teachers also saw assessments like the CTBS as a welcome check on the completeness of their own teaching. One noted:

> I think that without assessment we tend to muddle on and think that we are just doing such a wonderful job and we may very well be doing a wonderful job, in some things. But somewhere there are people with bigger pictures, who know what also is expected by state and national norms.

A teacher at a school with a high percentage of ethnic minority students wanted to keep getting CTBS data because she had doubts about the effectiveness of the new curriculum framework in teaching students who might not be exposed to standard English at home. "I think we need to see data on where our kids are. Because I think that our kids should be farther ahead than where they are." This teacher pointed out that many Latino children arrived at school without the background knowledge of standard English possessed by most Anglo children starting school: "They're not just seeing a word or a phrase in print and saying, 'Oh, that's what it looks like written down!'" She felt that students who arrived at school with a limited knowledge of standard English needed more direct teaching in phonics, spelling, and grammar than was provided by the minilessons that were taught as part of the whole language curriculum. This teacher argued that the CTBS data served as a check on whether minority children were being well served.

EFFECT OF BUDGET CUTS ON
IMPLEMENTATION OF CURRICULUM FRAMEWORK

Nearly all respondents agreed that the schools wanted more help from the Cottonwood district's curriculum specialists. A typical comment was, "We need to bring back curriculum specialists dedicated to each area. That was what made this district stand above the other districts. It's what made me come to this district." Coaches cautioned that teachers unfamiliar with performance-based teaching methods needed more than just a written manual. Too often, they read about an activity in the curriculum framework materials, misunderstood it or failed to visualize the activity properly, and thus did not succeed when they tried to implement it in their classrooms. The coaches at one school said it would be nice if district curriculum specialists came out to help with the support group they were planning for the fall: "Just add direction on where to go next and to keep the excitement level going."

Teachers and building-level coaches especially missed having the district curriculum specialists update them on new research and ideas. Literacy resource teachers reported that the individual research done by teachers at the building level tended to cover the same ground and thus lead to duplication of effort. They expressed a strong desire to have more research done at the district level:

> When you have schools that get further along, you need a different kind of education for those people. You don't need the basic skills. Now you have to go to a deeper level, just like at the college level, where people learn beyond the basics.

Several coaches spoke fondly of that era when the district had been able to spend the money to bring in recognized outside experts. These coaches expressed a desire to have more opportunities to connect with university researchers in their curriculum area:

> We have to be willing to bring people in who will be able to put us at a place where we need to be. . . . If we want these kids to continue on, with the excellence that they've obtained in elementary school, and we can even move them farther, you know, then there has to be a place to go.

Yet, with a statewide budget crisis limiting educational funds, there was little prospect of additional help. This caused widespread doubt about the district's ability to implement both curriculum frameworks in all schools by September 1995, as planned. Considering budget and manpower shortages, many informants predicted that a rather limited definition of "implementation" would have to be accepted.

PARENT REACTIONS TO CURRICULUM FRAMEWORK

Parent reactions to the new curriculum framework varied greatly. In most cases, when parents saw that their children were learning and enjoyed school, they became enthusiastic supporters of the experiential curriculum. A teacher noted:

> The parents, for the most part, have been absolutely supportive. For sixth-grade kids, and I knew this would be the case, every year I have kids come to school, and say, "My mom took the book, and she won't give it back until she is finished reading it." And I think that is wonderful to have moms and dads both enjoying the books and talking about them with their kids.

Yet coaches admitted that parents often went through an initial period of suspicion caused by the difference between the observed teaching methods they remembered from their own school days and the kind of teaching they observed at their children's school. A coach explained:

> One of the things that comes up with many of our parents is phonics. Phonics, phonics, phonics. They love to talk about phonics and basic math facts . . . because parents know what that means. We've decided, as a school, this fall we're going to have individual grade level meetings with parents, again to go over our curriculum and our philosophy and to answer questions for parents. . . . It takes a long time to get them to see the whole picture.

UNDERSTANDING THE COGNITIVE PROCESSES THE CURRICULUM FRAMEWORK SUPPORTS

An experienced math coach emphasized the need to make teachers aware that the math curriculum framework was not just about numbers, but meant thinking differently about math and "seeing that math can be talked about." In some cases a significant change of perspective was involved: "They [the teachers] need to see that it's not just a right answer or just problems out of the book." Coaches agreed that a major challenge they faced was the tendency for teachers to use curriculum framework activities in class, but not follow through and help children to draw the necessary connections.

An experienced math coach described the problem as "getting them to understand the importance of communication in mathematics and the debriefing part. For it to become a lesson rather than an activity, we have to debrief it and talk through the mathematics with the kids."

District curriculum specialists felt that a contributing factor was math anxiety on the part of teachers: "Math anxiety can block the ability to do the sort of thinking necessary to make connections." A curriculum specialist noted:

> Many older elementary teachers have lived rather comfortable, successful lives without a strong knowledge of math or science, and it may be difficult for these teachers to realize that the children they are now educating will face a different sort of world. . . . That's the aim of many of our staff development activities, to help teachers to make that cognitive jump.

One math coach enthusiastically described the value of dialoguing with high school teachers so as to better understand the math skills her students would need later on.

> We had the chance to dialogue and say, "We do all these wonderful little activities but what does that mean to you?" And they said: "You know, when you're teaching an algebraic formula or . . . This is what they have to come prepared . . . to put together down the line."

Problems reported by language arts coaches often appeared to be rooted in teachers' lack of understanding of the cognitive processes the curriculum framework was intended to support. As one coach observed "Those teachers who are bucking the curriculum framework are the people who were worksheet-oriented, skills-oriented in isolation. They can't see the connection between the writing and the reading process—and, actually, the writing and the reading strategies. The word 'strategy' just throws them for a loop, because strategy means that which you have to do metacognitively to get to a goal." Another coach saw the problem in terms of personal experience:

> If teachers are not willing to be writers and put themselves out, and understand what the writing process truly is, by doing it, themselves, and becoming better readers by analyzing them-

selves as literate people, then we can't move the kids along . . .
because you just get stuck. You don't understand the process
yourself and you get stuck in that and there's only so much
you can do at that basic level.

Like many others who had become deeply involved in the philosophy behind the new curriculum framework, this coach saw going
through a prescribed set of classroom behaviors as a very different
thing from perceiving the inner logic of what one was doing, so that
it became the thing one wanted to do, because it made sense. In
this, she was taking a position that was strongly at odds with the
kind of thinking that had supported the old system of criterion-referenced tests.

PHILOSOPHICAL IMPLICATIONS OF CURRICULUM CHANGE

Looked at in an alternative manner, Cottonwood curriculum
specialists and building coaches had stepped into a philosophical
debate which had been going on for centuries: Does our sensory
response to the outer world shape our thoughts? Or does the way we
habitually process the information coming to us from the outside
world cause us to perceive our environment the way we do? English
empiricists going back to Hume have held that sense impressions are
impressed on the mind, as on a blank tablet, and that these impressions have no connection with one another except the accidental
one of either following one another or appearing together in time. If
this is true, the connections human beings make between sense
impressions must be seen as somewhat arbitrary.

Seen from such a viewpoint, the skills-based, test-driven curriculum used in the Cottonwood School District between 1972
and 1982 makes perfect sense. Children were taught a series of
isolated skills. Little attention was paid to how these separate
skills might be tied into a larger whole. It was assumed that if children had all the necessary bits of knowledge, then they had all the
information needed to create a workable understanding of the subject matter being taught. This made perfect sense if it were
assumed that *all* learning is made up of similarly disconnected
experiences and perceptions. After all, the world does not explain
itself, and yet children gradually figure out how to maneuver about
within it. Why should learning about reading or mathematical reasoning be any different?

Those who pushed for adoption of a more integrated curriculum saw the learning process through a very different lens. As heirs to thinkers such as Kant, James, and Dewey, they assumed that learning is the process of synthesis that human reason performs on the raw data provided by the senses. According to this view, the mind does not "automatically" make order out of chaotic sense perceptions. Only when concepts are added to sense perceptions do we come to understand, for example, that one side of a house can look quite different from another. Only as we think about a problem do we come to recognize, bit by bit, where information is missing or that we may need to actively seek out additional information. Seen from this perspective, learning becomes a more complex affair. Just as possessing all the bits and pieces of a puzzle does not insure that the puzzle will be put together correctly, the teaching of academic skills in isolation does not insure that a child will be able to perform the complex activities that can be built up out of those skills when the need arises.

Advances in the field of psychology have, in recent years, given scientific backing to this second view. But, for much of the twentieth century this view was in disfavor. In *The Mind's New Science* Howard Gardner sketches how the study of behavior, as fashioned by scholars such as Pavlov, Skinner, and Watson, had discredited the introspective methods used by investigators such as Kant, James, and Dewey. In doing so, the behaviorists put forth two related propositions.

1. If a discipline were to be a science, its elements should be as observable as the physicist's cloud chamber or the chemist's flask.
2. Those interested in a science of behavior ought to focus exclusively on *behavior*: researchers ought assiduously to eschew such topics as mind, thinking, or imagination and such concepts as plans, desires or intentions. (Gardner 1987, 11)

Just as mechanics had explained the laws of the physical world, mechanistic models based on the reflex arc were assumed to explain human activity.

Kliebard has described the influence that behaviorism had on curriculum thinking at the national level, pointing out that in volume 3 of the influential report on the eight-year study:

"it was assumed that education is a process which seeks to change the behavior patterns of human beings" (Smith and Tyler 1942, 11). From that assumption, it was only a small step to link these behaviorist principles to the stating of objectives as the crucial first step in the development of a curriculum, a position that Tyler had been advocating for years. "The kinds of changes in behavior patterns in human beings which the school seeks to bring about," according to Tyler (in the part of the book he wrote), "are its educational objectives" (p. 11). Objectives, in other words, should not be stated in vague terms such as knowing, appreciating and understanding, but in terms that would describe in rather precise terms how a student would behave after a period of study. Moreover, the success of the program would be determined by the extent to which the behaviors embodied in the objectives would be achieved. (Kliebard 1987, 219-20)

Gardner points out that the behaviorist model was not effectively challenged until 1948, when psychologist Karl Lashley argued that an acceptable theory of human behavior ought to account for complexly organized behaviors such as playing tennis, performing on a musical instrument, or—above all—speaking. The explanatory framework offered by the behaviorists—that of simple associative chains between a stimulus and a response—could not possibly account for an action such as playing an arpeggio on a piano, where there is simply no time for feedback, no time for the next tone to depend upon the preceding one (pp. 12–13). What Lashley was arguing was that behavioral sequences had to be planned and organized in advance. In that case, behavior was not consequent upon environmental promptings. Central brain processes actually preceded and dictated the ways in which an organism carried out complex behaviors.

Gradually, a new science of cognition slowly took form, charting a scientifically respectable way between the "hard line" behaviorists and the unbridled conjecturing of the Freudians. Sir Frederick Bartlett first used the word schema (1932) to mean "an active organization of past reactions, or past experiences." Challenging the idea that remembering consisted of the passive retrieval of "fixed and lifeless" memories, he emphasized the constructive character of memory:

an individual does not ordinarily take . . . a situation detail by detail and meticulously build up the whole. In all ordinary instances he has an overmastering tendency simply to get a general impression of the whole: and, on the basis of this, he constructs the probable detail. Very little of his construction is literally observed.

This view of learning was strikingly different from that which had gained widespread acceptance under the aegis of behavioristic psychology. Indeed, such views at first made but slow headway against prevailing behavioristic views of learning.

At the time when Dr. Davis came to the Cottonwood district in 1972, the behavioristic underpinnings of the test-driven curriculum he put in place were still widely accepted. By the late 1970s, however, schema theory had become the driving force behind empirical investigations of basic processes in reading, spurred by the research of computer scientists doing simulations of human cognition. Processes such as reading comprehension became better understood through the study of how the reader's schema, or knowledge already stored in memory, functioned in the process of interpreting and storing new information. As researchers envisioned it, a schema was an abstract knowledge structure that summarized what was known about a variety of different, but related, experiences. Interconnections among integrated sets of memories facilitated retrieval and verification. The new integrated curriculum framework in the Cottonwood School District was based on this new understanding of cognition, which emphasized presenting material so that the relationship between one bit of knowledge and the next was made clear.

That the new curriculum was referred to as a curriculum "framework" implied recognition of the need for a conceptual framework that allowed separate bits of knowledge to be brought into meaningful relation to one another. Curriculum coaches involved in piloting the curriculum framework repeatedly expressed the view that the small particles of unrelated rote instruction imparted to students through the old test-driven curriculum had neither instilled a love of learning nor taught academic skills in a manner such that they were likely to be remembered and used. But, for those teachers who had not been actively involved in the curriculum change process—and who had learned a behaviorist version of educational psychology when they were in college—coming to grips with the theory of human learning that undergirded the new curriculum framework required considerable struggle.

CONCLUSIONS

Despite initial doubts by some staff members, the new curriculum framework proved helpful in raising the Cottonwood district's scores on the Comprehensive Tests of Basic Skills. The district had set a goal of increasing the number of students achieving at or above the norm on the total CTBS battery from 55% in 1991–92 to 64% by 1 July 1995. District students had increased their scores by 4.7 percentage points on the CTBS during the first year.

There remained some question about whether the new curriculum framework provided enough direct teaching for students who did not hear standard English spoken at home. The achievement of minority students is a matter of special concern in the Cottonwood School District because the dropout rate in those school communities with the highest minority populations remained substantially higher than the dropout rate elsewhere. Examination of test results of all non-Anglo students showed that they averaged at the 47th percentile on the total battery of CTBS, whereas the average score for Anglo students was at the 62nd percentile. If the district is to meet its stated goal of decreasing the achievement gap, attention would have to be paid to the most effective techniques for teaching minority children.

Teacher/coaches were seen by both teachers and administrators as the key to the success that the curriculum framework had enjoyed thus far. The area of need which stood out most strongly was greater assistance for these building-level coaches, especially the math coaches. Coaches were unanimous in calling for more support from district curriculum specialists, even though all were aware of the state-level budget shortfalls which made such support unlikely. The following exchange, which included two math coaches and two language arts coaches, focused on an often-expressed concern that present cuts in curriculum and instruction personnel would handicap the district in future years:

> *Math coach:* We've got to have someone who will lead. We don't have time to read all the research and things that we need to keep up on. It's really, really . . . it's extremely hard.
>
> *Language arts coach:* I think that's going to be where this district really falls down. You just write that in. In every curriculum area there's no one at the district level who is going to keep current with research. We are going to become, instead of a district that has been leading in the area of language, in the area of math, our social studies and science—we are just going to be . . . in a few years . . .
>
> *Math coach:* Treading water.
>
> *Language arts coach:* In a few years there won't be anyone to say "Hey! You've got to be trying some of this new stuff! You've got to keep up with what's going on."

If progress were to be made in implementing the curriculum framework at the secondary level, there would also be a need for district curriculum specialists to carry on a dialogue with secondary teachers. Unfortunately, the state budget crisis had left the Cottonwood School District with few options. If implementation of the math curriculum framework was to move forward at the elementary level, no extra personnel could be made available to assist at the secondary level. At the junior high level—where teachers appeared reluctant to throw away lesson plans they had used for years and experiment with an unfamiliar teaching style—there was a tendency for teachers to use the site-based decision-making apparatus, not to speed implementation of the curriculum framework, but to collaboratively decide not to rush into curriculum change.

The future of curriculum framework implementation at the secondary level remained in doubt, except at Sagebrush High, whose story will be told in the next chapter. Without intensive help from district curriculum specialists, successful implementation of the curriculum framework would require a kind of initiative and effort that most secondary teachers had thus far appeared unwilling to give. Therefore, the fate of the Cottonwood School District's curriculum reform effort on the secondary level appeared to depend upon whether budgetary decisions made in the state capital would allow the district to, once again, provide intensive support to schools experimenting with new teaching methods.

Put in terms of the geological metaphor, the Cottonwood district, with all its complex history, was no more independent of the larger political system of which it was a part than the land on which the school buildings sat could be seen as separate from the North American land mass. The extent to which a local school district could stray from the norm was limited by financial and legal limitations rooted in Western State's public education system. Thus, although Cottonwood had become, in many respects, an "outlier" among school districts, using limited resources to provide high quality educational opportunities, these achievements remained fragile, at the mercy of changes in the political wind.

CHAPTER 7

DIFFERING PATHS TAKEN
UNDER SITE-BASED MANAGEMENT:
THE COTTONWOOD HIGH SCHOOLS

This chapter will trace the evolution, since the introduction of site-based decision-making, of very distinctive cultures in the Cottonwood district's three comprehensive high schools. As has been pointed out in previous chapters, pronounced tensions had developed between the cities of Metroville and Suburbia. As a result of these tensions, intense feelings of competitiveness had developed between the staff and students at Metroville and Suburban high schools. When the new Sagebrush High School was built to serve outlying suburban areas of the Cottonwood district in the late 1980s, the two older schools became, for awhile, united in their opposition to changes associated with the new school.

The new high school was planned around the nine principles put forth by Dr. Ted Sizer and the Coalition of Essential Schools. Those secondary teachers who applied, and were accepted to teach, at Sagebrush High tended to be those who were most enthusiastic about the experiential teaching methods embodied in the evolving curriculum framework. An unintended result of gathering these teachers in a single school was that other secondary schools in the district were left with fewer teachers who were likely to pour their energies into successfully implementing experiential teaching. Thus the exodus of many energetic teachers to Sagebrush High has been associated with a comparative lack of progress toward implementation of the curriculum framework elsewhere.

This chapter will describe both the restructured program at Sagebrush and the reaction of staff members at the other two high schools. The first section will describe social tensions in the Cottonwood School District, prior to the opening of Sagebrush High School. The

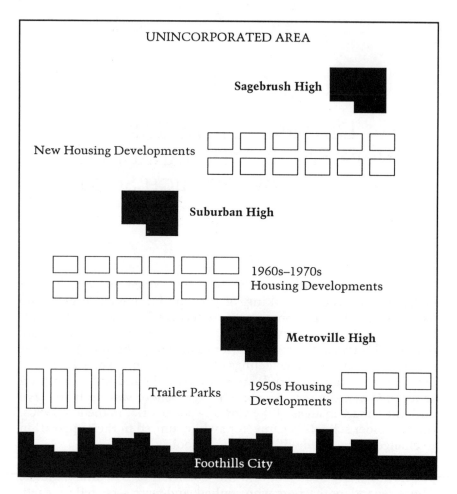

**Map of the Cottonwood School District
with Locations of the Three High Schools**

second section will describe the innovative programs implemented at Sagebrush High, a school that has been visited by educators from across the nation. The third section will investigate how Suburban and Metroville high schools have changed since Sagebrush opened.

SOCIAL TENSIONS WITHIN THE COTTONWOOD SCHOOL DISTRICT

Referring to the time when the cities of Suburbia and Metroville were each fiercely contesting one another's annexation and water policies, an informant commented: "They just didn't get along, and apparently didn't want to get along, and this animosity just seemed to mushroom." A school administrator noted:

> During the period of rapid growth there was a lot of boosterism going on, involving the schools, as well as everything else. At one time the mayor of Suburbia was on the school board. Then, when Suburban High was built, it was new and shiny and got a lot of attention, while Metroville was sort of left with this older building and the less desirable teachers. Later, when the new Metroville High School was built, it sort of shifted and there was talk about adding onto Suburban High to bring it up to the same standard.

A long-time resident mentioned the effect of ethnic tensions: "When Metroville was first built, that's where the younger people who came back from the Second World War moved. It had new housing and inexpensive homes. But it didn't take long, ten years, I suppose, before some Hispanics started moving in and Metroville's reputation as a model city declined." The present Metroville mayor blamed rumors of quality problems with the houses then being built: "Metroville was the victim of a negative image from the time the city was first started in the late 1950s. The bentonite soil here caused severe cracking problems in some houses and that was how the rest of the metro area thought of us. Once something like that starts, it takes a long time to recover."

Later on, more expensive homes were built, further from Foothills City, in an unincorporated area of Garfield County. Reacting to Metroville's unfashionable reputation, the residents of the new subdivision distanced themselves from Metroville. A school administrator remembered: "When they started building the subdivision called 'Suburbia,' they were a couple of steps up in the quality of homes and price of homes. So the people who moved there didn't want to be part of this sub-class city [Metroville], if you will."

Suburbia's expensive "water war" with Metroville and, later, a regional recession in the late 1970s and early 1980s, were a shock. Once an up-and-coming area, Suburbia found itself lumped together with Metroville. The chairman of the Garfield County Commission described the public perception: "Garfield County did have a lot of affordable housing, which attracted a lot of retired people and startup families. Consequently, the income level has been a little lower than some other areas." A manager for a regional utility company, now engaged in helping Garfield County rebuild its image, noted that when she had moved to Western State in the late 1970s she had not considered buying a house in Garfield County. "It definitely had a negative, blue-collar image."

A 1993 article in the *Foothills City Chronicle* pointed out the difficulty of altering public perceptions of Garfield County, "once renowned for its topless bars, massage parlors and adult bookstores." The article pointed out: "There are those in the metro area who think of Garfield county as a bunch of cheap homes occupied by blue-collar, beer-drinking, working stiffs and unmarried mothers struggling with too many social problems and too little money." Garfield County remained the site of many of the metropolitan area's landfills, gravel pits, and mobile homes, as well as an oil refinery and Western State's largest sewerage treatment plant. However, in recent years golf courses and fashionable new housing had been built in outlying areas of the Cottonwood School District. But this upscale housing often had the effect of exacerbating existing social tensions.

During the years when Suburbia was handicapped by the financial repercussions of its water policy, aggressive annexation policies were pursued by cities that could offer developers more water. Soon, Suburbia found itself surrounded, with no further growth possible. This made Metroville's relative success in the "annexation wars" all the more galling to Suburbia residents. During the time that Suburbia was paralyzed by water shortages, Metroville had annexed enough rural land to surround Suburbia on one side. Now, in addition to "old" Metroville, located between Suburbia and Foothills City, there was a "new" Metroville, connected to "old" Metroville by a narrow strip of land. On the opposite side of Suburbia from Foothills City, "new" Metroville occupied a semi-rural area that Suburbia had once expected to annex.

The history of the Metroville/Suburbia rivalry renders more comprehensible the fierce political battles over school attendance areas described in the following pages. The bitterness of these battles took many individuals within the Cottonwood School District by surprise. The shared decision-making structures put in place by Dr. Roberts during the 1980s depended for their effectiveness upon a certain amount of good will and amicable relations among the school district's constituents. Resentments and rivalries growing out of factors outside the school district's control made reaching consensus far more difficult. At times school district policies have been confronted with a kind of intransigent opposition that could only be explained by background issues such as those described above.

Resentment over the hard times their city had suffered caused some residents of Suburbia to perceive change, in general, as threatening. An article in the *Foothills City Chronicle* (April 1993) described city council reactions after Suburbia voters turned down a proposal to build a golf course:

> "Without the project, Suburbia will continue to stagnate," a councilwoman said. "Cities around us continue to prosper while we continue to do nothing."
>
> Some of the voter reluctance can be traced back to the city's ill-fated water bond project of the early 1980s, which residents are still paying for, said a councilman. "The people were sold a bill of goods on the water project. They are afraid to take another chance. I can understand that."

Privately, several Cottonwood staff members suggested that, had the municipalities of Metroville and Suburbia adopted, years ago, the collaborative approach to problem-solving that the school district was trying to model—instead of engaging in the economic blood-letting which had taken place—both the municipalities and the school district would be in much better financial health. But, ironically, the Cottonwood School District was still struggling to "sell" collaborative decision-making to constituents whose attitudes have been shaped by a competitive, politically oriented variety of decision-making that had encouraged mutual distrust.

By the end of the 1980s, Sagebrush High had been built to serve the new part of Metroville. The new school had a more modern building and a more affluent student body than Suburban High, heretofore considered to be Cottonwood's "academic" high school. Described by a respected researcher from the Education Commission of the States as "the most restructured school" in Western State, Sagebrush High was set up to encourage the integrated approach to learning embodied in the Cottonwood School District's new curriculum framework. In its first three years of existence, Sagebrush High was visited by educators from all over the United States. Yet Sagebrush's break-the-mold principal and staff have often found themselves to be "prophets without honor" among personnel at the other Cottonwood high schools.

SAGEBRUSH HIGH SCHOOL

When population growth in the Cottonwood district continued at a high rate during the late 1970s, plans had been made for a third high school. When Superintendent Roberts took the reins in

1982, much of the groundwork had already been laid. Dr. Roberts put great energy into making sure that the new school would be an institution of which the district could be proud. An observer explained:

> The district was insightful enough to go around to different schools with the architect and say: All right, what are good things about your school? . . . So they went to different places and got different views and said: What works? What doesn't work? What would you change if you had something to change?

As a result, the Sagebrush High building has gotten high marks for the many amenities it offers to students and staff—at minimal cost. The one drawback of this planning process was that, as frequently happens when public input is solicited, groups who responded enthusiastically ended up having a disproportionately strong influence on the planning process. A staff member noted:

> So you kind of see the influence, throughout this building, of who was really aggressive about saying what they felt should happen. For example, we have an extremely nice art department, fine and performing arts, which was a result, I think, of some dynamic people saying, "Look, we really need to be insightful about the arts in the future." The computers, all the computer rooms that you will see in our school, were started by that.

Suzanne Thompson was hired as principal two years before the school was to open, so that she could help with the planning. A core team of twelve (including administrators, teachers, a counselor, and a classified staff member) was released from other duties a semester early to work with Dr. Thompson in planning for the new school. A member of this core team recalled:

> Most of us came on board in January, and then we had January through the summer to prepare for getting the school opened. We worked at a little elementary school. We had tables and folding chairs in a kindergarten room. . . . This building [Sagebrush High] was still, you know, at the dirt floors and hard hat stage. But it was finished in time for school to open.

Another member of the core team described Suzanne Thompson's vision for the new school:

She was looking toward more of an integrated studies program, less of a shopping mall kind of high school, with a wide variety of selections for students. Simplifying the curriculum, keeping all the content intact, but not necessarily offering that content through lots and lots of courses. . . . I think the integration was the part that was probably the newest for this school district.

The core team used belief statements they had evolved, along with belief statements worked on by a group of students, to guide development of the curriculum. A teacher enthusiastically described the intense dialogue:

It was an opportunity of a lifetime. I think every new school should be opened that way. The time for intense dialogue, the opportunity to interact with each other, and to have a dynamic sort of creation. . . . I never have had an experience like it in my life. I do think it laid the foundation for a solid program here. . . . It wouldn't be the same if they would have just had an administrator and secretary and then they had hired a staff and got started.

A core team member described the obstacles that had to be overcome:

Both the other high schools were very, very traditional and the [secondary-level] curriculum in the district was very traditional. So this was a real nontraditional approach, and a real leap for those of us who had been working in the other schools. . . . [We] do a lot of reading, did a lot at the beginning and a lot of research so that people began to understand. I can remember reading tons of articles and books initially.

This core team arrived at a consensus about the importance of creating a personal, humane environment for students. A teacher described how they envisioned changing the traditional high school environment.

High schools are organized to be impersonal. There's no question about it. Teachers see 150 students per semester, 300 per year. Kids see five or six teachers a day. Teachers rush by each other, trying to get done all that they feel needs to be done. Nobody really knows anybody all that well.

A decision was made to pattern the Sagebrush High curriculum on suggestions put forth by the Coalition of Essential Schools. A staff member explained, "Sagebrush has pretty much followed the Coalition's Nine Principles like a Bible from the beginning. When decisions have been made about curriculum, they have been made with the Sizer principles in mind. . . . One of the principles is that no teacher should have more than 80 students. One way we have played around with that is through block scheduling. I see from 50 to 75 kids per day."

Published materials made available by Sagebrush High summarized the considerations that dominated the planning process: "Literature on learning and quality education identified the following interrelated strategic components as those essential to the educational environment Sagebrush staff members wished to establish: school-centered decision-making and accountability; personal sense of belonging; flexible use of time and space; integrated core curriculum; and changed roles with student as worker, and teacher as facilitator. All of these strategic components have been woven into the organization and curriculum of Sagebrush High."

Adherence to a clearly, stated philosophy gave the school a coherent vision around which to plan. As a teacher explained:

Sagebrush started with a specific philosophy. Those who became part of the school knew what they were getting into. There is great buy-in at Sagebrush. Last year our principal applied for a very prestigious position elsewhere. She was very up front about it. There was a lot of talk about what we would do if she left. One thing we talked about was self-government. People violently care about building administration.

Sagebrush principal Suzanne Thompson described how she saw her role:

The staff at Sagebrush sees me as the "vision keeper" who does the reading, gets materials out to people. Support from the superintendent is also very important. I came out here because of where Dr. Roberts said the district was going.

To understand the motivation behind innovations implemented at Sagebrush, it is helpful to review some problematic characteristics of "generic" U.S. high schools, as described in a book often alluded to by Cottonwood staff members: *The Shopping Mall High School: Winners and Losers in the Educational Marketplace* (Powell, Farrar, and Cohen 1985):

> Few characteristics of the shopping mall high school are more significant than the existence of unspecial students in the middle who are ignored and poorly served. Teachers and administrators talk a great deal about the problem. . . . Everyone agrees that the unspecial is a sizable group. One counselor first estimated that 70 percent of his school's student body fell into that category. (pp. 173–74)

One reason the "unspecial student" can slide through with only a cursory knowledge of the subject matter is the existence of classroom treaties that allow the "unspecial" to avoid work:

> Treaties for avoidance rather than engagement dominate classes attended by the unspecial. Little is usually expected of these students, and little is done to change their lot. High school attendance thus perpetuates and confirms unspecialness.

Students often bend their efforts to figuring out the least amount of work they can do and still get by: "For the middle students, a school's neutral stance on pushing students has the effect of making minimum requirements maximum standards" (p. 180).

The challenge that the Sagebrush staff faced was to move from a shared vision of what was wrong with the present system to create a school which avoided these pitfalls. As a member of the original core team noted:

> The kind of curriculum that was being planned . . . did not exist in that particular format in other schools, so . . . there's a lot of trial and error. And we went through that, particularly for the first year. I do think a real commitment on this staff's part to make that all work was very necessary.

Opening Sagebrush High

The seventy applicants who applied for the first twenty-five teaching positions at Sagebrush High (and passed the initial screening) were all observed teaching in their present classrooms. Dr.

Thompson did the observations. She pointed out, "There are always those teachers who look good on paper but are not good for kids." Dr. Thompson was also looking for teachers who were willing to take risks and wanted to get involved in school governance. After the school was established, hiring at Sagebrush became a committee affair. Hiring committees consist of two students, a parent, and two staff members, along with an administrative facilitator. Every time a job description goes out, even for custodians, the belief statements the school staff have agreed upon go with it.

The first year Sagebrush served 815 sophomores and juniors. Juniors who lived in the Sagebrush attendance area were given the choice of transferring to the new school. An integrated core curriculum was set up for the incoming sophomores. A unique advising system was set up to ensure that every student had an adult to talk to when the need came up. An article in the *Foothills City Times* gave an outside observer's view:

> Concepts considered futuristic in other schools—such as site-based decision-making, block-scheduled classes and integrated curriculum core classes—already are in place here. So are advanced computer technology, music synthesizers and theater lighting, all housed in a high-tech plant that reduces isolation by minimizing physical and mental walls. . . . Sagebrush's innovations have drawn more than 250 educational observers from across the country this school year alone.

American Studies Core

The tenth-grade American Studies Core met for three consecutive periods every day. The goal was to provide students with opportunities to understand relationships between historical events, scientific developments, artistic creations, and literary works. Teachers from three disciplines (social studies, English, and science, with the intermittent participation of an art teacher) planned lessons to help students to make connections. Also important to integration was the consolidation of teacher offices into two large work areas, which replaced the small, separated cubicles found at the other high schools.

Building on the philosophy that a school is a community of learners, the American Studies Core encouraged teachers (who often found themselves cooperating in presenting an activity outside their own special expertise) to model learning. Enthusiasm for the American Studies Core was not universal, however. During the first two years after Sagebrush High opened, a vocal contingent of parents made clear their distrust of a curriculum that differed so radically from courses they recalled taking in high school. An administrator recalled:

> In the first couple of years we fought tooth and nail with parents, some parents. You know, the majority of people were willing to give it a try and support a change. But we had a real problem with parents of gifted-talented kids saying, "My kid is far beyond that and doesn't need that." But we are saying, "Yes, but in the Core kids learn social skills, camaraderie, life skills, work ethic, all those kinds of things, they need to succeed. . . . Some of the content may not be as challenging as you would like it to be, but some of the other stuff, the methodology that goes along with it, is extremely necessary. So yeah, you have to take it and we are not going to let you opt out. But you can opt to go to another school."

Very few students ended up transferring. However, some ninth-graders from the Sagebrush attendance area opted to attend Suburban High because of the older school's traditional curriculum. Also, of the seventy students accepted into the selective International Baccalaureate program started at Metroville High during the final year of this study, many came from junior highs in the Sagebrush High feeder pattern. But the flow of students transferring out of the Sagebrush attendance area has been but a trickle, compared to the flood of students trying to transfer into the new school.

Advisory

Asked to name the most unusual thing about Sagebrush High, a member of the core planning team pointed to the advisory system:

> Every student is in an advisory; every teacher is an advisor. That was on our original job application, that you have to be willing to do this. It originally started meeting every day. That was too much; it was burn out. Now we meet two times a week . . . to deal with the affective part of kids; to deal with the social issues.

Most Sagebrush staff members, including some all the administrators, are involved in leading or co-leading advisory groups. Students remain with the same advisory for three years . The Sagebrush High philosophy statement says:

> The Sagebrush High Community believes that to meet the needs of the whole learner, educational experiences must extend beyond the academic classroom; our student advisement program is a team effort among students, staff, parents, and community. This program is designed to personalize education, complement the curriculum, and assist students in developing skills and attitudes necessary to their success.

Not all teachers ran their advisory sessions the same way. Some put considerable effort into creating a family atmosphere. Others felt uncomfortable playing the counselor role or unsure of how to fill the time. Dr. Thompson admitted there were still kinks to be ironed out, but said she was committed to helping teachers understand how advisory was meant to work.

Peer Writing Tutors

The Peer Writing Tutor program was introduced at Sagebrush in 1989. Students who act as tutors receive extensive training. Writing tutors specialize in the areas of revision and editing. They are available during the school day to help other students with writing assignments. Teachers see two main benefits: student clients show increased awareness of themselves as writers, more confidence in their own ability to communicate, and improved skills; and peer writing tutors improve their own writing and revision skills, while building communication skills by working with all personality types.

Wetlands

Through the Wetlands project, Sagebrush students transformed fourteen acres of school property into a wildlife sanctuary and outdoor learning center. Students hauled away truckloads of trash before planting over 1,000 trees and shrubs. Five acres were seeded with native grasses in order to stem erosion. Wildflower seeds were scattered throughout the area. Students also constructed a nature trail, which doubled as a cross-country racecourse. Bat boxes, bird houses, and feeders built by students were placed on the Wetlands. There were plans for a bridge, interpretive signs, park benches, even an outdoor amphitheater and classroom. Students in the Nature Guide Program prepared and gave presentations on wildlife to third-grade students throughout the Cottonwood School District.

Block Scheduling

Sagebrush provided a variety of scheduling options, including the traditional eight-period day, two-period blocks, three-period integrated CORE blocks, and a weekly three-hour evening seminar. Staff and students continued to explore using varying methods of instruction to maximize effective use of time.

New Directions Early Education Center

New Directions Early Education Center provided both training and dropout prevention for pregnant and parenting teens. Utilizing an on-site licensed daycare site, the center combined parenting education with skill development in problem-solving and decision-making. Students who used the center had to be enrolled in five regular credit classes per semester and follow program expectations, including: taking the New Directions class, maintaining acceptable grades and attendance, and carrying out a parenting practicum. Student comments included:

> This program got me back in school and keeps me in school.

> My child has matured faster by being around other kids and has learned manners.

> I now have a greater chance to get a job; it has also helped me gain more self-confidence.

The on-site licensed day care center and nursery also provided hands-on experience for Sagebrush High students taking childcare classes. A staff member explained that the daycare facility was self-supporting:

> The priorities are, parenting teens have first choice, then, if that doesn't fill it up, we have people from our own staff with their own children. That is second priority. Then we have district staff that have third priority, and then we open it up to the community. We have been full since the second year of operation. We were about 80 percent capacity by the second semester of the

first year that we opened. We had a good director, whom we hired to get the program going. She worked real hard getting it licensed.

Shared Decision-Making at Sagebrush High

Sagebrush High is characterized by a different set of power relationships than most American high schools. There are no department chairs. Teachers had noticed how, at other schools where they had worked, long-time department chairs used that position to enhance personal power and prerogatives, often in ways that did not serve the best interests of other teachers. To avoid such an outcome at Sagebrush, the duties traditionally given to a department chair were divided among the teachers in each department. Instead of letting a single department chair have an additional planning period everyday, substitute teacher coverage was made available, as needed, when department members needed time to carry out specific tasks.

During Sagebrush's first two years, roles were worked out by trial and error. Teachers reported a lack of certainty about who was supposed to do what. But, over time, more efficient ways of dividing responsibilities were worked out. Dr. Thompson described the administrative division of labor in her school:

> Every administrator is teamed with a counselor. They work with the same 350 kids from tenth to twelfth grade. Teachers have advisory groups. Job descriptions of administrators change. It is not a system where you have deans who just do discipline. Change is encouraged so that people are always developing, learning new skills. Those who wish to become principals are given the chance to round out their skills.

For Dr. Thompson, the first step in creating a more stimulating environment was changing the accepted regularities of schooling, so that staff members felt supported in their efforts, yet challenged to continually improve.

Sagebrush High personnel repeatedly pointed out that successful implementation of shared decision-making required more than learning new procedures. Shared decision-making rested upon different philosophical underpinnings than the top-down administrative system that preceded it. An assistant principal explained:

> I have had to change as an administrator. Where in the past it was kind of expected that you are the decision maker, now we have had to push that back on the teachers. And at the begin-

ning the teachers were saying, "Look, our administrative team is not very strong, because they can't make a decision." But we are saying, "You don't really want us to make a decision. It is going to take some time and you are going to have to work through this, but we want you to be a part of that decision, so don't look to us for all the answers."

A veteran Cottonwood staff member contrasted the decision-making process at Sagebrush High with what she had experienced at other schools:

> This school has a much higher involvement in shared deci-sion-making than other schools that I have worked in within the district. How we arrive at governing the whole building involves people in every single area: budget decisions, curricu-lar decisions. There are lots and lots of areas that we have decided on the shared decision-making model.

A teacher enthusiastically described the role of students in the shared decision-making process: "Kids also have lots of possibilities for input. Their input is actually sought after. Kids are on commit-tees." An administrator described the role of students within the school governance structure:

> The General Assembly is one representative from each advisory [home room], which then meets with student council once or twice a month and expresses their concerns.

Yet students had been reluctant to put in the time needed to become effective participants in the shared decision-making pro-cess. The general assembly had not been as active as teachers would have liked. A counselor explained the difficulty of getting students to see it as a serious commitment:

> Every other Wednesday we have zero hour, and during zero hour different clubs meet. One of the groups that meets every other Wednesday in zero hour is general assembly, and they are elected from advisory. We've had problems getting them to meet, because they have to come earlier that day.

Student council was an elective class, except for student body offi-cers, who were required to take it. A student council sponsor explained that the council had tended to show less interest in debating school policy than in organizing social activities:

> We meet every day fifth hour, and they . . . we haven't done as many governmental kinds of things as we would like to. I think next year it'll be much more of that. They do homecoming and that ends up, at the beginning of the year, being the only thing they can handle, and so it's hard to get anything going until we get that over with. And, then, they do all the assemblies. They're responsible for those and, they do a lot of other activities that they choose to do. Right now they're working on a spirit kind of thing.

One teacher noted there were differing opinions among students as to the weight their input was given:

> Kids are on committees. Some think their input is listened to. One boy I know is more cynical. He thinks kids are treated as children, not equally [when they serve on committees]. I'm not sure that's a fair opinion on his part. It could just be his personality. But he's voiced that opinion strongly.

More widespread, though, seemed to be a student reluctance to take on the added responsibilities. Some teachers hypothesized that the media-influenced U.S. popular culture communicated the idea that the adolescent years ought to be a carefree time, when young people ought to be able to leave community responsibilities to the older generation. In any case, Sagebrush students appeared not to see taking responsibility for the well-being of the broader school community as an attractive option. This attitude was similar to that of many Sagebrush parents, few of whom had chosen to dedicate time to the shared decision-making process going on at Sagebrush High.

Dr. Thompson, however, saw the real test as lying elsewhere: "If improved instruction doesn't occur as a result of what we do, I don't know what we have accomplished by being site-based." Most Sagebrush teachers did feel that shared decision making had affected what happened in the classroom. The following comment was typical:

> I suspect that teachers in a site-based building have more of a "we're in this together" attitude. That's part of the atmosphere. I suspect that they're more democratic in class, too, that they treat the students differently.

Has Sagebrush Succeeded?

In reply to enthusiastic descriptions of Sagebrush's restructuring efforts, the comment often made by teachers from the other high schools was: "They chose to be there." To some teachers at Suburan or Metro High, the Sagebrush staff looked like a self-selected group, busily patting themselves on the back. In fact, not all Sagebrush teachers had chosen to transfer there. Many administrative transfers had taken place during the second year after Sagebrush opened, as student and faculty populations rapidly shifted. Yet the team who had planned and opened the school had been volunteers who had "bought into" a specific vision, and of the teachers who had been administratively transferred, anyone deeply opposed to that vision could easily have transferred elsewhere. Very few did.

The sometimes fierce resentment expressed by staff members at the other two high schools might be paraphrased thus: "Sagebrush got to choose the best teachers, ended up with the best students, and was given an up-to-date, high-tech building to house them in. It would be strange if they *hadn't* come out looking pretty good!" In an attempt to get past such perceptions, and the sometimes merciless criticism of Sagebrush they generated, Superintendent Roberts invited a research team from Western State University to do an evaluation of Sagebrush High. During the spring semester of Sagebrush's second year of operation, four professors and several graduate students distributed surveys, interviewed a broad sample of staff members, held group discussions, and analyzed data from school records. They were clearly impressed with the programs at Sagebrush High.

"Nationally, the second wave of educational reform has yet to begin. But Sagebrush is leading the state and the nation in implementing meaningful reform efforts," the leader of the evaluation team concluded. The report also questioned whether Sagebrush High might be trying to do too much, too fast:

> While all these reforms have been tried and proven successful in other environments, few, if any, large suburban secondary schools have attempted them all at once, or during their first two years of existence. . . . It became clear to the visiting team that Sagebrush High wants to institute every major possible change for the better within its first three years, with the danger that in the process it might very well burn out its incredibly talented group of teachers, administrators and staff.

The visiting team pointed to the necessity of balancing Sage-brush's need for a period of consolidation with the staff's need to fight a definite tendency for innovative schools to "revert to the mean," becoming like every other "generic" high school. The visiting team perceived Sagebrush to be facing a critical period in its development: "History indicates that most [new high schools with lofty goals] jettison their ideals after two or three years, having burnt out their faculty, failed to get student buy-in, or alienated their parent-community."

Sagebrush High's strength lay in the exceptional quality of the teaching staff, which included many recipients of outstanding teaching awards. Student teachers reported arriving at the school at 6 a.m., only to find many veteran teachers there ahead of them. Returning for evening programs, they found teachers still at their desks or working on various student activities. But Sagebrush's students took all this effort for granted. Researchers were surprised by the lack of respect the school's upper-middle-class students sometimes showed for their teachers, each other, and their school. A visitor commented:

> While the kids are appropriately dressed and generally well behaved, they seemed to lack a focus or a genuine desire to learn. With the exciting teachers and creative core curriculum, I expected much more intellectual excitement in the class-room, more active learning, and creative use of time than I found.

One teacher quoted quoted in the study suggested that affluent neighborhoods in the Sagebrush High attendance area seemed to produce some "spoiled, materialistic kids." Another teacher suggested that undisciplined Sagebrush students represented "the worst of New Age parenting." The research team pointed out that Sagebrush "appears to be faced with the dilemma of how to maintain a student-centered environment while not being run over by the students." Sagebrush students did not seem to know what the boundaries were, or the consequences for crossing those boundaries.

Questions posed by the visiting team included:

• Who makes what decisions?
• Which decisions is it important to have teacher, staff or student input on, and which ones should be made by administrators?

- Are there areas of management and administration which are falling through the cracks because no one person/group is responsible?
- Are students really being empowered, or are staff members doing too much to and for them?

A year later, when this study began, duties and responsibilities of staff members at Sagebrush High were more clearly defined. Discipline had been tightened. There was no longer a feeling that everything was up in the air or open to question. There was now a full student body at the school. The first students to arrive at Sagebrush as tenth-graders were now seniors and accustomed to the system. Little was said about disruptive student behavior. However, Sagebrush had still not solved the problem of creating an atmosphere which encouraged students to strive for excellence, within a school based upon an egalitarian philosophy.

One quote in the visiting team's report was echoed by several respondents in the present study:

> We have too much mediocrity here at Sagebrush on the part of students. It appears that in our desire to treat all kids equally . . . we have an inability to create an atmosphere of excellence or competitive drive.

Yet staff members pointed to exciting things that were happening at Sagebrush High. A teacher enthusiastically described the school's strong points:

> Mutual respect and value are pretty big, lofty goals, but I think people have really been empowered to make those things happen. . . . For example, you say, "All right let's really go for it. How can we get a really strong computer program going?"
>
> Well we have [a teacher who is] a real computer guru, who has gone out to the trash dumps at AT&T and has pulled lines in, free line, and he has run lines throughout the whole underneath of the building to link all of our computers, to network all of our computers. He is really on the cutting edge. He has kids operating networks.

Staff members noted, with considerable justification, that Sagebrush offered great learning experiences to highly motivated students who seized the opportunities this unique school offered.

Students who knew what they wanted had a good chance of getting it. Those who had trouble tended to be those accustomed to being guided, who had trouble stepping forward or committing, those unprepared to answer the question: "What would you like to do?"

Ironically, the area where Sagebrush High most noticeably fell short of its original vision, was in addressing the needs of the "unspecial" student. *The Shopping Mall High School* (1985, 191) described the outlook typical of such students:

> These self-proclaimed average students thought that friendly and tolerant relationships were the most important thing about high school. "The school is relaxed," one said, and others chimed in that "the social life is great" and that "Enjoy yourself" best captured the local mood.

Such attitudes remained prevalent among students at Sagebrush High. A veteran teacher admitted, "We overestimated the changes that could be produced in kids' attitudes and behavior, simply by fiddling with what they experienced during high school, during the school day." A counselor, talking about the difficulty of getting the student general assembly to meet, admitted:

> They have to come earlier that day, and kids just don't do that. You know, if it's a day that they can stay home later, or meet their friends and hang out in the student center, that's more fun than going to general assembly.

Nor did faculty attempts to build a welcoming, multicultural atmosphere outweigh the influence of the larger social context of the school in the minds of minority students. A teacher noted:

> I remember a girl who had transferred to Sagebrush from a Foothills City high school. She wanted to transfer to Metroville High because it was more "low class" in contrast to "high class" Sagebrush. This is a very "blond" school. Some kids just don't feel comfortable here.

As this research project ended, Sagebrush High was ending its fourth year of operation. Shared decision-making among staff members was running smoothly. Many Sagebrush programs had been copied by other school districts. Yet there appeared to be a dimension of the "generic" U.S. high school culture that the restructuring carried out at Sagebrush High was unable to significantly alter. As the visiting team from Western State University had noted: "We are concerned that if a teaching staff as talented and committed as that found at Sagebrush High School cannot generate such a [intellectually exciting] learning environment, there may be little hope for other secondary institutions."

Why was it that what Sagebrush high teachers and administrators were trying to accomplish was invisible, not only to many other Cottonwood staff members, but to a sizable percentage of their own students? In the case of many Sagebrush students, their lack of interest in putting forth the effort needed to pursue a personal vision of excellence or self-realization, may have been tied to the peer relationships they openly pursued. Perhaps they did not feel that pursuit of a personal vision of excellence was their most immediate need. Such a hypothesis would be in agreement with Maslow's widely accepted theory that there exists a hierarchy of human needs. Until more basic needs—physical needs for food and shelter, social needs for feelings of belonging—have been met, people are unlikely to pursue self-realization as a goal. Thus, if the sense of belonging these teens crave was most efficiently achieved by informal socializing, the school's attempt to interest them in higher-level pursuits might be doomed to failure, unless far larger changes were made in their cultural environment.

That the solutions they sought might be outside the walls of the school was also suggested by the teachers who had thrown their energies into the restructuring effort at Sagebrush. Often, in interviews, Sagebrush teachers expressed nostalgia for the sense of community solidarity that had characterized the Cottonwood district in its early years. By reversing the process of impersonal bureaucratization that had overtaken Cottonwood during the Davis era, these teachers hoped to make their school a more personal, caring place. Similarly, by honoring the unique character of the families and neighborhoods that made up the sprawling Cottonwood School District, reformers at the district level hoped individual schools would be able to create a greater sense of community among students, staff, and parents.

Going back to the geological metaphor may help to clarify what these reformers hoped to accomplish: Just as the universe was formed out of a rotating cloud of gas and small dust particles that attracted one another, collided, and formed larger particles, what became the Cottonwood School District had originally been a series of small, rural schools. Local families had put forth considerable effort to build and support these isolated schools. In the years before these rural schools had been consolidated into the Cottonwood district, children had routinely walked or ridden miles to go to school. But, as the importance of education came to be more widely recognized at the state level—and efforts were made not only to secure better financing, but to regulate and control what happened in schools—many children (and their parents) came to take more of a "draftee" attitude toward their local schools.

Yet simply offering to give some control back to the community a particular school served did not reverse this process. Shared decision-making, as implemented at Sagebrush High, offered students and parents direct input into the decision-making process. Relatively few chose to take advantage of this opportunity. By the time students got to high school, their habits, attitudes, and expectations had become ingrained. As one Sagebrush teacher observed, with a shrug, "The junior highs have changed very little. Riverside Junior High, which sends us more students than any other school, is the most traditional of the lot. So the kids' expectations on what schools are like are pretty much set before they get here—and we've had only limited success is changing those expectations."

The most optimistic teachers at Sagebrush argued that, once children whose elementary experience had been formed by the hands-on curriculum put in place by the new curriculum framework began arriving in the junior high schools, the schools would change their curriculum. Then the tenth graders arriving at Sagebrush High would be better prepared to take advantage of the curriculum. But others doubted that Sagebrush could even become what the original core team had envisioned, unless the politics of the district changed enough for it to become a true magnet school, attended by students whose families had willingly bought into the school's vision.

Since, as things stood now, student attendance at Sagebrush had been largely determined by where students lived, not by a conscious choice to attend a break-the-mold school, the students tended to minimize the ways in which Sagebrush differed from other schools. In characterizing their school, students mentioned the impressive physical plant and the success of the sports teams, but seldom mentioned their own voice in school governance. Asked for suggestions about how to improve their school, student suggestions tended to center on bigger dances and better social events.

Resentments Directed at Sagebrush High

In 1991, when Sagebrush High School received a prestigious award, the member of the state board of education who presented the award, said: "Sagebrush High School's real reward is that students are growing in good citizenship, lifelong learning, and service to the community." But, so far, the ideal of service to the community has proved elusive. A major disappointment for many Sagebrush High staff members has been their school's relative isolation. Sagebrush's integrated core curriculum has yet to be copied by any other Cottonwood secondary school. The largest junior high in the Sagebrush High attendance area clings tenaciously to a highly tracked academic curriculum.

Cottonwood teachers pointed out that part of the reason for the lack of communication between Sagebrush and other Cottonwood schools is historical:

> When Sagebrush was first planned, Cottonwood was a growing district, but when it was finished, growth had stopped. The local economy was down. We have limited open enrollment in Cottonwood. The result was a loss of population at Metroville High, when students went to Sagebrush. Metroville's athletics went down. There was great anger among some people. Later the same thing happened at Suburban. They thought they were losing the better students to Sagebrush. There were rumors of Sagebrush robbing the best teachers from the other schools.

> Those teachers who didn't get "instructional leader" [core planning team] positions at Sagebrush were resentful. As educators we're not used to direct competition. Losing out is hard to take. Also the equipment was thought to be better at Sagebrush, the computers, etc.

Philosophical conflicts added to the tensions. Some well-respected high school teachers had not applied for positions at Sagebrush because they did not feel comfortable with Suzanne Thompson's vision for the school.

> People were suspicious of the [Sagebrush] approach. They'd say "A core curriculum is OK for middle school, but is it OK for high school?" There was a certain amount of chaos at Sagebrush in the first two years. Some people hoped this was an indication that the whole thing would fall apart.

Other teachers, who were relatively indifferent to Sagebrush High at first, but became resentful when the recognition accorded Sagebrush appeared to lessen public regard for their own schools.

> When Sagebrush was built, Suburban lost its glamour. It also lost population. It had teachers who had been there "forever." After Sagebrush was built, Suburban began to look very staid. It seemed to stay a school of the 1970s and didn't know what to do.

As a consultant who had worked with the Cottonwood district noted, jealousies pop up whenever a school district builds a new high school. The new school—just because it is new—has new equipment and a certain aura of excitement. The resentments that arise can sharply limit diffusion, to other schools, of innovative programs and techniques. In Cottonwood, unexpected political and socioeconomic changes also deeply affected Metroville and Suburban high schools. For example, an alteration in state law limited the Cottonwood School District's options in reacting to school attendance area disputes.

Schools of Choice

In May 1990, the governor of Western State signed into law a bill mandating open enrollment within public school districts. Students could choose to attend a school besides the one in whose attendance area they resided, so long as there was space available in the school they requested. Accordingly, a plan was approved by the Cottonwood Board of Education, outlining how students could apply to attend a Cottonwood school other than their "home school." If the number of applications exceeded the space available in a given school, determinations would be made by lottery.

A Cottonwood administrator described the attraction he saw the choice program holding for students and parents:

> A sign of the times is that people like choices, even if the choice is that I could stay here. Even those that have allegiances [to their local schools] like the idea, they like the flexibility.

Students who chose a school other than their home school were responsible for their own transportation. Western State High School

Activities Association athletic eligibility rules stated that ninth-graders may choose to attend any high school without affecting their eligibility, but on a one-time basis only. Current high school students who changed schools, except as a result of a bona fide family move, became ineligible for participation in all sports for one year.

Districtwide, a relatively low percentage of Cottonwood students took advantage of the choice option. In 1990–91, 96 percent of the Cottonwood district's elementary students and 91 percent of the secondary students chose to attend their home schools. However, transfers could translate into significant gains and losses for individual schools. A district level administrator mentioned the tensions caused:

> The district also had to consider the problem that you would have if you had a building where—not so much, say Sagebrush, because the projected growth is out in that area, that's a high growth area—but at Metroville and Suburban, either one of them, it would not be a wise use of space to allow them to really be depleted. The fear was that would happen to Metroville, that they might have more students leaving. There was fear on the staff's part.

By the spring of 1992, Metroville High had shrunk to under 1,200 students—a third less than the number the building could comfortably hold. Both Metroville and Suburban high schools had to struggle to attract highly motivated students. New programs were put in place. An administrator explained:

> As the whole idea of innovation and creative approaches is nurtured—and I do think that really is one of the hallmarks of our school district—you find that, whatever it is that is of particular interest to a kid, that often times becomes the basis for them to choose a given high school, especially if that is out of their attendance area. Each one of the three schools has kind of got their following.

As this district-level administrator saw it, under the system of site-based decision-making put in place in Cottonwood, each high school had developed a distinctive character, well suited to the community it served. The following sections offer descriptions of the differing cultures that evolved at Metroville and Suburban high schools.

Metroville High School

The present Metroville High facility was already in the planning stages in 1956, when the original Metroville Junior/Senior High was constructed. That school had been designed as a junior high, even though it housed both junior and senior high students. The ground for the new Metroville High was acquired through a fifteen-acre public land dedication, made by a developer to the city of Metroville. The Cottonwood School District purchased an additional ten acres, bringing the total to twenty-five. Revenue from a $12 million voter-passed bond issue in 1970 financed construction. A vocational center, housed in its own building, was built after the academic facilities were completed. The vocational center has now been organized as a separate vocational high school, offering classes to students from throughout the Cottonwood district.

The neighborhood around Metroville High School was built in the 1950s. During the 1991–92 school year, approximately 1,100 students were enrolled at the high school, in grades 10–12. In the fall of 1992, Metroville became a four-year high school, serving grades 9–12. This change brought the Metroville High population up to a level more in keeping with that of the district's other two high schools, while also relieving pressure on the elementary schools in the Metroville High feeder pattern, which were experiencing overcrowding.

Socioeconomic Factors Affecting the Metroville Area

When community members were asked to compare Metroville High with the other Cottonwood high schools, they usually mentioned the socioeconomic and ethnic composition of the Metroville student body. The school staff saw Metro's diversity as an advantage. A teacher pointed to the atmosphere of openness, friendliness, and adaptability which characterized the school. An assistant principal noted: "There's a sense of family. If kids are here long enough, they find a friend or an advocate. Parents comment on it, too, the way teachers here really care about kids."

A former Metroville High administrator pointed out that Metro had, early on, "acquired the reputation of being a 'rough school' in a 'tough neighborhood,' things like that." The construction of the new building in the early 1970s did not erase that reputation. Middle-class parents put enormous pressure on the school board to draw attendance area boundaries that allowed their children to go elsewhere.

There was a great brouhaha because the attendance areas had to be changed in order to fill up the new Metroville High. Finally, the boundaries ended up being gerrymandered along what seemed suspiciously like socioeconomic lines. Later on, when Sagebrush High was built, the same thing seemed to happen. Those boundaries were gerrymandered, again, along similar lines.

The Metro High Feeder Pattern

Some Cottonwood elementary schools, located near Foothills City, had yearly student turnover rates in excess of 100 percent. Of course, not every student moved. Instead, the turnover rate reflected the very rapid movement, in and out of the school, of a certain group of students. Staff members noted that some students repeatedly moved on a three-month cycle. They explained that single mothers on welfare were able to move into local apartment complexes on the strength of government rent guarantees. However, if they were not able to keep up on the rent, they would be forced to move after three months.

Interestingly, in Cottonwood, this was largely an Anglo problem. A principal explained that the minority students at his school were often among the most motivated. For their families, Metroville had been a step up from strife-torn Foothills City. The hardest children to reach were most often Anglo:

> The white single mothers on welfare are in some ways the most beaten down and hopeless. They really feel like they've hit the bottom of the barrel. There's no cultural community that they can turn to for support, or for alternative explanations of what has happened to them. So many just withdraw. It's easy for the kids to pick up a feeling of "It's just no use."

After being repeatedly uprooted, many children became withdrawn and unresponsive. Teachers reported having great difficulty in getting oft-moved children to put forth the energy needed to build affective connections with their new teacher and classmates. Other children exhibited debilitating emotional or physical problems. While interviews were being carried out at one elementary school, a child with fetal alcohol syndrome had a seizure in the principal's office. The boy had been removed from class for disruptive behavior; the seizure occurred while the school secretary was calling his home to see if he had taken his medicine. The mother had not been able to afford to refill the prescription that prevented the boy's seizures. The principal drove to the Garfield County Social Services building to refill it.

Earlier in the week, at the same school, a child who had been diagnosed as manic-depressive by doctors at the Foothills City Children's Hospital had to be taken out of his classroom. His mother had never refilled the prescription that controlled his mood swings. The principal shrugged: "You do what you can." Later, this well-respected elementary principal pointed out that many tensions between staff members in different parts of the district were, at bottom, tied to questions about the distribution of resources.

Increasingly nervous about grumbling from taxpayers in the outlying suburbs, Cottonwood's elected school board held to a policy of providing the same per-pupil funding for all elementary schools. Staff members at schools serving low SES neighborhoods had long argued that their schools needed more per-pupil funding because of the extra services they provided to needy families. However, as things stood, schools that served needy populations were forced to seek help from outside social service agencies. The principal of another elementary school in a low SES area discussed programs that his school had set up:

> We started, this year, a foodshare program that distributes over 140 packets of food each month. I don't know if you're familiar with the Western State Shares program or not, but it meets the needs of a community that is, to some degree, in poverty. We also wrote a grant and got $410,000 to hire a community relations specialist for our [Metroville High] feeder school system down here . . . and are working with families to improve the lives of kids.

Needless to say, writing grants and opening lines of communication with social service agencies takes considerable time, energy, and patience. Yet the results are not "splashy." Indeed, an outsider, unaware of the obstacles a given child had to overcome in order to learn to read, might see nothing to brag about in that child's "average" level of achievement. Yet the effort teachers had put forth to enable that child to read at grade level might have been far greater than the effort required to teach a more privileged child to read at an "above average" level. Frustration at not being able to explain the daily struggles that lay hidden behind the "average" scores of their students understandably influenced the reactions of teachers in low SES schools when they heard about teaching awards given to staff members at schools that served more privileged populations.

An elementary principal, whose strong support for the use of innovative curriculum had been mentioned by a number of respondents, commented on the limitations put on restructuring efforts at a low SES school. As he saw it, the goal of the curriculum framework was to meet children where they were, developmentally speaking, to help them to advance. That would meant something different in a school where the basic needs of many children were not being met in their home environment than it meant in an elementary school where most of the students had been given a head start by attending private preschools.

The same principal pointed out that shared decision making was based—at the most basic level—on cultivating an attitude of collaboration. This meant meeting teachers where they were and not requiring them to put energy into issues they preferred to have the principal attend to. In an environment where decisions were often crisis-driven, being true to the spirit behind shared decision-making might mean holding fewer formal meetings and having more quick conversations in the hall. Often, when asked if they wanted to have input on a given decision, his teachers said they didn't have the energy to think about it. A teacher in a school with a similarly low SES population observed, "All most of us want to do after school is to just go home and 'crash.'"

However, building administrators were less sincere in their commitment to shared decision making, flexibility could shade over into manipulativeness. One teacher explained: "Our principal would say, 'The decision is yours. What do you want to do?' The teachers affected would talk it over and come to an agreement among themselves. Then he'd sort of backtrack and say 'Well, that's not what I had in mind.'"

Metroville High as a School Community

Student turnover at Metroville High School did not approach the turnover in some of the feeder elementary schools. Staff members gave two reasons for this: (1) severely troubled students often dropped out of school during their junior high years; (2) teenagers who were committed to finishing school often stayed in Metroville, supporting themselves with minimum wage jobs, even though their families moved on. Nevertheless, student turnover at Metro High remained a challenge. An administrator, who had acted as registrar at Metroville High before Sagebrush High opened, described the problem at that time:

> We had about 1,700 kids at Metroville High School. Out of 1,700 kids, we had 800 kids that turned over in one year. So you had a 40 percent mobility rate. Maybe 400 kids left and maybe 400 kids came in new, or maybe 500 kids left and 300 kids came in, because the dropout rate was pretty high. How do you deal with such a transient population?

After Sagebrush High opened, the student turnover rate became even higher because many of the Metroville students who chose to attend Sagebrush High were longtime residents whose families had middle-class incomes and values. The student population at Metroville High plummeted to about 1,100, at times dropping considerably below that toward the end of the school year.

Student turnover was greatest among sophomores. A university professor deeply involved in dropout intervention efforts at Metro High noted:

> Most of the kids who are going to drop out will have done so by time they're a day or so over 16. So the junior and senior classes are relatively stable. But turnover [in the junior and senior classes] may still be as high as 20 percent.

Discussing reasons for that dropout rate, the professor described the changes he had observed in the Metroville area in the last twenty-five years.

> Old Metroville Junior/Senior High was not that way. There were a fair number of dropouts, but it was academic failure. My impression of Metroville High is that most kids who drop out these days do so for affective reasons, rather than cognitive. I found very few students dropping out because they couldn't do the work or because of failure to understand concepts.

Anecdotal accounts of the day-to-day challenges some Metro High students face abounded. Problematic situations mentioned by Metro High staff included: emancipated teens who skipped class because they had to work thirty-five hours a week at fast food restaurants in order to support themselves; teens who had to depend upon their mother's boyfriend [who was not always present or willing] to drive them to school; teens who fell asleep in class because they had to work nights in order to help their mothers make ends meet; teens who saw no advantage in getting a high school diploma, yet kept showing up at school in order to be with their friends; teenage mothers with no dependable childcare for their babies.

Although Sagebrush High housed an excellent childcare facility for parenting teens, comparatively few Metro High girls chose to transfer there. Transportation was a problem, but seemed less of a barrier than perceived social differences and the desire to remain in familiar surroundings. So, Metro High student mothers mostly got by as best they could.

Metro High teachers showed deep concern over the challenges their students faced. Community members familiar with Metro High spoke movingly of its warm, caring atmosphere. An educational consultant commented:

> I've never seen a bunch of teachers work so hard to try to get a bunch of kids to understand . . . and be so understanding. It was the most amazing thing. During their free periods many spent their whole time with kids instead of planning. A couple years ago, a kid came in and said he had nowhere to stay. The teacher invited the student to stay with her . . . for a whole year . . . and she had two kids of her own.

Yet the good will and helpfulness of the faculty could not free the school from tensions imported from society at large.

Students attending Metro High brought social norms they had absorbed outside of school. In a "tough" area like the older part of Metroville, many teens spend evenings and weekends within a neighborhood culture in which compromise was seen as a sign of weakness. Teens living in such a culture had a tendency to see problems in terms of interpersonal conflicts. Solving a problem easily became identified with searching out an "enemy" and bringing him down. Living within a socially constructed reality that defined "toughness" in terms of scouring the horizon for enemies—whom they would then feel required to try to defeat—even teens who had benefited from teachers' helpfulness and concern could react in unpredictable ways. Thus, teachers needed to exercise caution to keep from being drawn into explosive conflicts. A veteran teacher contrasted this sense of caution with the way he had handled discipline in the Larimer era.

Once, years ago, I caught a big, burly farm boy harassing a girl in the hallway after school. I mean, he was laughing and treating it like a joke, but he was pawing at her and trying to stick his hand down her blouse. She was trying to get away. I grabbed him by the front of his shirt, slammed him back against the lockers, and yelled in his face, "How dare you do that!" Physically, he was bigger than me. But he flushed beet red and slunk away. The girl wiped away some tears, murmured a "thank you," and ran off. . . . The girl didn't have to appear and face skeptical questions in order to "prove" anything. I just made a point of keeping an eye on that boy, and he knew it. I never saw him act that way again.

He described how options for intervention had changed.

Misbehavior often starts out sort of tentative. They're probing to see what they can get away with. If they find that those around them will not put up with certain things, they stop and grow up to be better people because they stopped. But that *in loco parentis* thing that allowed us to discipline kids in that way has gone by the boards. These days I wouldn't dare discipline a kid like that. Chances are, I'd either get sued or he'd pull out a knife and stab me.

Fear had become an aspect of daily life in many neighborhoods around Metroville High. These days, tough talk and a "take no prisoners" attitude had been adopted as protective coloring by many Metro students. Outside the school doors lay a world in which ordinary courtesy and civility could be taken as a sign of exploitable weakness. As in similar neighborhoods in urban areas across the United States, wearing the wrong clothes could get you hurt. So could language or behavior that brand you as passive and vulnerable. Inevitably, such experiences color relations between students when they are in school and must be dealt with by the staff.

Yet it would be misleading to give the impression that Metro High faculty did their jobs in a climate of fear. Stern district policies vis-à-vis gang-related attire had made Metro High into an island of safety for many students. Teachers seemed confident that most students had hopes that transcended their dissimilarities and provided a basis for mutual understanding. Yet there was an undercurrent of uncertainty about the future. There was an acute awareness of the school's limited ability to fill the gap left by the breakdown of the neighborhoods, churches, and families that had provided structure in students' lives outside of school.

Nostalgia was a recurring theme in Metroville High interviews. Veteran staff members spoke wistfully of the years when open fields, now hidden under parking lots, had stretched to the horizon. In less than forty years, the area surrounding Metroville High had been transformed from farmland, to suburban housing developments, to a neighborhood suffering from urban blight. Yet, despite uncertainties, Metroville High was experimenting with innovative programs that built upon the school's strong points.

Metroville High embodied a different approach to restructuring adaptation of an existing site. Despite the close association between site-based management and shared decision-making elsewhere in the district, that association had yet to take place at Metro High. Kent Evans had proved eager to chart an independent course for his school, but had made little effort to share power with teachers. In an effort to break the deadlock and a explore new directions, Metro High had invited the outside facilitator who had worked with the attendance area boundary commission to guide the discussion as the Metro High staff discussed the options open to their school.

Eventually, the Metro High staff identified two immediate challenges they wished to address: (1) Metroville High's loss of academically oriented, middle-class students to Sagebrush High, and (2) a decline, in the neighborhoods served by Metro High, of the sense of community that had been a hallmark of Metroville, back when it had been a bustling new suburb which served young families buying their first home. Various programmatic options were explored. Eventually the two approaches Metro High staff members agreed on, they saw as likely to be effective in meeting the challenges that lay ahead.

The Plaza Concept

Close attention to student needs had long been part of the Metro High culture. The Plaza concept focused on by creating cooperative ventures that linked the high school with a nearby junior high and elementary school. The intent was to provide that sense of cross-age community that many students lacked in their neighborhoods. Thus far, the successful links that had been established have grown out of the initiative of individual teachers, and who had reached out to colleagues at the feeder schools.

Taking advantage of the close proximity of Metroville High, the Cottonwood Vocational Center, Hildebrand Junior High School, and Metroville Elementary, the Plaza concept had as its goal the closer integration of all levels of education, from kindergarten through high school. One enthusiastic supporter explained that cross-age student tutoring and mentoring were seen as a way to cultivate a sense of mutual responsibility, by cultivating a recognition that being an integral part of a community meant not only being able to depend on others, but also showing others that they could depend on you. As a high school computer teacher put it, "You've got to carry out your part of a bargain. If a first-grader is expecting you to come, write out his story, and bring it back typed up, you have to do that."

The Western State Department of Education had awarded the Plaza a waiver so that, when necessary, Plaza teachers could teach students at any age level, from kindergarten through high school. Another aspect of the long-range plan was upgrading the buildings that housed the Plaza schools, to bring them more in line with facilities in other parts of the district. The Metroville Elementary principal described how the Plaza program affected his school:

> Metroville Plaza is an attempt, and a fairly new attempt, to try to put together a kind of K–12 continuum. We have a lot of high school kids who come down here now. A writing class comes down on Tuesday mornings. They read to kids, interview kids, and write stories that are "published" and given to the kids. It's part of our literacy program. Work-study kids from the vocational center come down and do a big-brother, big-sister sort of thing once a week. We have a high school teacher who has our kids dictate stories to her computer class. Also, a lot of things happen by serendipity. That's the best stuff.

The foreign language departments at Metroville High and Hildebrand Junior High had offered a list of options to teachers at three nearby elementary schools. Elementary teachers could request mini-lessons in Japanese, Spanish, French, German, Russian, or classical Latin; travel presentations and slide shows, or lessons that centered on geography, cultural influences, songs/dances, or daily living in the culture of their choice. High school students visited eighteen elementary classrooms and worked with 455 students. Enthusiasm for the program was high. As one fifth-grader, writing a thank you note to the high school students who had visited his class, put it, "Bonjour, Dude. Thanks for everything!"

International Baccalaureate

Aware of the dissatisfaction some parents in the Sagebrush High attendance area had expressed over the lack of honors classes at Sagebrush, Metroville High had interpreted this dissatisfaction as a felt need, on the part of some Cottonwood families, for a selective academic program that would test the talents of even the most gifted students. By setting up such a program, Metro High could offer Cottonwood students a rigorous academic option and, in so doing, bring a highly motivated group of students to Metro High.

In 1992, Metroville High School became the fourth school in Western State (one of fewer than 200 schools nationwide), to offer an International Baccalaureate program. Based in Geneva, Switzerland, the International Baccalaureate (IB) was unique in its combination of depth, scope, and international emphasis. Aimed at the motivated and successful student, the IB was structured to provide students with the intellectual, social, and critical perspectives necessary to succeed in an increasingly complex world.

Since the IB was so rigorous, U.S. school districts advised students to enroll in a Pre-International Baccalaureate program in grades nine and ten, then advance to the IB in grades eleven and twelve. Unlike other honors programs, the IB required each student to take courses in all six academic areas (English, foreign language, the study of man in society, experimental science, mathematics, and fine arts). To earn the International Baccalaureate Diploma (in addition to the regular Metroville High diploma), a student had to:

- Complete the required sequence of courses in each of the six subject groups.
- Earn an acceptable score on an examination at the higher level in three or four subjects and an acceptable score on an examination at the subsidiary level in the other subjects.
- Submit an extended essay in one of the subjects in the IB curriculum.
- Complete a course in the Theory of Knowledge.
- Engage in an approved creative or service activity.

A Metroville High administrator explained that the International Baccalaureate had originally been developed to serve international businessmen and diplomats whose children had experienced problems being admitted into schools in their home countries after going to school abroad. By the end of the four-year program, IB students were supposed to demonstrate considerable breadth and depth in their knowledge in literature, science, mathematics and other fields, as well as an ability to communicate in writing with a high degree of competence. Students were also expected to become proficient in research and independent study, and to engage in service to others.

Any eighth-grade student in the Cottonwood district could apply to enter the International Baccalaureate program. Initial response was encouraging, with a majority of the first seventy students admitted to the International Baccalaureate program coming from junior high schools outside the Metroville High attendance area. However, debate over the program continued among staff members. Some teachers saw the IB as stratifying the school.

Clearly, in sponsoring the IB, Metroville High had chosen a path radically different from that chosen by Sagebrush High (where staff sentiment against ability grouping was so strong that students who wished to take advanced placement history had to do so in an evening class, outside the regular school day). A Metro High staff member who had been instrumental in bringing the IB to Metro defended this choice:

> It really, really challenges kids. You can only challenge kids that way if there is a buy-in. It's not that the kids that go to that class are brighter, but that they signed up for it knowing that they were volunteering for some heavy duty. You can't do those things if you can't have special courses, where they buy in.

Although the IB did select out an elite group of students, who spent much of their day segregated from the rest of the student body, he felt strongly that the availability of such choices was necessary, if public schools wanted to encourage the pursuit of excellence. For those who wanted it, a very strong academic curriculum was available at Metro High.

Shared Decision-Making Has Progressed Slowly at Metro High

Kent Evans, the Metro High principal, had pushed hard for specific changes, such as block scheduling, that he felt would benefit Metro's student population. He argued that at-risk students typically attended fairly regularly during the first half of a semester, then attended less and less often as Christmas or summer vacation approached. Evans pointed out that, because block-scheduled courses would run for two periods a day, students who hung in there for just half a semester would end up with some credit toward graduation. He also suggested that intensive exposure to fewer subjects might facilitate learning among those students who already had all too many distractions in their lives.

Many Metroville High teachers were wary. Questions abounded: What about kids who transferred in, during the semester, from schools that didn't have block scheduling? Don't the Metro staff need time to digest the extensive changes already being attempted with the Plaza and IB? What if students forget their math skills during half-semester break between math classes? Backers of the principal's proposal argued that Metro High was faced with a crisis, in the form of a dropout rate that remained stubbornly high. Further changes had to be made. Disgruntled teachers remained unconvinced. Resentful of the principal's heavy-handed approach, they complained: "He shares his decisions with us and calls that 'shared decision-making.'" Eventually, the teacher's union filed a grievance, on the grounds that block scheduling would require Metro High teachers to teach more hours per day than their contracts allowed.

Shared decision-making remained rudimentary at Metroville High. Kent Evans, the Metroville principal, had been in the district for thirty years. His reputation as an old jock (a college football stand-out and former high school football coach) left many staff members disbelieving in Evans' present incarnation as educational reformer. Indeed, Evans delighted in playing the role of "good ol' boy," a public persona popular among male Metro High teachers. To such veteran staff members, the phrase "good ol' boy" meant someone who held to old-fashioned values, even though these values were no longer accorded widespread respect.

As this research project progressed, it became clear that differences in how the phrase "good ol' boy" was used served as an indicator of certain cultural divides among Cottonwood personnel. Elsewhere in the district, a very different meaning was attached to the words "good ol' boy." When staff members at Sagebrush High referred to someone as a "good ol' boy," the implication was that this was someone who relied on personal ties, rather than on talent and professionalism, to get ahead. Thus, the words "good ol' boy" were used to describe a mindset that did not lend itself to the sort of inclusiveness necessary to schoolwide consensus building.

In fairness, it should be noted that Kent Evans had, more than once, proven better at predicting the responses of Metroville area parents than his teaching staff had. Despite predictions that no one would come, he had instituted a yearly "open house" during which parents could visit Metro High and talk with teachers. Although bringing parents into the school for other sorts of meetings had proven difficult, the open house had proved popular. "These aren't people you can expect to form a committee and support the school," an Evans ally explained. "Many of these parents look to the school for support. But they care about their kids." By all accounts, Kent Evans was popular with Metro High parents, as well as with key members of the school board.

However, elsewhere in the district, staff members committed to the principles of shared decision-making often pointed to Metro High as an example of the sort of "us versus them" face-off between faculty and administrators that shared decision-making was meant to avoid. Despite rhetoric about the need for bold initiatives, the climate Evans had created at Metro was more conducive to cautious adaptation. Despite the professional conscientiousness of many teachers, the Metro High staff had been able to reach only a narrow agreement on adoption of the Plaza and IB programs. As this research project ended, adoption of block scheduling continued to be negotiated.

If ambitious programs like the Plaza concept and International Baccalaureate are to be successful, a committed effort by the teachers "in the trenches" will be required. Political maneuvering had squandered much energy and good will. Metro High remained a school at risk, not just because social and economic challenges had transformed the neighborhoods it served, but also because lack of solidarity among staff members continued to limit Metro High's ability to adapt. The promise of site-based decision-making—the possibility of tailoring solutions to the needs of individual school communities by bringing to bear the special talents and resources available in each community—had yet to be fulfilled at Metroville High.

At the same time, there was a palpable feeling of "in the trenches" camaraderie at Metro High. As a Metro staff member, arriving back at his school after a meeting at Sagebrush High, said with a kind of battered pride: "Meanwhile, back in the real world . . ." Striding across the cracked Metro High parking lot, he expressed an attitude shared by many Metro personnel, a sense of doing a job teachers in easier schools might not be capable of tackling.

Suburban High School

Although economic woes have beset the city of Suburbia in recent years, this has not resulted in the dramatic demographic changes that have, since 1983, so altered the older part of Metroville. Suburban High lost population after the opening of Sagebrush, but it lost far fewer students than Metroville High. Thus, there was less impetus for change. An observer close to Suburban High commented that, after Sagebrush opened:

> If anything, the curriculum at Suburban became less dynamic, more [centered on survey courses]. The Suburban faculty is a fairly conservative group. There has been less variety in English classes, more year-long classes. Instead of a revision, there's been a backward movement.

Yet many of Suburban High's teachers considered their school's highly structured curriculum to be an advantage. They described Suburban as a fairly traditional place, whose older staff that had been around long enough for teachers to have learned what style of teaching fitted them best.

A counselor noted that every year parents visited her, shopping for a high school. Their opening words would be: "I hear that you're the college prep high school." She replied that, although Suburban High had a strong academic curriculum and a good college placement rate, it is not a college prep high school. Half the curriculum, and more than half the school's resources, were dedicated to the non–college prep student. Yet only sixty Suburban students took classes at the Cottonwood Vocational Center. A Suburban High administrator explained:

> I think convenience is a lot of it. A Metro High kid might think, "I guess I'll try a course in commercial art because, I can just run out the back door." Suburban kids really have to make a decision, because it affects two hours of their day, if they take the bus.

Like the other Cottonwood high schools, Suburban put a strong emphasis on making sure students knew that their teachers cared about them. However, at Suburban students were expected to search out the adults they wanted to advise them. "What makes Suburban High unique," a teacher insisted, "is the diverse staff, which includes teachers with enough different styles and attitudes that any student should be able to find adults he or she can relate to well."

The Legacy of Past Experiments

Suburban's older staff was wary of what they perceived as mere changes in educational fashion. Comments about "new" ideas were routinely met with a question: How did the "innovation" differ from a similar intervention which had failed to achieve the expected result? Such skepticism could convey the impression that Suburban teachers were unwilling to try anything new. Yet their queries were often thought-provoking: Why should this innovation succeed where a project very like it had failed, for reasons that we now consider obvious? Following is the summarized account of one such failed experiment, conducted at Suburban in the 1970s. Recounted by a respected social studies teacher, this narrative shows how prior experience has shaped the attitudes of Suburban teachers toward the innovative curriculum at Sagebrush High.

Seven American history teachers volunteered to work on a project that the American Historical Association was trying to push at that time. Back in the seventies there were attempts to try to get more connections between the university and the high school. We got money, college credit, and meeting space at Western State University. We divided the teachers so that each essentially had a home room, and then we did unit teaching, with students able to choose any two-week units that interested them.

For the four or five years that we had this operating, we tried to get as many student teachers as we possibly could. So we had a lot of people to do the work. Part of our concept was that this would give us a chance to work with writing skills, reading skills, analysis skills, all of that sort of stuff. We had students do projects, book critiques, reaction papers, five or six different kinds of things, so we could keep a finger on how things were operating, what they were thinking about. We were dealing in many ways with the affective side of it, because that was the buzz word in the seventies.

All the teachers had a common planning period. We met virtually every day and talked about what we were doing. Student contact time was similar to what Sagebrush has got; we did episodic or segmental kinds of things. But the whole issue of sequence and continuity and completeness, thoroughness, was sort of lost in the process.

So that was one of the problems: what are we really covering and how well are we doing it? Then the second question was a logistics question. Part of our expectation was, given the number of people we had, we would be able to intervene and do all that sorts of stuff for students who were sort of at-risk. But we could never do a very good job of that. Much of that was our fault. We were really sort of setting up the system so we had to have autonomous learners and, you know, we basically just had kids. So for those who were prone to say, "Well I don't know what to do," we didn't really think that was good for them. They were better off in a contained class.

So, just to complete the circle, when Sagebrush was doing its planning and they were going to orient their operation around American history, or common historical problems, it didn't seem to be very unique or new.

A counselor recounted Suburban's earlier attempt to implement an advisory system similar to what Sagebrush had set up:

We did that here. At the time, I was really involved in that I really believed in it, and I still do. Teachers really fought that system; they didn't want to do it at all. . . . Advisor to them means "shrink," counselor, that kind of thing. Some of them are a little leery about doing what they call "touchy feely stuff" with kids. . . . Well, the people who were comfortable doing it did a great job, and the people who weren't, didn't. Eventually it just got to the point where there were too many people who said, "We don't want to do this anymore. We don't like it." So we disbanded it.

Many Suburban teachers see the innovations at Sagebrush High as more the reflection of current "fads" than as educational "breakthroughs." They proudly point to the slightly higher scores that Suburban High students have achieved on standardized tests. Yet Suburban staff members insisted that it would be wrong to infer that Suburban High had not changed at all.

Shared Decision-Making

Suburban remained very much a "shopping mall high school," proud of its diversity. Yet, by the standards of its staff, Suburban was also a restructured school. The School Improvement Team was made up of six staff members and a similar number of parents. Committees were created to deal with specific problems with standing committee memberships opened up at the beginning of the year, and those wanting to participate were required to make a commitment at that time. People could not join a committee in mid-year to participate in a specific decision. However, the most important decisions would be presented to the faculty assembly before they are finalized.

Teachers were forthright in saying that they had "no wish to do the principal's job for him." Yet they were pleased that, since the advent of shared decision-making, the relevant facts were presented to them before major decisions affecting their building were made, and their assent solicited. John O'Neill, Suburban's principal, described the consensus-building process he used:

> We go through a process that basically says: "If we were to do this, what are the best possible outcomes? What are the worst possible outcomes?" As we go through and discuss those, things start to fall out. We start to see agreement on things. It's a lengthy process, but eventually you get to a point where the majority of people in the room see where, basically, it's going to have a negative outcome and we want to "can" that idea, or it has a lot of merit.
>
> The more you talk in these types of terms, the best and the worst, the more you dislodge people from representing their department or their individual needs. . . . [But] to make a decision like that may take three or four meetings. If you go in and want to make a major decision about your school and expect to bring closure in one three-hour meeting or one after school meeting, it won't happen. You'll end up with a lot of frustration.

O'Neill admitted that many members of his staff were reluctant to put much energy into solving problems they defined as "what the principal is being paid to do."

> I think we are at a point in the decentralization process where we need to speed up the decisions that are being made. It's causing a lot of frustration, almost to the point of saying, "You make the decisions.". . . When I get that comment, which I got recently on a really big issue, I say, "I will accept that challenge." But I will say at the same time, "I'm willing to draw up what I think it should be, but I'm going to come back to the staff for consensus."

O'Neill explained that, on any given issue, there was a tendency for the three or four people who cared most about that issue to meet separately with the principal and develop a proposal, which would then be presented to the faculty assembly for discussion and modification, or approval. An administrator who had worked at both Suburban and Sagebrush compared the way shared decision-making had worked at each school:

> At Sagebrush they had what's called staff governance, which is somewhat of the decision-making group for the school. All different issues cross that committee, and so they make decisions on many different things. Then they have a budget committee. But, after that, if you're a staff member— and not on staff governance and not on budget—then you're not so much involved, which is okay for some teachers who choose not to be involved.
>
> Here at Suburban, if we have a registration meeting it could be these ten people here. Then we'll have a meeting to decide food and drink policy and it's going to be a whole different group. So we have more faculty involvement, not on the big scale, but based on what they choose to be involved in.

A teacher described how John O'Neill had gone about building consensus on an important issue that had been brought before the entire faculty, yet had remained unresolved, after extensive discussion. Before bringing the issue before the full faculty again, the principal had engaged in extensive discussion with smaller groups:

> He went to primary groups, the faculty, the school improvement team, parent advisory council, and got input from them. The way I understand it, he designed the focus [for further discussion] based on all that input. Then he went back to those groups and said "Okay, did I hear you right?" Rather than trying to have a whole committee decide where the focus is, which is a very long process, he went to the key groups ahead of time to find out common elements in each group.

Interviews with administrators and faculty indicated that, at Suburban High, the widespread sentiment was: "If it's not broke, why try to fix it?" Yet there were individuals who saw a need for further change. The teacher who chaired the committee in charge of budget and staffing allocations pointed out a need for better communication:

I think we are still trying to figure out how all those pieces fit together. For example, in the resource committee a lot of times we feel like we are making decisions we shouldn't make. We've got a curriculum committee, but communication between those committees hasn't jelled well enough that we're making decisions based on priorities established by curriculum. Sometimes we just go ahead, because we've got to make a decision, and make a decision.

A veteran teacher asserted: "Just talking to people around the district, I think we've got as good a shared decision making process, right now, as any place." However, shared decision-making at Suburban High seemed to have been handicapped by the necessity of building a consensus among diverse faculty members, with widely differing views.

When no mutually satisfactory compromise was reached, the default solution was to keep things as they were—even when the status quo did not really satisfy any one. As Sarason cautioned in *The Predictable Failure of School Reform*, "changing power relationships is no guarantee that those alterations will lead to improvement in educational outcomes. One seeks those alterations because one has a special vision about what people are and can be" (1990, 8). Yet staff members at Suburban High insisted that their school had changed. They talked about the feeling of having a voice, of knowing what was going on. In varying words, teachers asserted: "We're the ones who are closest to the kids, and it seems like common courtesy to consult us about policies which will affect us and affect our students."

The changes that had taken place at Suburban had been facilitated by the fortuitous placement of the Cottonwood district staff development office in empty classroom space at Suburban High. Cottonwood's talented staff development director, who trained staff members throughout the district in shared decision making methods, frequently passed through the Suburban High office. Her proximity made her a ready resource for O'Neill and others with an interest in shared decision making. A counselor observed, "In those days when Suburban and Metroville high schools were forced to be the same, you know, we ended up with something that nobody liked. Now we can make this school what we want it to be, theoretically. We'll see if it really happens."

Whereas Sagebrush High had used shared decision-making to create a dramatically restructured school, at Suburban High shared decision-making led to a much more subtle realignment of power relationships. The change in attitude was succinctly expressed by Suburban's principal, John O'Neill: "I'm not taking that monkey back, that says 'I'm going to be the sole decision-maker and, whether you agree with me or not, this is the way it's going to be.' Because then you've got a portion of your staff that never supports you." Significantly, the two programs that were most often mentioned as examples of innovation at Suburban High School had grown out of the initiative and/or grant-writing ability of individual staff members. This appeared to be symptomatic of the ethos of the school, which emphasized letting teachers invest their out-of-the-classroom energies in whatever activities interested them, rather than attempting to build a consensus for broader change. A teacher explained, change at Suburban High was an entrepreneurial affair.

Pascal Center for Concentrated Studies

Available to all Cottonwood high school juniors and seniors, the Pascal Center was based upon the idea that learning is a natural process. The Pascal Center allowed students to integrate aspects of literature, writing, history, social science, and the arts. Materials, activities and methods were determined by the student's own abilities, interests, and goals. Work in the student's major area resulted in preparation of a portfolio of original work. The center operated for a three-hour block of time during the school day. Students earned the same credit as they would earn for any three-period series of classes. Credit was distributed among English, social studies, and fine arts according to the nature and emphasis of each student's work.

The Bridge Program

This two-year grant, funded by the Drug-free Schools and Communities Act, was designed to help students experience success in school and to reduce the incidence of high-risk behaviors and lifestyles. The project addressed the 20–40 percent student turnover at Suburban and its feeder schools. One feeder elementary had a turnover rate of 50 percent per year. There was a 30 percent turnover at Suburban High. Although these rates were considerably lower than those in the Metro High feeder pattern, they still left may students feeling uprooted and adrift. Support groups and timely staff intervention were designed to help students stay in school. As of spring 1992, none of the students in the Bridge Program had yet dropped out of high school.

Contrasting Attitudes

Spontaneous comments made by Suburban High teachers about the changes that had taken place since 1982 tended to be very positive:

> Dave Roberts is the best thing that ever happened to this school district in my opinion. Absolutely. He's put the power where it needs to be, he's put the decision-making where it needs to be. I feel like I really have a voice here.

Yet there was an air of resignation in the comments many Suburban teachers made about the larger problems they faced. There was a sense of frustration over the incommensurability of resources available to schools and the problems of a more diverse generation of students. As one staff member pointed out, "Some of the best teachers in this school, the ones that are willing to help kids, can't. They have thirty-five kids in a class. They can't help a kid who comes in and doesn't know how to read."

Teachers expressed a deep sense of frustration over being forced to spend much of their time coping with the problems of a minority of their students. The following sentiment was widespread: "If there's any concern that I have about the direction we've been going the last couple of years, it's that so many resources, so much staff time, so much of everything is going into this at-risk deal, because it's the buzz word right now. I'd like us to do more for the good students at this school. They've got concerns; they need information; they need guidance; they need help, maybe in a different way, but they need it as much as anybody else. They have conflicts with teachers; they have test anxiety; they have stress. But we tend to think they're self-reliant and they can deal with it on their own, and they can't always do that."

CONCLUSIONS

As a Sagebrush High staff member pointed out: "In some ways you're comparing apples and oranges when you compare shared decision-making at an established school and at a new school." A member of the original core team at Sagebrush explained:

> That unusual kind of planning, I think, was easier because we were a brand new school. We have visiting groups that come

through, and I find that it's much more difficult for schools who want to make those changes if they have an existing curriculum and an existing staff. So I do think, in a way, that it was easier for us even though we went through a lot of difficulties in just being a new school.

Sagebrush High's staff had "bought into" a single, coherent vision. Led by a principal who believed passionately in the school's vision, staff members were never allowed to forget the theory behind school governance structure at Sagebrush High. When disagreements arose, the school's vision statement became the unifying standard against which new ideas were measured. Suzanne Thompson's sense of mission remained pivotal in keeping Sagebrush's innovative vision fresh. Referred to by her staff as the "vision keeper," Dr. Thompson continued to impart to her staff her own conviction that their joint vision could be made a reality. Over and over, when teachers were unable to suggest alternatives to the way things "had always been done," she urged: "Let's think about it." Often the rethinking led to change.

At the elementary level, where schools were small enough so that the teachers interacted with each other fairly regularly, shared decision making had resulted in innovative programs, many of them based on the new curriculum framework. Many elementary-level teachers reported experiencing a less professional isolation and a greater sense of collegiality since the introduction of shared decision-making. Yet the great majority of Cottonwood's junior highs and high schools still lagged far beyond. All had adopted vision statements, but most of these expressed only broad, generally acceptable goals. With so many individuals pulling in opposing directions, the energies of those people who desired change often canceled one another out. In the end, the compromise most frequently arrived at was to stay with the present structure, which at least had the advantage of familiarity.

This helped explain why the Cottonwood junior highs, in particular, had changed so little after a decade of shared decision-making. Like the subtle classroom treaties described in *The Shopping Mall High School*, unspoken agreements which allowed the "unspecial" student to get through the school day with a minimal amount of work, many teachers who taught in "unspecial" secondary schools seemed content to negotiate de facto shared decision-making treaties that allowed them to become involved only when an issue was of particular interest to them.

Individuals committed to bringing about change emphasized the fundamental shift in perception that was necessary if restructuring was to be effective. Sharp contrasts in attitudes were evident. Principals who had felt most comfortable with the hierarchical school governance arrangements of the Davis era now reported that they felt as if they had the responsibility—but not the power—to keep staff members at their schools moving toward declared district goals. Principals who were comfortable with the shared decision-making approach stated a clear preference for having the site-based decision-making teams at their schools reach a concensus on a new policy, even if the policy might not be quite what they, as principal, would have preferred. They reasoned that this was much better than getting the policy they preferred, but then having to deal with the ongoing passive resistance of a disgruntled staff.

Those principals who were most successful in using the shared decision-making model also tended to be comfortable with a give-and-take communication style. It is interesting to note that when, during the Davis tenure, staff members were asked (on anonymous questionnaires) to name a professional characteristic on which they thought Dr. Davis might be in need of improvement, they named "ambiguity tolerance." This was defined as the quality that is present when a manager is able to suspend judgment until as much evidence as possible is available—thus avoiding impulsive decision-making. Of course, "ambiguity tolerance" was not of primary importance under a system of management-by-objectives, where each employee's goals and duties were carefully spelled out. As a seventeen-year veteran of the Cottonwood district recalled:

> During Davis's administration I was a brand new teacher. Everything was very normal to me because you were taught in school that you have a principal that's your boss and you're told what to do. So I never even thought about questioning or being part of the decision-making or anything. Nobody ever questioned anything. You just did it.

Under the administrative philosophy in force during the Davis era, to question the goals set by one's supervisor was to risk being labeled "not a team player." For an aspiring administrator, such a label could be a career-ending epithet. Since the present principals at both Suburban and Metroville high schools received their formative training as administrators within the Davis-era administratie culture, both absorbed the expectation. But, since then, they had chosen different paths. A former guidance counselor, John O'Neill at Suburban had evolved a management style that was built not only upon the Davis-era administrative culture, but also on his own more collaborative professional experiences as a guidance counselor.

Kent Evans of Metroville High, a former football coach whose conception of teamwork centered more on the need for decisive leadership, found it considerably more difficult to adopt the leadership style required by the shared decision-making model. During the Davis era, when Evans had gained his initial experience as an administrator, his personal strengths had been congruent with established expectations concerning the administrative role. Possessed of an unending supply of amusing yarns, Evans contributed to the strong sense of esprit de corps among principals that was assiduously cultivated during the Davis era. Keeping tests scores up and discipline problems down was, at that time, valued considerably more than developing a collaborative building-level culture.

During the Roberts era, expectations for principals have shifted away from cultivating relationships with other administrators, toward establishing collaborative relationships with teachers in one's own building. Perhaps feeling himself ill-suited to this new role, Evans chose instead to focus on the real challenges Metroville High faces, plugging hard for adoption of bold new programs. Building on his long-standing connections with the community, Evans also cultivated close relationships with influential school board members. In a sense, Kent Evans opted to substitute one kind of risk for another. His relations with many of his teachers remained tense. In subtle ways he defied district shared decision-making mandates, implicitly portraying them as inappropriate to the culture of Metroville High. Yet Kent Evans remains Metro High's principal. How has he pulled that off?

Evans' assiduously cultivated "good ol' boy" persona allowed him to inject social class overtones into the debate. He played upon the connection many residents of the older part of Metroville saw between the integrated teaching methods introduced at Sagebrush High and the "yuppie" social milieu associated with that school. In so doing, Evans put Metroville teachers who opposed his autocratic management style on the defensive. A long-time associate of Evans pointed out:

> A lot of people don't take Kent seriously because he comes on like he's just this good ol' boy and he's always telling jokes. But he's a very smart guy, with a mind like a steel trap. When it

gets down to discussing who made what decision in the district and why they made it, even if it was years ago, he can tell you as well as, maybe better than, anybody else.

Kent Evans represented the challenge that old-style administrators present to meaningful districtwide implementation of the shared decision-making model. As long as Evans remained in control at Metroville High, he would continue to frame the issues at that school in a way that suited his own leadership style. On a superficial level, he said all the "right" things, about valuing consultation and collaboration. Yet Evans continued to run Metroville High in a manner that left many able teachers with strong feelings of impotence and frustration. However, since Dr. Roberts was, himself, an employee of the school board—several of whose members saw Evans as providing the kind of leadership that a school like Metro High needed—the superintendent's options were limited vis-à-vis dealing with Kent Evans.

At Suburban High John O'Neill represented a more subtle challenge to the thorough-going implementation of shared decision making. O'Neill had been at Suburban High from the first day it opened: first as a science teacher, then as a guidance counselor, finally as principal. Proud of his school and respected by his faculty, O'Neill attempted to deal with the districtwide change to a shared decision-making philosophy by trying to figure out what Dr. Roberts wanted and giving him that. Such an attitude led to initiate enough changes to satisfy Suburban High teachers, but not to the kind of rethinking of a public high school's essential mission that committed advocates of restructuring insist is needed.

Under the prior two superintendents, administrative knowhow had been perceived to be something that was brought in from the outside and placed within the school. Among those for whom the assumptions of the Davis era had become the norm, any falling away from maximization test scores and careful attention to district goals was interpreted as a sign of poor administrative performance. Thus it was that Kent Evans continued to see those teachers at his school who pressured him to channel more time and energy into collaborative decision-making as troublemakers. John O'Neill had responded to the changing Cottonwood district culture by expanding the attention given to interpersonal responsiveness at his school. However, at Suburban the fostering of personal growth continued to be perceived as a private concern, beyond the school's power to significantly influence.

Given the relative lack of student buy-in in response to Sage-brush High's attempt to incorporate personal growth into that school's mission, it could be argued that O'Neill's assessment was essentially correct. Yet, in one respect, the restructured environment at Sagebrush had strikingly fulfilled an important part of its initial promise: recognition of the need of faculty members to learn, change, and grow—so that their ability to create and sustain optimum conditions for students would not be impaired. As a district curriculum specialist put it: "You look at the Sagebrush faculty and in whole departments, like English or Science, you don't find a single teacher that you wish would just retire." A teacher who had worked in Cottonwood since Ed Larimer was superintendent described the atmosphere at Sagebrush:

> Teachers get a feeling of being trusted and treated very professionally. The more input teachers get, the more they care and are professional . . . and the more they are exhausted. But the alternative to exhaustion is terrible. I would not want to be in a building where the principal made all the decisions. I've seen situations elsewhere, in schools where the principal is authoritarian, and the teachers resist however they can.

The importance of this feeling on the part of teachers was routinely downplayed by staff members at other schools, who took for granted the unverbalized axiom that schools do and should exist primarily for students. Yet, as Sarason has pointed out: "What are by conventional criteria considered our 'best' colleges and universities are those that have assigned equal importance to the development of both faculty and students" (1990, 137). Insensitivity to how the structure and culture of schools affects the professional and personal growth of teachers can have the effect, over time, of powerfully undercutting the motivation, creativity, and professional-intellectual growth of those people upon whose energy, skill, and commitment educational quality depends.

Superintendent Roberts has attempted to create an environment in which all stakeholders within a school community participate in inventing mutually acceptable solutions to shared problems. This chapter has investigated the extent to which this shift could be observed in the three Cottonwood high schools. Evidence shows that the challenges that stood in the way of achieving such a shift have been multiple:

1. _Time Crunch_—Staff members were so busy with their usual tasks that asking them to participate in finding solutions to problems once routinely left to administrators was often seen more as a burden than as an opportunity.
2. _Personal Initiative vs. Team Approach_—Throughout their careers most teachers had been accustomed to both the isolation and the freedom of the closed door. Administrators had been accustomed to having a relatively free hand within their assigned realm of authority. Many found these things hard to give up.
3. _Playing It Safe vs. Risk-Taking_—Under the previous superintendent the doctrine of accountability had been based on the premise that control could be exercised over every employee and every building block of learning. Now staff members were being asked to trust a process whose outcome was uncertain, and to take risks to change a system that many found relatively satisfactory as it stood. Some found the lack of certainty deeply unsettling.
4. _Self-Expression vs. Dialogue_—The shared decision-making model demanded that personnel not only "go through the motions" but also entertain ideas that were at variance with those they already held. When willingness to do this was lacking, the shared decision-making process tended to produce only slight variations on what already existed.

Success had been uneven so far. Even at Sagebrush, where a wide array of reforms had been implemented, the shared decision-making structure had not succeeded in motivating students or parents to put in the time and energy to become prominent "players" in the shared decision-making process.

The one time when students, parents, and school staff members from all parts of the district did become actively involved in debating school policy was when deep budget cuts—made necessary because of a revenue shortfall at the state level—threatened valued programs. The use of a shared decision-making process to address such districtwide concerns will be discussed in the next chapter.

CHAPTER 8

SHARED DECISION-MAKING
AT THE DISTRICT LEVEL:
LIMITATIONS INHERENT
IN THE SOCIAL CONTEXT

Since the early 1980s, the site-based decision-making model has allowed the Cottonwood School District to serve an increasingly diverse population through enabling individual school communities to adapt programs and curriculum to fit their needs. Other kinds of decision-making have been necessary to address challenges affecting the district as a whole. This chapter will examine how the Cottonwood School District has used shared decision-making to address districtwide issues. Special attention will be paid to social contextual factors. Tensions arising from social and economic issues beyond the district's administrative control often made it difficult to cultivate attitudes of openness and collaboration, with the result that shared decision-making at the district level became particularly challenging.

The use of shared decision-making in regard to two specific issues will be examined. The first issue was touched upon in the previous chapter: How should the attendance area boundaries for the new Sagebrush High School be drawn? A second issue grew out of the large funding shortfalls at the state level: How would the Cottonwood district cut expenditures in order to bring its budget into alignment with the reduced funding that Cottonwood would receive from the state during the next school year (a projected loss of approximately $10 million of the $91 million initially budgeted for district programs and schools)? However, before discussing these issues in more depth, it is necessary to gain an understanding of the demographic changes that made these issues so volatile.

The Impact of Demographic Changes

Earlier chapters have discussed how changes in the balance of political power among various community groups—for example the shift in perspective that took place during the Larimer era when businessmen succeeded local farmers as the most influential group on the school board—have affected the operations of the Cottonwood School District. Before describing how the district addressed specific districtwide issues, it may be helpful to put the discussion into a broader historical perspective. This section will briefly sketch broad demographic trends that significantly altered the cultural context within which the Cottonwood School District operated.

Growth of the Black Community in the Foothills City Metropolitan Area

Although black fur trappers and cowboys had played a part in Western State history since its early days, until World War II the black population of the Foothills City metropolitan area remained small. Indeed, the population of the United States did not become primarily urban (meaning more people lived in cities than in rural areas) until World War I. Blacks became primarily urban dwellers during and after World War II. Foothills City's black population almost doubled during the 1940s, from 7,836 in 1940 to 15,059 in 1950, when blacks comprised two percent of the city's population.

Social attitudes changed slowly. In 1950 the *Foothills City Times* hired its first black reporter. Yet when he attempted to swim at the Foothills Amusement Park pool, he was refused admittance. The same thing happened at the YMCA pool. Although Foothills City might have been socially advanced compared to places in the South where blacks were prevented from attending white schools, eating at white restaurants, or drinking from white drinking fountains, it was far from being an integrated city.

In 1952, blacks living in Foothills City remained concentrated in the Industry Junction area. Although the U.S. Supreme Court had made restrictive covenants in property deeds, designed to keep minorities out of white neighborhoods, legally unenforceable in 1948, other barriers remained in the form of custom, the reluctance of banks to lend to blacks, and real estate agents' unwillingness to show homes in white neighborhoods to blacks. Such informal stratagems became less effective, however, after Western State toughened its anti-discrimination laws in 1959 and strengthened its fair-housing statutes in 1965. Gradually blacks began to follow other ethnic groups to the suburbs.

The traditionally black neighborhoods were fast becoming overcrowded; black population in the Foothills City area more than doubled in the 1950s, reaching 30,251 in 1960. By 1970 the metropolitan area counted 50,191 blacks, of whom 94 percent were in Foothills City, mainly in the Industry Junction area. During the 1970s more blacks settled outside the city limits but predominantly black neighborhoods persisted, both in Foothills City and in the surrounding counties. In 1980, 76 percent of the metropolitan area's 77,779 blacks still lived in Foothills City. But in the early 1980s economic problems in working-class areas such as Metroville made homeowners and landlords more open-minded about selling and renting to minorities. Black population in the Metroville area began to climb.

Growth of the Foothills City Area Hispanic Community

Although Spanish settlements in the southern part of Western State predated the founding of Foothills City, most of the settlers who came to the Foothills City area between 1860 and 1900 were from the Eastern and Midwestern parts of United States. A historian noted:

> Before 1930 it was easy for most people to overlook the city's small Hispanic community. The 1910 [*Foothills City Directory*] listed only twelve persons with the common Hispanic surnames of Gonzales, Lopez, and Martinez. By 1920 there were 113 with those names, by 1930 over 300, by 1940 over 600, and in 1950 over 1,100. That year the [Foothills City] Area Welfare Council guessed that there were between 30,000 and 45,000 Spanish-Americans in [Foothills City]. The 1960 federal census gave a more exact picture, recording 43,147 Spanish-Americans in the city. By 1970 the number had risen to 86,345 and by 1980 to 91,937. Since the city's total population changed little between 1960 and 1980, the dramatic increase in Hispanic numbers meant more than a doubling of the Hispanic percentage of the total population.

Since the 1930s, the agricultural areas of Garfield County had been home to relatively large numbers of Hispanic residents. Hispanic residents began moving into the Metroville area when the subdivision that later became Suburbia was still under construction. However, the number of Hispanic families living in Metroville increased substantially during the 1980s, when the impact of a regional recession made housing there more affordable. As pointed out earlier, the minority families moving in often had more middle-class values than their Anglo neighbors. But to people from the outer suburbs who were driving through, the demographic changes made Metroville look much more like Foothills City.

However these factors, alone, do not explain the ethnic tensions and parental fears that complicated the Cottonwood School District's attempt to encourage more open and honest communication among all stakeholders through a shared decision-making process. Local media coverage did much to harden attitudes.

Media Coverage Exacerbates Tensions

"The problem," as one Cottonwood administrator put it, "is that many suburbanites see the darker faces at Metro High and automatically assume this has to mean more crime and more drugs." During the two years when data for this study was being collected, a number of similar comments were made by Cottonwood personnel. The existence of unvoiced tensions and fears among parents living in the outer suburbs was also suggested by comments made in the spring of 1992, during a series of neighborhood meetings about the overcrowding in Sagebrush High's junior high feeder schools. Cottonwood administrators had pointed out that there was extra space in some of Metroville High's feeder junior high schools.

Since there was no money available to build new schools, the easiest solution to the overcrowding problem was to bus some Sagebrush-area students to junior high schools that had extra space. The only alternative was to have the overcrowded junior highs go on split session, a solution local parents opposed. However, it soon became clear that Sagebrush-area parents would accept split sessions far more readily than having their children bused to a Metroville school. A husband and wife, strongly opposed to busing, explained the strength of their feelings later:

He: We grew up in L.A., in a really poor area, so there were gangs all over.
She: I used to get jumped all the time on the way home from school—and raped, once I got raped. We were in a very

Hispanic area and I was white, so I got picked on. I got in serious fights as early as elementary school.

He: The reaction of the law was so slow, it was like they weren't even there.

She: That's why when they talk about things like the Rodney King beating, I see it differently. People elsewhere ask: "How could that happen?" But the cops out there are more like soldiers. They never know what they'll be up against. They stop a car and maybe some more cars with gang members in them pull up behind and beat up the cop. . . . I mean, now that this stuff is spreading here, where are we going to have to go to get away from gangs? To Alaska?

For these people, issues connected with their personal experiences were clearly of primary importance. However, there was reason to believe that other parents took their cue from news reports and other media coverage.

The Media Coverage Increases Sensitivity to Crime

Although causality in such cases is exceeding difficult to pin down, many Cottonwood personnel clearly felt that local media coverage had created preconceptions about the older part of Metroville that made open-minded discussion of the quality of the education offered by the schools there exceedingly difficult. A common complaint had to do with the way in which emotional images communicated through the media overpowered the more reasoned discussion in which school district teachers and administrators attempted to engage. When protests were made to media representatives, the reply usually was that this particular story, the one mentioned in the protest could not possibly have made much difference. One story can, however, be of interest as an example of the sort of images Cottonwood personnel referred to.

After a heated public meeting, a Cottonwood teacher commented that many Sagebrush-area parents had, very likely, never spent much time in the older part of Metroville. Asked why these parents were convinced it was such a dangerous place, the teacher pulled out the current issue of a weekly tabloid available, free of charge, at supermarkets, drugstores, and newsstands in the Foothills City area. The cover was dominated by a full-color picture of the tombstone of a junior high student who had been murdered in Metroville ten years earlier. The headline announced "Ten Years

After: Karen Todd's Murderer Took a Long, Strange Trip to Justice."
Inside, pictures of a fresh-faced, smiling Anglo girl appeared alongside
mugshots of the Hispanic murderer. The heading implied conspiracy:

> I'VE GOT A SECRET
> Pablo Sanchez told his family he was a killer.
> Nobody told the cops.

Although widely dismissed as a "scandalsheet," this free
weekly newspaper had stayed afloat and profitable by focusing on
that layer of the human psyche where anxieties and superstitions
often resist rational control. Scanning the first paragraph of the title
story, Sagebrush-area residents would have read the following:

> Pablo Sanchez was always a ladies' man. At fifteen, the slender
> kid with the piercing brown eyes was seen running up to first-
> grade girls [sic] on the playground of a Metroville elementary
> school and kissing them on the mouth.

There was no way that the caring and able staff at Metroville
Elementary School, a bright and cheerful place where children's art-
work is prominently displayed in classrooms and corridors, could
reply to the picture these words painted of their school. Nor could
they moderate the description of the Metroville social environment:

> Karen's life was far from pampered. Her parents were divorced,
> the family was on welfare and she was having trouble in school,
> depressed that her father had stopped writing. . . .
>   The kids naturally gravitated to the park, a nondescript
> field that stood less than a block from the apartment. Better
> known as "Pot Park," it was an outdoor bazaar for illegal drugs
> and a popular hangout for neighborhood kids. . . . It was no
> secret that Karen liked smoking pot. She was seen there in the
> evenings, getting high with whoever had a joint.

What parents would want their children bused into Karen's
world, knowing how membership in that world had ended for Karen
Todd? Even the more respectable Foothills City media organizations
had consistently emphasized emotion over reflection in covering
the issues of youth crime and illicit drugs, in the process creating a
picture of certain areas—like the old part of Metroville—that was
both more frightening than reality and exceedingly difficult to

humanize. This often meant that local issues were often presented against a backdrop of frightening images formed, not by thoughtful analysis of events, but by media coverage aimed at building up readership through delivering dramatic stories.

At public meetings it became clear that parents who lived in the outer suburbs did not see themselves as privileged. Instead, they saw themselves as struggling to provide adequately for their children's present and future needs during difficult times. Often, with both parents working, they seemed anxious about the small amount of "family time" they are able to set aside. They worried that they were not able to spend enough time with their children to overcome possible demoralizing influences encountered at school. In interviews parents expressed concern that their attempts to teach moral values to their children might be undermined by constant exposure to peers who belittled those values. Repeatedly parents communicated a feeling of being stretched too thin, with the specter of college costs looming ahead.

School district personnel were visibly straining to retain the support of those middle- and upper middle-class parents who voted in large numbers and whose taxes, in this industry-poor district, provided the primary financial support for the local schools. Early on, it became apparent that busing would be dropped as an option if a strong majority of parents opposed it. However talk continued, with many parents expressing a generalized feeling of unease, a distress at the continued growth of social problems they found difficult to define. Yet a pervasive anxiety—unconnected with any actual incident that had taken place in the Cottonwood schools—that public schools could no longer guarantee the safety of the children who attended them remained the keynote of the night.

USE OF SHARED DECISION-MAKING TO FORM DISTRICTWIDE POLICY

Formation of citizen panels has been the most effective tool used by the Cottonwood School District for addressing controversial issues on a districtwide basis. The school district invites prominent community members to work with parents, students, and school staff in finding solutions to shared problems. Law enforcement and social service personnel may be invited to give information and/or cooperate in finding a solution. The objective is to develop as broad a consensus as possible, so that all involved are committed to the same goals and have "signed off" on the specific actions which will be taken. Negotiating the specifics of such an agreement has, on occasion, taken as long as a year of regular meetings.

By inviting all interested parties to participate, the school district strengthens its hand in regard to enforcing the rules agreed upon. There will be those who choose not to participate in the decision-making process, and who later complain about the decisions reached. But, having chosen not to contribute, such individuals cannot expect to come along afterward and overturn the result of months of dedicated work by individuals who showed their concern by showing up. School district personnel also pointed out that much care is taken to make sure that all points of view are represented on a citizen panel. Important points of view cannot be left unrepresented just because no one initially volunteered to act as a spokesperson. Once a group is constituted, however, its deliberations are expected to be taken seriously.

Cottonwood personnel described the "balancing act" which was required because more affluent parents living in the Sagebrush High and Suburban High attendance areas tended to vote and to show up at public meetings in greater numbers than parents living in the Metroville High area. Articulate and often politically well-connected, Sagebrush parents "sometimes throw their weight around." A Metroville teacher observed, "Sometimes our parents just assume that they can't possibly win, that certain individuals will end up getting their way, no matter what." The remainder of this chapter will describe the school district's struggle to overcome such imbalances of power, and other social context factors, in order to reach fair settlements regarding controversial issues involving the district as a whole.

High School Attendance Area Boundary Dispute

When Sagebrush High first opened, the school district had planned to let the school fill gradually as more housing developments were built in the outer suburbs. However intense political pressure soon built up from taxpayers who wanted to know why the beautiful new school built with their money should not be used to its full capacity. Since Sagebrush High had been built to accommodate the continued growth expected in the outer suburbs, in a certain sense it could be seen as having plenty of "extra room." Cottonwood students had always had the option of changing schools, as long as they could get the agreement of the sending and the receiving principal, and provided they were willing to provide their own transportation. Through most of the school district's history, this policy of limited open enrollment worked well. But after Sagebrush High opened, the sheer number of students wishing to transfer to the new school began to create problems.

With the end of the regional recession, population growth began again in the Cottonwood district. New housing was being built in the outer suburbs, and housing that was empty elsewhere was filling up again. Yet the teenage population in the area immediately surrounding Metro High had shrunk. The population in the older part of Metroville had aged, so that it now included more older couples with no children. At the same time, many families with teenage children had moved to the newer part of Metroville, further from Foothills City. All these factors contributed to the fear of many Metroville High staff members that their school might wither away and perhaps eventually close down if too many students were allowed to transfer to Sagebrush High. As one interviewee explained, "The Metroville High population had been dropping like a stone thrown into a pond."

The Cottonwood School District originally tried to remedy this situation by announcing that the Metroville High attendance area boundary would be extended and that all students who lived within that new attendance area would have to attend Metroville High. Apparently no one on the school district staff anticipated the violent opposition which this decision encountered. A respondent who had attended a meeting where this issue was discussed recalled:

> The parents were mad. There were maybe 1,000 people at that meeting, ready to bring down the administration, the school board, whatever.

A Cottonwood administrator gave a more detailed account:

> There were some interesting board meetings where parents expressed their dislike for what was being proposed and said that they felt they had not had a chance to be heard. So they decided to go with a broadly based boundary commission and bring in a highly skilled facilitator and . . . you might say, go back to the drawing board. But prior to that they had come up with a proposal . . . they met at Metro High School. They met at Suburban High School. They met out at Sagebrush. They invited the parents. But the parents did not like their proposal, for a variety of reasons.

A district level administrator explained the problems the Cotton-wood district faced:

> One of the [district's] concerns was the number of students that were in attendance at Metroville High School. They had a problem of flight, so to speak. Of the three [high] schools, it has the largest minority population. There was this . . . image of Metroville High School which was one that is often associated with those schools which have a high proportion of minority students.

Another observer saw the ensuing confrontation as similar to the struggle in Foothills City when busing had been instituted for purposes of racial integration:

> Metroville is now 30–35 percent Hispanic. Although Kent Evans, the Metro High principal, has tried to maintain a safe, solid school, among some whites the feelings of uneasiness about the number of darker faces at Metro High are still there. Busing between the inner and outer suburbs has many of the same over-tones that [court-ordered] busing does in Foothills City.

The period of intense "white flight" that had followed court-ordered busing in Foothills City had dramatically altered the city's demographic composition. But some observers played down the importance of ethnic tensions, insisting that the attendance area controversy in the Cottonwood district was best understood in class, rather than ethnic, terms. A respondent close to the debate explained:

> Many middle-class people, including many middle-class His-panics, moved up to the section which was expected to be part of the Sagebrush High attendance area because they wanted their children to go to the new school. They had been promised a new school when the bond issue to build Sagebrush High was passed. Now this $25 million school was built and the district wanted to bus them back to Metroville. Many of these people had moved away from the old part of Metroville because they didn't want their children to go to school there.

An informant familiar with the Metroville area explained that, historically, the close-in part of Metroville had been where people went when they moved out of Foothills City. Then, when they became more affluent, they moved further out. Once they had moved further out, whether they were minority or not, they didn't want their children bused back to where they came from.

The Boundary Commission

Affirming that he was in favor of offering choices for parents, choices for teachers, and choices for kids, Superintendent Roberts arranged to set up a boundary commission to study the matter of high school attendance area boundaries. Everyone who cared deeply about the issue was invited to join this committee, which ended up including activist community people, as well as the more activist teachers. A former boundary commission member described the membership:

> There were students, there were parents, there were community members, teachers. There were ministers. Naturally there were the three high school principals, since it was their boundaries. And there were central office administrators.

A staff member who had been actively involved remembered the guidelines boundary commission members had been given:

> We were given four guidelines that had to govern whatever proposal or boundary changes we came up with:
> First, that they should be in the best interests of kids.
> Second, that the students would be assigned according to something that we would define as the capacity of the building. Later on, that was a hot topic of debate because, before Sagebrush High School was built, Suburban High School, for example, had 2,400 kids. Although that might not be the ideal size, we had to come to grips with what "capacity" meant.
> The third thing was, whatever proposed boundary changes there were, we would minimize requirements for bus transportation. Whatever we were looking at, we had to come up with something that didn't cost more for transportation.
> Fourth, we had to stabilize attendance areas so as to minimize future change and student disruption.

The district gave the boundary commission information about projected enrollments, architectural capacity of buildings, busing costs, and so on. Looking at proposals one by one, commission members listed advantages and disadvantages and identified the major issues involved in each of the proposed boundary changes. The process was not a smooth one. A boundary commission member recalled:

> It took three months for us to be able to talk together. But I liked the people, the blunt working-class way some members had of making a statement, like "This is how I feel right now about a certain kind of people." When you get it out in the open like that, it can be worked through. I find that working-class people, those who live and work with minority people— are actually more tolerant in practice, even if not in their way of speaking.

Boundary commission members also went out to the various school communities in order to gather input from parents. Some of the concerns expressed had to do with tradition, with making sure that if a brother or a sister had graduated from a certain high school, younger brothers or sisters would have the option of graduating from that high school. Others wanted to make sure that, whatever boundaries were drawn, their children got to go to the new school. The district was concerned with not overloading the new high school. But it proved difficult to come up with a way to determine whether the growth anticipated in the new high school's area—the reason Sagebrush High was built—would fill the school within ten years. "That uncertainty added a lot of fuel to the fire," a boundary commission member remembered.

An outside facilitator was brought in to moderate discussions. An administrator recalled: "He was superb. He would look at what the proposals were, brainstorm [with commission members], and list—without any kind of judgment—the advantages and disadvantages." The compromise eventually reached affirmed that people living in the debated section could choose to go to Sagebrush High, although the official change to the Metroville attendance area stood. The facilitator who had moderated the boundary commission meetings explained, "A bottom limit was put on each high school's enrollment, that no high school could go below. A top limit was also established, that no school could go above. By putting top and bottom limits on the student population at each high school, they guaranteed that Metroville High would not just disappear, which was a real fear at the time."

Managing the Building of a New High School

Although sociological factors strongly affected the high school attendance area debate, it would give a false picture to imply that they were the only factors at work. As one key informant pointed out, "That's an important question faced by many districts: How do you manage the building of a new high school? You have to rebuild the old schools, too. They all need to have a vision, to feel comfortable with their function and mission. Every district which builds a new building has the same problem. The new building steals the best teachers, or those that have a certain perspective. It has new equipment. Jealousy develops."

A strong contributing factor to the boundary dispute was the pressure put on the central office by personnel at the older high schools to prove it was evenhanded and would move to protect their interests. As a respondent familiar with the conceptual framework being used for this research pointed out:

> Sarason says that everything is a system. If you upset one part, unless you redesign the other parts, you screw the thing up.

There were also tensions having to do with the kind of school culture which evolved at Sagebrush High. As an observer at Sagebrush noted:

> Before Dave Roberts, the Cottonwood schools had been run by a "good old boy" network, had been for years. Suzanne Thompson was the first woman high school principal, and she had to deal with all that.

Several informants had indicated that, at the elementary level (where there were more female principals, diluting the possible influence of personal idiosyncrasies), power-sharing had seemed to come more naturally for female principals. One informant speculated that, having never been part of the old boy network which had been the center of power in the district under Superintendent Davis, female principals "had less of a vested interest in the way things used to be." Another speculated that power sharing was more a part of the accepted feminine role. As one respondent said admiringly of Suzanne Thompson, "She doesn't get pushed around, but she doesn't play the same games as men."

Differing Ways of Interpreting Boundary Commission Results

Looked at from a pragmatic perspective, the boundary commission was a triumph of district responsiveness to community concerns. Looked at from the social meliorist perspective, it was a triumph for articulate, determined middle-class parents who did *not* want their children going to school with "poor kids." Certainly, the way the attendance areas were finally drawn made socioeconomic differences between the Metroville High population and the population of the high schools further out in the suburbs more pronounced. As one teacher pointed out, "Metro High wasn't the suburbs any more. What you were left with started to look more like a Foothills City school run by the Cottonwood district."

Arguably, given a situation where school board members were acutely aware that middle-class parents voted in far greater numbers than parents from less affluent areas, such a result was unavoidable. However, many staff members at Metroville—and also at Suburban High—felt that their interests had been slighted by the decision to allow Sagebrush to "siphon off" their students. Over time, some came to talk as if other Cottonwood personnel, specifically those at Sagebrush High who had seemingly benefited from this decision, must have been involved in some kind of secret maneuvering aimed at bringing it about. Although objective evidence indicated that this was not true, there were staff members at Metroville and Suburban high schools who seemed to take comfort in sharing conspiracy theories. Such talk appeared to gain acceptability among some staff members simply by hint of repetition. It took several years for the bitterness caused by such gossip to subside.

EVENTS LEADING TO WESTERN STATE'S SCHOOL BUDGET CRISIS

Educational policy in Western State has been complicated in recent years by changes in the way schools within the state are funded. Under the school finance act in effect before 1988, education funding varied dramatically among districts, according to how much each district was able to collect in property taxes. Legal challenges were mounted, charging that the unequal and inferior education available to children in property-poor districts made this way of funding schools unconstitutional. Although the state supreme court did not find the system unconstitutional, the justices warned that it was unfair and needed to be changed.

In an open letter on 9 September 1991, the Western State treasurer explained that the legislature had responded to the supreme court's warning with a major reform of the school finance act, designed to equalize both the property tax burden and the resources available per student among Western State's school districts. A secondary goal was to reduce property taxes statewide. The new law enacted in 1988 had set a maximum property tax mill levy for school districts, thus meeting the legislature's goal of reducing property taxes. At the same time, the state pledged to make up the difference between what school districts were authorized to spend and the lower statewide property taxes.

Since the cost of the new school finance act was substantial, the legislature decided to defer decisions on funding the 1988 act fully. However, balancing the amount collected through local property taxes with that contributed from the state's general fund—and distributing the cost of education fairly—turned out to be an ongoing dilemma. Writing on 8 October 1989, the year after the legislature had decided to defer decisions on funding the 1988 act fully, the editor of the *Foothills City Times* editorial page described what he perceived to be the cause of the continuing financial crisis plaguing Western State schools:

> The problem stems from the political game-playing that went on in the Western State Capitol during the boom years of the 1970s. Blessed with ever-increasing budget surpluses, the legislators decided to give the money back to the taxpayers instead of banking it for Western State's future needs.
>
> These "golden gimmicks" were quite popular with the voters, and they helped the politicians get re-elected time and time again. If the gimmicks had been temporary refunds, it wouldn't have been so bad. But the shortsighted legislators made permanent changes to Western State's tax laws which have shrunk the state's tax base.
>
> As Western State entered its economic recession, the lawmakers found themselves with insufficient tax money to meet even the basic Western State needs. But they weren't willing to restore the tax structure that had existed earlier and, instead, began playing more games with the system.

During the last days of the 1990 session, the legislature projected that an extra $70 million per year would be needed to meet the requirements of the new school finance act. To provide this large amount of money without raising taxes, the legislature resorted to some creative accounting. They passed a bill that changed the schools' fiscal year from a calendar year to the state's fiscal year. The transition would occur in January of 1992, when schools would have a six-month fiscal year. Sponsors of the plan surmised that school districts could collect all of 1992's property tax revenues during the first six months of 1992 (the "short" year). The state could therefore reduce its financial aid to school districts and put the savings into a "property tax reduction fund," which would amount to $270 million. It was argued that these savings could be used to fund the projected $70 million shortfalls of the next few years. However, unexpected circumstances intervened.

Far more new students enrolled in Western State schools in the fall of 1990 than had been expected. In 1989 Western State school enrollment grew by 2,000 according to the assistant education commissioner. In 1990 school enrollment grew by 12,000, and in 1991 it grew by 18,000 (*Foothills City Times*, 3 December 1991). That 3.3 percent enrollment increase was the biggest gain in twenty-seven years. Since the increase was distributed across all grades, it was attributed to in-migration from other states, brought on by improving economic conditions in Western State and sagging job markets elsewhere.

At the same time, a decline in property values throughout much of the state had resulted in the fixed property tax rates generating fewer dollars than expected. The resulting fall in property tax revenue deepened the financial crisis when the state was suddenly faced with spending much more for school financing than it had budgeted for. Also, because of recent changes in federal guidelines, Medicaid was costing far more than expected, cutting deeply into the discretionary funding the state could use for schools. The interaction of all these factors left Western State, which by law must balance its budget, facing a serious deficit.

Further problems were caused by the state-mandated change in the school fiscal year. As long as school districts had operated on a calendar year, the property tax revenues had come in during the first half of their fiscal year, giving school districts cash to pay their bills throughout the year. Under the new law, property tax revenues would come in during the last few months of the fiscal year, forcing most school districts to borrow to pay their bills during the first seven to eight months of the fiscal year. Such borrowing added to the costs of school district operation without contributing anything to educational programs. It was to avoid having to borrow in this way that the school districts had traditionally operated on a calendar year basis.

In September 1991, Western State found itself facing a total budget shortfall of approximately $260 million. Just as school started, long after they had hired teachers and signed contracts, school districts were faced with the prospect of having their budgets severely cut. Two-thirds of the state's budget already went to education. Available options for raising additional revenue, either by giving up on property tax relief or by raising sales or income taxes, were not popular. To balance the budget, the governor proposed a mixture of budget cuts and tax increases. But, despite calls for a long-term solution—for deciding which government services were most important and devising a dependable way to pay for them—no such solution was worked out. School districts across the state were forced to cut their budgets.

Shared Decision-Making on
Budget Expenditures in Cottonwood

Each year the Cottonwood district's proposed budget is brought to the board of education for review. This review is followed by public budget hearings. Citizen members of the District Budget Review Committee perform a critical role in the review process. Citizens ensure that the budget accurately reflects the shared values set forth in the District Strategic Improvement Plan. There are two sources of funds for district operations: the general fund and the building fund. General fund dollars come largely from Western State allocations (69% in 1991) and local tax receipts (28% in 1991). The operating budget for instruction and supplies is paid from the general fund. The building or construction part of the budget is funded by a school bond issue which was approved by the voters in 1986.

Noninstructional costs are reduced through intergovernmental joint-use and purchasing agreements with local cities and county agencies. For the past several years, the Cottonwood district has made extensive reductions in its level of central office support. Additional budget reductions were made in 1990 to counteract the loss of funding due to adjustments in the local property tax. At the same time, expenditures were projected to increase during the next few years due to an influx of new residents with school-aged children.

FUNDING CHALLENGES FACED BY THE COTTONWOOD DISTRICT

Cottonwood School District has built a reputation for being fiscally responsible while providing high-quality programs. Due to its lack of an industrial tax base, the Cottonwood district operates with the lowest per-child funding of any of the fourteen school districts in the Foothills City metropolitan area. At present, the bonded indebtedness of Cottonwood is at the statutory limit and the district's inability to issue bonds is projected to continue until January 1995. Yet most schools in the outer suburban areas of the Cottonwood School District are either at capacity or will be within one or two years. Three elementary schools were over capacity in 1992, as was Riverbend Junior High. Sagebrush Senior High will be above capacity in 1993. Yet the district has no funds for further building at this time.

Debating the Fate of Goose Pond Alternative Junior/Senior High School

This section will discuss how the Cottonwood school board's reaction to the budgetary shortfall illustrated the limitations of shared decision-making, given the existence of strong political pressure, as well as sharp differences of opinion among various groups of stakeholders concerning the mission of the public schools. At the center of the debate was future funding for Goose Pond, Cottonwood's well-respected alternative junior-senior high school, which had served at-risk and other secondary students since the 1970s. Negotiations over the future of Goose Pond Alternative Junior/Senior High School also demonstrate the tension between the model of participatory democracy represented by the shared decision-making process and the model of representative democracy exemplified by the school board.

The educational philosophy of Goose Pond Campus had been to provide each student with an opportunity to develop the skills and support systems necessary for a productive future. Important to this concept was establishing a delicate balance of appropriate emotional support, complemented by clearly defined and consistently enforced limits. Goose Pond staff members felt it was important that students show commitment to their own academic success. Commitment was shown by attending classes regularly, having the appropriate materials, and completing the work assigned, as well as by respecting self, teachers, and other students through using appropriate language and cooperative behavior. Compared to the other secondary schools in the district, the Goose Pond program was very structured. However, the rules have been evolved to suit the needs of the predominantly at-risk population Goose Pond served.

Attendance policies for Goose Pond high school students were strict. In the M-W-F classes a student could have three absences per quarter and still pass. (Goose Pond did not distinguish between excused and unexcused absences for the first three absences.) The fourth absence resulted in an F for the quarter, unless it was excused. In the T-Th classes, a student could have two absences per quarter. The third absence resulted in failure unless excused. The only way to excuse an absence was to present a doctor's note or a court subpoena. In any class, three tardies equaled one absence. A tardy was marked after the first ten minutes of class. Junior high students dropped a letter grade for each unexcused absence after three on M-W-F or after two on T-Th.

Goose Pond Campus offered an individualized, student-centered program that included required basic skills classes, electives, and a variety of support offerings. Class size was approximately fifteen students to one teacher. Most classes were multigrade level and reflected a 2/3 to 1/3 ratio of high school to junior high school students. In addition to the course offerings at Goose Pond Campus, off-campus classes were available in the community, at Suburban Community College, and at other Cottonwood District schools. An education at Goose Pond Campus was open to all high school–aged residents of Cottonwood School District. Total high school enrollment per quarter was limited to 100 students.

As a high school of choice, Goose Pond made it understood that, upon enrollment, both students and parents must accept the conditions and rules that governed the program. Students must have attended their home school for at least one semester before making application to Goose Pond. Prior to the start of each quarter, student applicants were notified of the date for an intake interview. A panel of teachers and students presented the Goose Pond program and listened to each applicant's motivation for wanting to be a part of their school. In addition to the interview, the Goose Pond program and expectations were presented at a group orientation, where curriculum offerings and course prerequisites were discussed.

Students who were enrolled at Goose Pond campus had to pass six classes (including at least two T-Th classes, and three M-W-F classes) to avoid being recycled for the following quarter. Students on recycle could interview for reregistration at Goose Pond Campus for the school quarter following the recycle quarter. Students on recycle were, in effect, suspended from school, in that they could not enroll at Metroville, Suburbia, or Sagebrush high schools. If a student was recycled twice, Goose Pond Campus was no longer an educational option. Options for such a student might include, but were not limited by: Lone Tree Adult High School (minimum age 18 years); enrollment at another Cottonwood school (with the principal's permission); Suburban Community College; G.E.D.; Trade/vocational school; seeking employment while considering other options.

Housed in a historic rural school building, Goose Pond Alternative Junior/ Senior High was widely respected but expensive to run, given its 15:1 student/teacher ratio and the relatively small number of students the Goose Creek campus served. The historic building the school occupied and the land on which it sat were both, in themselves, valuable. Yet the building was in need of repairs which the Cottonwood district could ill afford. Goose Pond did not meet present state requirements for school buildings, but remained open because it had been "grandfathered" under a clause in the state law which exempted schools in continuous service from building code revisions put in place after those schools had first opened.

THE TENSION BETWEEN PARTICIPATORY AND REPRESENTATIVE DEMOCRACY

Discussion of the fate of the Goose Pond alternative school took place in the spring of 1992, at a time when there had just been a significant shift in the membership of the school board. The previous year the relatively liberal school board president, who had headed the hiring committee that had selected Dave Roberts as Cottonwood superintendent, had retired. The agenda of the new school board was set by fiscal conservatives. Noting that the district was in a period of general financial retrenchment, board members questioned the amount of money the district was spending on the Goose Pond facility.

Board members argued strongly that the district's primary mission was to offer high-quality programs to all students. They rejected the argument that more funding should be assigned to help those most in need, arguing that social work should be left to the social service agencies. According to their view, achieving the greatest good for the greatest number meant maintaining strong programs districtwide. In a time of financial austerity, they argued the district could ill afford to keep open what they saw as an inefficient school. Despite a strong consensus among Cottonwood staff members that the alternative school should be kept open, the school board decided to close the Goose Pond school after the 1993–94 school year.

Although, on this issue, the opinions of personnel at other schools had not been solicited by the school board, it was clear that most secondary-level staff members opposed closing the alternative school, both for the altruistic reason that it offered a last chance to troubled teens and for the less-than-altruistic reason that it gave other schools a place to send some of their most difficult students. Interviews with Cottonwood teachers during this period of time made it clear that they saw this as an example of a situation where widespread consensus on the value of a program had made no impression on the school board. Teachers further noted that there was a definite connection between the amount of energy they, personally, were willing to put into shared decision-making around a given issue and the perceived likelihood that the school board would "do what it wants to do, anyway."

There was also a values issue involved, which posed a special challenge to the superintendent's shared decision-making paradigm. In chapter 6 it was mentioned that Dr. Roberts had stated in school district materials that, in examining the values of an organization, it was critical that perceived values be put to a test. A value was to be measured against the following criteria:

1. Does it permeate the organization?
2. Does the value drive decisions?
3. Is there a strong reaction when the value is violated?
4. Is the value something that you won't give up?

Dr. Roberts had used the value "success for all students" as an example, stating "If a school district has a high dropout rate or certain groups of students consistently score below others on standardized tests, [success for all students] may be a perceived value but, in reality, it is not happening." He went on to say, "If 'success for all students' is important, are resources allocated with that thought in mind? Using the above example of students performing below grade level, does the school district, school and individual teacher consistently look for ways to improve student achievement for those at risk students?"

In the debate over closing the Goose Pond campus, it was exactly this issue of success for all students, long proclaimed to be a major goal of the Cottonwood School District, that lay at the center of the debate. Through its resource allocation decisions the current school board had by implication announced that, by Dr. Roberts' own criteria, the issue of success for all students might be a perceived value but it was not likely to be given high priority while the present school board held office. Of course, differences between public rhetoric and political practice are by no means unknown among elected officials. However they may present special difficulties when an organization is trying to institutionalize shared decision-making mechanisms that depend for their effectiveness on openness and trust.

As one teacher pointed out during a building-level school budget meeting the following year, "I feel like Dorothy in *The Wizard of Oz,* saying 'I believe, I believe, I believe.'" She was replying to a parent who had wondered aloud whether the gathering of budget input from all the buildings was not "just for show," whether all the work being put in at the building level was simply being wasted. Ironically, the detailed budget process in which they were involved appeared to have been set up in such an elaborate, formalized fashion in order to insure that people in the individual buildings did have some discretionary power in regard to how their building's funds would be used. Yet the many uncertainties inherent in the political context surrounding the budget process left ample room for doubts to grow.

THE IMPACT OF BUDGETARY POLITICS ON SHARED DECISION-MAKING

On an abstract level, the need for mutual support between a school board and school district personnel is clear. Each has too much to lose if cooperation breaks down. The school board is made up of people who are, in one respect, outsiders to the school system, individuals who have a generalized interest in education but often possess little knowledge of the problems faced by classroom teachers. Board members hold the ultimate power, but lack the knowledge of day-to-day operations necessary to manage a sprawling educational enterprise. On the other hand, school district personnel are in a position similar to that of long-time employees of a publicly owned corporation. They might have put in decades of service to the organization, but if they find themselves at cross purposes with a large stockholder who bought his shares the day before, he could vote to cancel a project on which they had spent years.

Unnecessary arbitrariness on the part of those with decision-making power can cause the morale of the frontline staff to deteriorate to the extent that neither a corporation nor a school district can operate up to its true potential. Indeed, performance levels may slide disastrously. Evidence suggested that such a situation had come about in the nearby Foothills City School District when deeper budget cuts were required in the spring of 1993. An editorial in the *Foothills City Times* described the budget negotiation process in that district:

> The task of trimming $30.1 million from next year's Foothills City Public Schools budget would be difficult enough if the school board, parents, administrators and teachers were working together in good faith. But the raucous name-calling and snarling turf wars that have so far derailed the budget process are a disservice to the children the various combatants profess to serve.

Optimally, the knowledge of educational professionals is respected, while school board members take seriously their duty to consider the interests of the wider community, bringing with them a breadth of knowledge and/or a specialized expertise which educators who have spent much of their working lives within a single school district may lack. In a climate of continuing budgetary crisis, the Cottonwood School District would soon face a greater challenge to its commitment to collaborative governance procedures characterized by decision-making.

THE 1993 SCHOOL BUDGET CRISIS

The governor had insisted that Western State lawmakers faced three choices if they failed to vote new tax money for education: dramatically cutting state funding for public schools, dramatically cutting other services to pay the state share for public schools, or retreating from the goal of reduced property taxes and letting these taxes rise to fill the gap. No agreement on raising more money for schools was achieved, nor were other services cut. By default, given the continued rise in school enrollment, school districts found that they were faced with dramatic cuts in per pupil funding.

Throughout the 1991–92 school year, the debate over how Western State would manage to fund its schools continued. If nothing was done, a shortfall of almost $300 million was foreseen during 1993–94. In November 1992, an initiative introduced by the governor was on the Western State ballot. The proposed amendment to the state constitution would have raised the state sales tax by one cent, earmarking the resulting funds entirely for education. Exasperated by the legislature's inaction, the governor campaigned hard for his amendment, asserting such an amendment was needed to insure adequate school funding on an ongoing basis. However, the governor's amendment was defeated and another amendment, that required elections be held before any new taxes were put into effect, was passed. This second amendment greatly restricted the legislature's ability to raise new tax money.

School districts across the state faced significant budget shortfalls for the 1993–94 school year. The Cottonwood district faced a projected shortfall of $10 million, out of a total budget of $91 million. Clearly the process of deciding on budget cuts would be difficult. The district had been cutting back for several years and was already very lean in terms of central office staffing. To decide how the district could best absorb the projected loss of approximately 11 percent of its operating budget, nine critique groups were asked to conduct an analysis of Cottonwood programs and services and to make recommendations for budget reduction and redesign. In reaching their decisions, they were asked to use a shared decision-making and consensus-building process.

Critique groups included: Citizen Advisory Committee (includes one parent from each school in the district); Classified Employee's Association; District School Improvement Team, and its subcommittee, District Budget Review Advisory Committee; district administrators; Cottonwood Educator's Association (teacher's union); Learning Services Team (Office of Curriculum and Instruction); Principals' Association; student leaders; Support Services Team. Each of the thirty-one district programs or departments, ranging from athletics to utilities and energy, were asked to submit a budget showing what the program staff felt ought to be kept and what ought to be cut if the program were funded as 95%, 85%, 75%, or 50%. These recommendations were given to the nine critique groups, which in turn recommended a level of funding for each program, so as to reach a target of $4.5 million in total cuts for the 1993–94 school year.

Subject to final decisions by the school board, this would be central administration's portion of the budget cuts. Those cuts that were not made at the district level would be left up to the schools, which would be given reduced building allotments and asked to use a shared decision-making process to decide where their budget cuts would be made. However, teacher contracts limited the possible options at the building level. Since cuts of the magnitude of those being considered could not be made without dropping FTE (full-time equivalent staff positions), seniority requirements in the union contract made it likely that the younger, untenured teachers would be the first let go.

The way the district budget-cutting process had been set up, any budgetary relief which might come through higher-than-expected tax revenue during the spring semester would go to the buildings. If no relief was forthcoming, once the district-level cuts had been made, the schools would decide on a building-by-building basis which personnel, programs, and supplies they would choose to forego in order to keep their spending in line with their lower building allotment. As it turned out, initial rumors that all probationary teachers (those who had spent less than three years in the Cottonwood district) would be RIFed (let go due to reduction in force) proved unfounded. An upswing in the Western State economy generated enough new tax income that the buildings were largely relieved of the onerous prospect of dropping FTEs. But the district level cuts, which will be discussed in the following pages, largely remained.

PUBLIC MEETINGS HELD TO DISCUSS BUDGET CUTS

The suggestions made by the nine critique groups regarding district-level budget cuts were presented to the public at evening meetings held at each of the three Cottonwood high schools: Suburban High on Monday, 22 February; Metroville High on Tuesday, 23 February; and Sagebrush High on Thursday, 25 February. These widely publicized meetings were held in the auditoriums of the high schools, from 7:00 to 9:00 p.m., and were presided over by the superintendent and the school board.

These public meetings turned out to be highly emotional, offering a kind of "snapshot" of the deep social divisions which existed in the Cottonwood district and of the challenge the district faced in trying to bring about community consensus. For this reason, they will be described in some detail. The divergent cultures that have evolved at the Cottonwood high schools often showed up in telling details: Sagebrush High not only had permanent directional signs showing visitors how to find the office, gymnasium, and auditorium, but had also put up student-drawn paper signs to direct parents to the budget meeting; Suburban High had neither permanent signs nor paper arrows, causing considerable confusion to parents unfamiliar with the school's complex floor plan.

Most striking, however, was the indifference of individuals who were undergoing rough times in their own lives to either logical analysis of the financial problems besetting the Cottonwood district or discussion of state-level budget decisions that had led to the current crisis. During the public second meeting, at Metroville High, the atmosphere at times crackled with the frustration of hard-pressed parents, who had lost jobs, or had to do without insurance, or had no money put away for retirement, demanding to know why the schools kept threatening to cut programs. In such an atmosphere, the venting of generalized anger often interrupted attempts to engage in thoughtful discussion of how best to solve common problems. The school district came under attack, not because it was the direct cause of these community members' woes, but because it had become a more satisfying target than the faceless state and federal bureaucracies whose effects on local affairs were harder to pinpoint.

Suburban High Meeting

Suburban High is often described as resembling "a small college campus." The high school is made up of several buildings, on different levels. Parking lots surround the school on three sides. Since the school had been built on a gentle slope, visitors who parked in the student parking lot actually entered on the second floor and had to find their way from one of the half dozen entrances on that side of the complex, down a flight of stairs, and around a U-shaped central courtyard in order to make their way to the auditorium on the far side of the campus. Although the buildings were attractive and well-lit, there were no visible signs showing visitors the way to the auditorium. Clearly, many of the arriving parents were unfamiliar with the high school's rambling floor plan, and some grumbled loudly as they searched.

The inward-facing design of the school, impressive when seen from the central courtyard, had been approved during Superintendent Larimer's tenure. At the time, the school's college-like setting had seemed a natural environment in which to prepare the school's middle-class students for the university environment most were expected to encounter shortly after graduation. The educational philosophy of the time emphasized helping students to become responsible citizens through giving them responsibility. Parents did not usually show up in the building, except when invited as audiences for school events or when called in to discuss disciplinary lapses.

Although the school district's philosophy had changed, with parents now encouraged to participate in each school's decision-making process, Suburban High continued to be an inwardly focused school. "Why can't these modern schools have something you could identify as the main entrance?," a mother mumbled as she made her way down the hall from the gymnasium wing. Another parent sniffed: "I heard they patterned their architecture after their site-based management policies. You can never grab the head of the beast, but just have to start wherever you are and feel your way along!" There seemed to be a noticeable tendency for community members disgruntled with a wide range of both educational and social phenomena to see the school district administration as monolithic, assuming that whatever displeased them was somehow characteristic of the present administration's policies.

Outside the Suburban High auditorium, new arrivals were given a four-page handout that described the budget crisis the district faced:

> Following the November 1992 election, the Board of Education challenged citizens and staff to help determine ways the district could begin living with Amendment 1's tax and spending limitations and estimates of a substantial decline in state funding.
>
> The most recent information indicates the district will face a shortage of approximately $10 million from the $91 million allocated to district programs and schools. Ninety percent of the district's funding is driven by the 1988 School Finance Act, which enables Western State's Legislature to determine the level of support based on state revenues and local property taxes.

Proposed cuts were listed, along with a detailed description of the process which had been used to arrive at the proposed cuts. The procedures for discussion of the proposals were also explained. Final decisions about budget cuts were to be announced at the 15 March school board meeting.

Little casual conversation was heard as people filed in; few smiles were visible. The atmosphere was tense. The demeanor of many parents hinted at feelings of irritable helplessness in the face of rumors that programs they valued might be cut. Most were dressed in casual clothes. Administrators and school board members sitting on-stage wore suit coats and ties, as did teachers sitting in the audience (most specifically identified themselves as such during the public input phase of the meeting). During the evening several parents pointedly identified themselves as being "working class," "lower middle class," or "working poor." Subtly, the difference in dress added to an overall impression that the school personnel were among the more affluent individuals in attendance.

The large auditorium had a single, gently rising bank of seats, divided into three sections by two wide aisles. Microphones had been set up at the midpoint of each aisle. About 200 people were present as the meeting began, bunched toward the middle and rear of the auditorium. The president of the Cottonwood School Board opened the meeting, introducing her fellow board members and emphasizing that the board had made no decisions. Nor would the board make any decisions during the meeting, which had been set up specifically to gather public input to be used in later decision-making. The board president then turned the meeting over to Superintendent Roberts, who explained that the Cottonwood School District hoped to minimize the impact of the projected budget cuts by taking into account community views.

Dr. Roberts again emphasized that the board had made no final decisions yet, and that the recommendations listed in the handouts were no more than a composite of the recommendations of the nine critique groups. The percentage reduction listed for each program was simply the reduction most frequently suggested by all critique groups. For this reason, the figure for the total cuts was only $3,484,640, although the superintendent thought it prudent to be ready with as much as $5.5 million in possible cuts should it turn out, after the state legislature had made its final decisions, that this size reduction was needed. Dr. Roberts suggested that a closer look might have to be taken at central administration, where it might be possible to cut more than the 15 percent currently recommended, and also at special education, where no budget recommendations had been made because no consensus on the amount of budget reduction had been reached.

Before turning the meeting over to the district's communications director, Dr. Roberts emphasized that never before, in the ten years he had been in the district, had they faced such drastic cuts. He said he hoped that staff and community members would look at this as an opportunity to deliver programs differently and more efficiently. He also expressed his hope that all present would listen respectfully to each other's views and values as they all searched for a solution.

The district communications director briefly reviewed the "Norms for the Public Meetings" listed on the last page of the handout:

- We will listen to each other with respect.
- Speakers will state their name and the name of their child's school or the school nearest them.
- Each individual will be allowed two minutes.
- A timer will hold a stop card at the end of that time.
- Speakers may be asked to give up their time if their specific concern is addressed by someone else during the meeting.

If individual comments were longer than the two minutes allowed, speakers would be invited to put them in writing for board members to read after the meeting. At the end of the meeting the superintendent would answer as many questions as possible. However, to get as much input as possible—and also to enable Dr. Roberts, where possible, to answer several related questions at once—no answers to specific questions would be given until the end of the evening. Those in attendance were then invited to come up to one of the two open microphones and share their concerns with the school board.

The first speaker who stepped to the microphones represented the largest interest group present: supporters of the elementary band program. When an elementary band teacher, who traveled among five schools, asked how many band supporters there were in the room, about 75 percent of the audience raised their hands. Of forty-four people who came forward to speak during the meeting, ten spoke of the importance of music education, most emphasizing its importance to a segment of the student body that might not find much else in the school curriculum to be enthusiastic about. There would have been more speakers on this subject had not the district communications director asked, half way through the meeting, that band supporters allow other people present to bring up additional issues that might be of concern.

Five parents spoke in support either of the community swim team, which served as a "feeder" for the high school swim teams, or of school athletic programs in general. The budget recommendation in regard to sports gave no specifics, saying only: "Eliminates 7th grade athletics and five high school sports. With an increase in fees, no reduction in sports would be necessary. Current fees are $25 per sport." Parents emphasized their readiness to pay fees to preserve school sports, as well as the readiness of the community swimming team to pay fees to preserve its access to the high school pool.

Six speakers addressed various aspects of the special education issue. A kindergarten teacher, who had taught special education for most of her thirty years in the district, spoke of an inclusion program she had started recently, which had gained some national attention but needed continued support. The Garfield County educational advocate expressed her concern that the district's widely respected special programs not be lost. A father made an emotional plea:

> I have had four children who attended school in this district. Two have graduated. One graduated last year without being able to read. That sort of thing still happens. Kids slip through. I'm now spending $200 a month on a nine-month literacy program for him. But I am here to talk about another son. Without the help of a special education teacher he got hooked up with in junior high, I honestly think he might now be in jail. Instead, he's now an "A" student.

A mother spoke of her adopted daughter, who required occupational therapy, speech therapy, and special education, and asked why her child was not mainstreamed. A school social worker spoke of the benefit his two children had gotten from helping the less able children who attended a special program at their elementary school. Unlike supporters of the music and sports programs, parents who spoke about special education appeared to have come independently, rather than as an organized group. Parents who spoke in opposition to the arguments put forth by supporters of music and special education also appeared to do so on the spur of the moment. For example, two parents commented (following unrelated remarks) that transportation arrangements or special needs students seemed exorbitantly expensive.

A few parents argued that, to keep classroom size down, the district should eliminate all professional FTEs who were not regular classroom teachers. A father of an elementary school student said he did not think nonclassroom certified staff earned their keep. Another parent suggested that, instead of eliminating 1.2 reading resource teacher slots, the district should get rid of all reading resource teachers and use that money to keep the student-teacher ratio down. Two parents suggested getting rid of the outdoor education program which allowed sixth-grade classes to take a three-day camping trip. Strongly objecting, an elementary physical education teacher spoke eloquently of how the students looked forward all year to their class trip. A junior high boy came forward to declare: "I really liked outdoor ed. You guys shouldn't cut it."

A mother suggested that the outdoor education fee, which had been dropped the year before in order to insure equal access to all children, be reinstated and children be encouraged to engage in fundraising activities to finance their class trip. About a third of the parents who spoke advocated charging fees for various programs, with sliding fees available to those who could not afford to pay or who had multiple youngsters in school. Two parents brought up fees in connection with transportation, one saying that she would be willing to pay a fee for her children's bus transportation if this would leave other programs intact. A special education parent said she would be willing to transport her daughter to the school to avoid program cuts.

Two individuals (both of whom spoke early in the meeting) took an openly confrontational attitude. One remarked "Everyone up there [the school board and superintendent] knows me," the other "You've heard from me before." A mother who said she "had kids all over the district" wanted to know about $2 million that had been added to the district's general fund in November: Where did it come from? What would happen if the state legislature was able to come up with more funding than anticipated? If the shortfall was not as great as anticipated, would the money currently being cut from programs be spent on students or on administrators? Her comments were met with scattered audience applause. At the end of the evening Superintendent Roberts explained that the $2 million had come from the before- and after-school programs available in almost all of the Cottonwood elementary schools.

A man in a cowboy hat and Western leather jacket, who said he had a son at Metroville High, demanded to know whether the district's administrative salaries had ever gone down to reflect the downturn in the local economy and the decrease in local real estate values. Loudly, he declared: "I'd like to get some answer right now! Yes or no! Although I know I can't count on getting any!" There was a small amount of applause. The district communications director replied in measured tones, "We will respond to as many questions as possible at the end of the evening." "No answer then!," he shot back. "You have five board members and the superintendent up there. You should be able to answer this!"

The next speaker was a father who said he was grateful that the school his children attended was in as good shape as it had been when his wife had attended it twenty-five years before. He said that he only wanted to emphasize the importance of remembering intangibles, like keeping up the facilities and keeping down class size.

After the twenty-sixth speaker, the Suburban High band teacher, the man in the cowboy hat came up to the microphone again. Although the district communications director asked him to respect the norms that had been established and to submit further comments in writing, he refused to step back, insisting that two other people in attendance had given their time over to him. He pointed to an older man and woman sitting nearby. The communications director pointed out that such exchanges of time were not part of the norms which had been established. Another speaker was recognized, at the other microphone. But the man in the cowboy hat remained where he was, forcing other speakers to go to the microphone on the other side of the auditorium. After five speakers had made their remarks at the other microphone, the school board treasurer picked up the microphone in front of him and said that he would like to hear from the man in the cowboy hat, who responded:

> If you double the cuts to central administration, from $213,895 to twice that, you can do away with cuts to band, athletics, and some other things. You say this is a site-based district! Then why do we need to spend so much money on central administration?

Speaking at the end of the meeting, Dr. Roberts explained that, of seven central administration positions that had contained the word "superintendent" when he came to the district, only three were left—and there might be fewer than that the next fall. Cottonwood had already, since 1988, cut $180,000 from the central administrative budget. Even though it was close to the bottom of the districts in the metropolitan area in per-student funding, Cottonwood maintained programs which were of comparable quality to any in the state. If critics would compare Cottonwood to other school districts, they would see that it was already a very lean district.

Metroville High Meeting

All parking was on one side of the school and the main entrance was directly opposite the parking lot. Parents found their way into the school more easily than they had at Suburban High. The auditorium was straight ahead, across an open lobby area. More compact than the space at Suburban High, the auditorium had steeply rising banks of seats on three sides. A television camera was set up and bright lights lit the area. At the start of the meeting, it was explained that the film crew was associated with a national professional organization and was making a documentary about site-based management. If any speakers preferred not to be taped, they should make a motion to shut the cameras off and their wishes would be respected.

More students were present than at Suburban High. Although Metroville High had a higher percentage of minority students than the other high schools, there were no black and very few Hispanic parents at this meeting. One procedural difference was announced: If there was time, after all who wanted to speak had a chance to do so, individuals who wished to speak a second time would be allowed to step up to the microphone again. There were about 150 people present when the meeting began.

The father of a Metroville High student was the first to step up to the microphone. His remarks were carefully prepared. He said that in 1992 the total district payroll had been $68 million. If everyone on that payroll would agree to a three year wage freeze, no one would have to lose their jobs. No programs would have to be cut. No one would go on unemployment. His remarks sounded the keynote for the evening.

The next four speakers touched on themes similar to those sounded the night before. An elementary band teacher stepped up and asked band supporters to stand. About half the audience stood. A mother with two sons on the swim team pointed out that swimmers bought all their own equipment, while the district paid thousands of dollars for football equipment. A junior high music teacher noted out that, because of class size, secondary-level music teachers carried a student overload equal to seven FTEs, which more than made up for the salaries of the five elementary band teachers. Two girls on the Metro High gymnastics team asserted that, without sports, many students would see nothing in the school day that made it worthwhile not to skip school.

The sixth speaker was a mother who had been at the meeting the night before. She again brought up the $2 million which had been added to the general fund in November, passing over the explanation offered by Dr. Roberts the evening before. She also pointed out that the school system was presently in salary negotiations with the unions and said, "If I were you, I'd insist that my employees were with me instead of against me. Why not demand that they take a cut in salary rather than cutting programs for our children?"

Next, the Metroville High band director compared the elementary band program to the Little League sports teams, which make it possible for high school athletic teams to excel. Then, an elementary father got up to insist that the handout he had been handed did not deserve the title given to it, "Redesigning the Future:"

> I would like to see a proposal that did not just shave around the edges of existing programs, but that really did redesign how programs are delivered. From what I can see, you chose all of the nine groups which critiqued this proposal. What have you done to include other groups that might disagree with what you have here?

Later, the father of a student from a Sagebrush High feeder school took an even more confrontational attitude, saying that he had done an independent audit of his daughter's school, using the Western State open records act. The way he saw it, the school had two illegal cash "slush funds" and had used them to finance student outings, as well as to buy a large screen TV and computers for the school. The school had also sent staff members to Las Vegas for a conference on year-round education.

Then, the man with the cowboy hat, who had spoken at the Suburban High meeting, stepped up to the microphone to announce that he was the co-founder of a parent group that was independent of the school district. He invited all the parents present to attend a meeting at the Metroville Town Hall at 7:00 p.m. that Thursday (the same time as the district's scheduled budget meeting at Sagebrush High School).

The president of the Cottonwood teacher's union stepped up to the microphone next. He explained that the budget dilemma the district faced had been caused by the nonfunding of the 1988 School Finance Act by the state legislature. Trying to take the shortfall out of the teachers' pay was not the answer; people had to pressure the legislature to act. Then, a thirty-year veteran teacher stood up to say she intended to help with the shortfall by contributing part of her salary to the Cottonwood district's nonprofit foundation. She called on others to join her in doing so. A young junior high teacher spoke in an emotional tone about all the extra time he and other teachers put in that they didn't get paid for, adding:

> A lot of teachers feel belittled right now, by people and by the media. Freezing teachers' salaries and benefits hurts morale.

As soon as he sat down, a mother came to the microphone and said that her husband's wages had been frozen for eight years. "We survived! It was tough, but we survived. We all put in extra time at our jobs. Teachers aren't the only ones! I recommend a wage cut." Another mother hit a similar note:

> Teachers are worried about a pay freeze. They should be thinking more about the kids than about themselves!

A high school girl came to the microphone to take issue with her remarks:

> I don't want my teachers' salaries to be cut. I'd like them to know that. The focus should be on the administrators. There are lots of people out there making it on much less than the administrators make.

After this comment, no more speakers came to the microphone, so the floor was opened for further comment from those who had already spoken. The mother who had first suggested that teachers take a salary cut came forward to insist that, although teachers seemed to think parents were out to get them, "teachers only spend 1,000 hours on their jobs in a year and the average person works 2,000 hours. Others have experienced freezes or cuts." She informed the audience that she had recently lost her job. In her view, parents asking teachers to "bite the bullet" did not differ from teachers asking parents to participate more in their children's education.

Another mother, who had a teen at Metroville High and one which had just graduated, came to the microphone to challenge her: "They have good teachers here. What makes me sort of sick is the small number of people who came out tonight. People sit around and bitch, but they don't get active."

The head of the teacher's union came forward again, to defend the teachers:

What's happened in other states is that the best and brightest are not going into teaching. College kids are thinking twice about going into a profession that is constantly being bashed. Teachers here (in Cottonwood) have done things in the past like taking a 1% salary increase. But we have a long-term problem. We need to let legislators know we need adequate funding.

The last speaker of the evening was a mother who directly challenged the teacher's union president:

We run a small business. In the past few years our insurance costs have gone up tremendously. Right now we pay 20% of our take-home income for insurance. We don't have any retirement. What are your benefits like? I bet you don't pay anything out of your take-home income for insurance. You have retirement. In the last two years, the amount that taxpayers have shelled out for your benefits has gone up 53%. I say we should be looking at cutting benefits, not cutting kids.

After the meeting several Cottonwood staff members noted how different the atmosphere at the Metroville High meeting had been from the one the night before. No one at this meeting had said they were willing to pay fees to support sports programs. Talking of toll on the superintendent and board members presiding at such meetings, a longtime staff member said resignedly, "I suppose they're used to it. This budget cutting has been going on for years now."

Sagebrush High Meeting

The budget meeting at Sagebrush High coincided with a basketball game, but despite the large crowd in the gym, about three hundred parents were present when the budget meeting started. Many wore business suits. After the confrontational, emotional atmosphere of the Metro High meeting, the Sagebrush High meeting seemed somewhat anticlimatic. Again, the band and swim team were well represented. More students spoke than at the other public meetings, many reading carefully prepared remarks which appeared to have been written with parental help. Parents gave their support to instituting fees for sports and other programs, with sliding scales attached so that students who might not be able to pay the fee would not be excluded.

Parents spoke in measured tones, often from written notes, and many offered practical money-saving suggestions—from the use of special valves to cut down on water bills to the contracting out of custodial services. Cost-saving measures that had been taken by local businesses were described and the possibility of cost-saving cooperation with other institutions was mentioned. Several parents mentioned pet peeves: schoolrooms with bad thermostats which overheated on warm days and the lighting of the sign outside the district's administrative headquarters at night. Some concerns appeared to be based on environmental considerations rather than the possibility of significant monetary savings. Although the tone of a few speakers was peevish, no one took a confrontational stance. The part the state legislature had played in causing the current budget crisis seemed well understood.

At the end of this last meeting, after answering questions and replying to comments, Dr. Roberts made the first personal comment he had made during these public meetings. He talked of the public's loss of confidence in the public education system, which had been reflected the November before both in the defeat of the governor's sales tax amendment and in the passage of a tax limitation amendment which had squeezed public school budgets even more. Cottonwood's superintendent spoke earnestly of the need for educators to regain the public's confidence. He urged anyone in the audience who was not already actively involved in their neighborhood school to "come onboard and help us out."

FINAL BUDGET CUTS

At its 15 March meeting, the school board announced its three-year budget reduction plan. Most of the district's programs would be funded at the 85 percent level. Of those categories that were funded at less than 85 percent, assistant principals and school secretaries were among the hardest hit. Approximate cuts (across 35 schools) would be: 14.5 FTEs at the elementary level, 11 FTEs at the junior high level, and 10 FTEs at the senior high level. Central administration took the biggest percentage cut, with the superintendent's office funded at 65 percent, giving up 4 FTEs. However, Curriculum and Instruction, entrusted with implementing the curriculum framework, was funded at 95 percent.

Support services were hit hard. Custodial operations lost 19.82 FTEs. Transportation lost 10 FTEs. The number of health aides was reduced by 10 and school media specialists by 5.3. Psychological services lost 6.8 FTEs. The number of school counselors was cut by 4.

The program that would see by far the most dramatic cuts, however, would be special education, which lost 36.7 FTEs. Many of those let go would be aides, but without the paraprofessionals there was a real question as to how the mainstreaming of severely handicapped students could proceed.

PROSPECTS FOR THE FUTURE

Sarason (1991) has highlighted the futility of attempts at restructuring that do not alter power relationships within schools. My findings suggest the effectiveness of restructuring will be limited unless power relationships in the social context within which public schools are embedded are also transformed. When the Western State legislature failed—for the fourth straight year—to come up for a plan for fully funding the 1988 School Finance Act, even the most well-run school districts were thrown into a budgetary crisis. Efforts at responsible planning on the school district level cannot overcome financial mismanagement at the state level, given the state's power to regulate the public schools. Indeed, in Cottonwood it did not prove possible even to make clear to all stakeholders the political genesis of the budgetary crisis the school district faced.

The use of shared decision-making allowed Cottonwood to survive the year with less damage to educational programs, or to professional and community relationships, than nearby school districts like Foothills City, where tales of political in-fighting were splashed across the headlines of regional newspapers. However, as the school year ended, Cottonwood staff members talked anxiously of their feeling that the district was losing ground. The financial shortfall had turned out to be less than initially feared, but the required cuts were still painful and the disruption to normal school operations and site-based planning processes could not be undone. In the area of special education the inflexible nature of the needs which had to be met, combined with the strict guidelines the district was required to follow, forced upon the Cottonwood district a painful dilemma. A principal pointed out:

> We're running into legal things. Our sign interpreters are running into that tendonitis thing. They're overloaded, going morning and afternoon. A doctor told one kid who's an interpreter, "You can't do that."

A five-year plan for mainstreaming special needs students had to be shelved. At a principal's meeting, a district administrator explained, in reference to the inclusion program: "It's on hold. . . . We're not moving forward with inclusion. If needs can't be met, why do it?" This news was greeted with relief by building administrators, who perceived their teachers to be in no mood to have additional demands made of them. One principal asserted: "If I could tell the special ed team that they're not going to get severe kids next year, that's the one good thing I've told them all year." Another administrator, worried about the budgetary bottom line, observed, "I read in *Education Week* about an inclusion thing back East that cost an outrageous amount of money. So now the regular kids' parents are suing the district because there's no money left for *their* kids."

Among staff in the Cottonwood district, there was uncertainty about the future. Shared decision-making is an energy-intensive method of school governance. Proponents argue that it is worth the effort because of the higher-quality programs a collaborative approach can produce. Still, the extra work becomes harder to justify when people begin to worry that the programs so laboriously built up will be struck down, without warning, because of possible changes in the direction of the political breeze at the state level. In the Cottonwood district the tension caused by the budget crisis was unmistakable. At a district meeting, two principals commented on the mood created at their schools by the prospect of drastic budget cuts:

> There's plenty of defensiveness going on at my school right now. I've got some pissed off people running around my building.

Nor were teachers the only ones whose nerves were on edge. One principal from a large elementary school insisted at a meeting of principals:

> If they take my assistant principal, I'm going to the board to say, "You just try to manage this alone!"

Although building level cuts turned out to be less severe than had been feared, a question still hung in the air: Does the state legislature intend to put us through this wringer every year? School people reported feeling disoriented and exposed to fickle political crosswinds that could, at any time, force them to divert large amounts of energy away from educating children in order to cope with unpredictable decisions handed down by legislators—who often appeared more concerned with immediate political fallout than with how their decisions affected Western State's public schools.

CONTINUING FRUSTRATIONS AND CHALLENGES

The emergency districtwide budget process, initiated in response to drastic cuts expected during the 1993-94 school year, worked in tandem with the deliberations of Cottonwood's elected school board. The process was necessarily somewhat rough, given the short period of time in which a large amount of work had to be done. Not till after the governor's sales tax initiative had failed in the November election did the process kick in. In a short period of time, which included Christmas break, heads of district programs had to estimate the services they could deliver at various levels of funding; the central office had to get these estimates compiled and given to the nine critique groups; the critique groups, in turn, had to make their recommendations in time for the February public meetings.

All these deadlines had to be met in order for the school board to announce its final decisions at the 15 March meeting. This date had, in turn, been fixed in order to give the individual buildings time to decide on their own budget cuts before the end of the school year. There was considerable frustration over both the time the process took and the uncertainty many stakeholders felt as to how much weight the school board would give to the recommendations they arrived at. As a principal put it: "I feel like we go to all these meetings and we don't know anything yet . . . till we hear from the board."

Some politically active parents tried to take matters into their own hands, becoming adept using the formal consensus-building process at the building level to gain predetermined ends, rather than to engage in an open-ended search for a win/win solution. After describing the successes experienced by a nearby school district, which had just begun implementation of the shared decision-making model, two principals discussed this problem at a district meeting:

Since our people are used to shared decision-making, it doesn't work so well. They've figured out how to position themselves.

Parents decide beforehand what they're going to say, and everyone says the same thing. So instead of it coming from one group, it comes from six. They've gotten really good at positioning themselves.

Another principal noted, in regard to parent members of her school's planning team: "Many parents don't know what happens in a school and have no real basis for voting."

However, some principals commented that school board members tended to be more removed from the immediate concerns of a given school community than were the local parents. At least parents whose children went to a particular school had a strong motivation to learn about that school's needs. School board members often had less child-centered preoccupations, such as using board membership as a stepping stone to local prominence. Thus, involvement of parents in site-based decision-making had the advantage of giving individual schools a stronger voice. Parent involvement in building level decisions created a political environment in which it became difficult for the school board to reverse building-level decisions.

In the present site-based environment, principals saw the school board as far less likely to question building-level decisions than the teachers union. In fact, a frequently voiced frustration on the part of administrators at all levels was the union's hesitancy about going along with building-level plans that were not strictly in accord with districtwide agreements. These feelings are exemplified in the following exchange, which included a district-level administrator and three principals. While brainstorming session ways to keep instructional quality high, despite expected budget cuts, a suggestion was made that a college-style lecture hall format might be used to present some academic material, freeing other teachers to work with smaller groups of students:

> At the secondary level, you might have two history teachers volunteering to take 100 students, with the help of two paraprofessionals.

> The Association [teachers' union] would go crazy!

> The [partial] block scheduling at Metro High works well, but the Association . . .

> I've said [to teachers] at our school that increasing class size might allow us to keep programs, and they do want to keep programs.

There was evidence that the advent of shared decision-making had created an identity crisis for the teachers union. During the decades that the social-efficiency approach had reigned supreme in U.S. public education, teacher unions had helped teachers to assert themselves within a hierarchical administrative structure in which they had no other effective voice than the one they could make heard through collective bargaining. The union had justified its existence through the concessions it wrested from the school district. Within a shared decision-making environment, the Cottonwood teacher's union wavered between collaboration with the district and continuing in its accustomed role, attempting to wrest from the district concessions that it would defend, in a territorial manner, against any attempts to bend the rules.

Classified staff repeatedly voiced concern that positional bargaining on the part of the teachers union would render their input into the shared decision-making process a waste of energy. At a district-level shared decision-making meeting for classified staff, talk centered on the relationships that school secretaries, paraprofessionals, and bus drivers had built with students, their dedication to their jobs, and their worry that the attitude of "we're all in this together" that the Cottonwood district had strongly encouraged somehow seemed to break down when it came to discussions of whose job would be cut. A custodian described the rumors going around among classified employees who felt helpless before the perceived insider connections of administrators and the power of the teachers' union:

> In the initial phases of the cuts, it's classified staff who are being cut. From what I've seen, you don't get to admin. and certified until you get down to 75% or 50% [reference is to the amount of this year's funding retained by a specific department]. The rumor is that decisions have already been made. People ask "If that's so, why are we doing this?"

In this, classified staff can be seen as differing only by matter of degree from fears expressed by other stakeholder groups. Principals feared being left in a position where they were held responsible for decisions made by site-based planning teams over which they had limited control. The teachers union feared that site-based decision-making might turn into a kind of divide-and-conquer mechanism that worked to dilute the bargaining power of teachers. Parents feared that they were wasting their time in going to meetings where their input was solicited, but the real decisions were made elsewhere. For the members of each of these groups, judgments about whether the time and energy put into shared decision-making had been well spent often came down to a question of trust.

DRIVE-BY PARENTS UNDERMINE PARTICIPATORY APPROACH

Shared decision-making in this age of telecommunications does not take place within a closed system. Principals trade anecdotes about happenings in other school districts. Teachers network with peers across the country who have been experimenting with similar sorts of curriculum reforms. The Western State Education Association, with which the Cottonwood teachers union is affiliated, is influenced by speculation about how site-based decision-making might affect union strength nationally. Parents, many of whom see their children's school primarily from the outside, when they drop their children off or pick them up, often pick up ideas about how well public education is working from media stories about large urban districts.

Widespread public cynicism, influenced by media accounts of crises elsewhere, made it more difficult for the Cottonwood School District to cultivate the climate of confidence and trust necessary to successful shared decision-making. Cottonwood residents read newspapers and watched television news shows based in neighboring Foothills City. Often they knew more about what was going wrong in the urban Foothills City School District than what was going well in the Cottonwood schools. Speaking on the campus of Western State University, a highly placed official in the Western State Department of Education noted that the undue weight news organizations gave to events in Foothills City was the biggest obstacle to passage of the governor's one-cent sales tax for education:

> I've stopped in tiny rural towns and heard that people there intended to vote against the sales tax because they disapproved of what was going on in the Foothills City schools. They didn't even think of what the amendment might mean for their local schools.

In the suburban Cottonwood School District, many people came to budget meetings ready to complain about the sort of top-heavy administrative structure media commentators had criticized in the Foothills City School District. Only those parents who were actively involved in school-related activities in Cottonwood were aware that Cottonwood had made deep cuts in district administrative staff since 1982. During the Davis era, Cottonwood had been a heavily top-down administrative structure. This had led to an expanded staff at the central office. When Dr. Roberts arrived in Cottonwood, there had been seven people with the word "superintendent" in their titles. Ten years later, there were only three, and there was serious talk of eliminating one of these positions. Yet many community members did not know this.

Such misunderstandings point to an important stumbling block to collaborative decision-making: the difficulty of carrying on a meaningful discussion in the absence of a common frame of reference. Three decades earlier, during the "make do" Larimer years, when it had seemed quite natural to call up farm families with tractors to plow the snow from a football field before a big game, parents had been in and out of the schools on a regular basis. One effect of the increased focus on professionalism during the Davis years had been an attitude on the part of educators that parents should "Leave school matters to us." This, along with the increased inclusion of mothers in the workforce, meant that parents had much less first-hand knowledge of what was going on in their children's schools.

Cottonwood administrators involved in the restructuring effort repeatedly mentioned frustrations arising out of the continuing need to explain to new groups of parents the rationale behind building- and district-level policies that had been extensively discussed with stakeholders before they were adopted. The mobility of families, the continual arrival of new cohorts of students at each grade level, the number of parents who paid attention to communications from the schools only when emotion-laden issues were involved, meant that site-based decisions and policies had to be continually reexplained. A consensus arrived at with one group of actively involved parents and community members did not extend to other discussions, in which other individuals were involved. Despite the effort Cottonwood put into getting parents involved again, parental disengagement proved difficult to reverse.

The cynicism of some parents came out clearly during the large public meetings described in this chapter, where the public was invited to give feedback on proposed budget cuts. Some stakeholders openly doubted whether their comments would be taken seriously by the school board. Yet many of these same community members had, themselves, come to the meetings with fixed ideas that were all but impervious to being influenced by arguments put forward by others. Not only were they unaware that Cottonwood was, in fact, a very lean district, but they paid little attention when presented with evidence that, although close to the bottom of the all districts in the metropolitan area in regard to per-student funding, Cottonwood maintained programs which were of comparable quality to any in the state. Despite such evidence, they accused the Cottonwood district of extravagant spending.

Personal stubbornness might explain part of this, but other contributing factors should also be considered. Clearly, the great majority of those present had gotten their information about schools from the news media. Quite possibly, information about the Cottonwood district presented at the meeting was so out of line with what they had been hearing on the news about public schools, in general, that they found the information presented by Cottonwood School District personnel hard to believe. After all, to people who do not spend much time in schools, one public school may look pretty much like another. To parents who do not know where the border between one school district and another is, it might be hard to see how this invisible boundary makes much of a difference.

Given this relative lack of differentiation (in the thinking of many parents) among public schools, the skittish feelings expressed by some Cottonwood parents about their public schools become more understandable. For, if public education across the United States is considered as one relatively undifferentiated whole, then some rather frightening things have been written about it in the last decade or so. Since A Nation at Risk (1983) asserted that the average high school graduate of the 1980s was less well-educated than the average graduate of 25 to 35 years before, an avalanche of reports have been published, not only questioning whether the schools are doing an acceptable job of educating students, but pointing out that many public schools are becoming more tense and violent places, where students show less respect both for their teachers and for each other.

It is not difficult to imagine how parents familiar with media coverage of such reports—and not particularly knowledgeable about the particulars of their local school district—might act somewhat like nervous travelers who have heard there has been a rash of air accidents, but who can't remember just what airlines were involved, or the causes of the accidents. They find themselves with no other choice but to fly, but their confidence in the whole idea of air travel has been shaken. They repeatedly demand reassurance that the airline they plan to use is dependable; yet some remain jittery, unable to get the images of the scattered wreckage shown in news accounts out of their minds. Nor is the comparison to air travel frivolous. Just as an airline passenger must trust the pilot with his life, parents must trust schools with the lives of their children.

The participatory approach adopted by the Cottonwood School District was intended to rekindle a lost sense of trust, to bring parents and other community members back into the schools in such a way that they would not only have a first-hand knowledge of what was going on, but would have a real voice in how the schools were run. Behind the move to site-based decision-making was the vision of creating individual school cultures that not only nourished the growth and learning of students, but were strong and coherent enough to become centers of community, forging new links between home and school. At the elementary level, many buildings did become community centers, serving children and parents in new and imaginative ways. At Sagebrush High, a high level of shared decision-making was achieved among the school staff. But no such vision, or culture, existed districtwide.

As mentioned earlier, the tension between representative democracy, as represented by the school board, and participatory democracy, as represented by the shared decision-making process, existed in an unresolved state of tension at the district level. When political pressure mounted, as it had when the fate of Goose Pond Alternative Junior/Senior High School had been decided, even a strong consensus among school district staff—and those community members who knew teens who had benefited from the program—could be set aside by a school board interested in winning the favor of that vocal and affluent group of voters who went to the polls regularly and in large numbers. During the budget meetings, the number of supporters of band and the swimming team who showed up demonstrated a widespread awareness that the school board could be swayed in this way.

As things stand, local control of schools in the United States means political control. The public knows that school policy can be swayed by political means. For decades, those who wanted a particular program adopted, or discontinued, by the public schools have used rhetoric as a primary weapon in their arsenal. Therefore, even when the schools do accomplish one assigned goal, they face a situation such that what constitutes success to the partisans of one educational goal often constitutes failure to the partisans of another. Thus, when the tide of public opinion causes one of two competing goals to be strongly emphasized, the partisans of the goal which has been ignored tend to do their best to focus media attention on this perceived failure, turning the tide of public opinion in their direction. This has given the recurrent crises in education a cyclical nature (Kirst and Meister 1985; Cuban 1990).

It may also have worked to undermine public trust. As has happened in politics, those who have wanted to put forward certain points of view have found that "negative campaigning"—using sharp language to point out the weaknesses of those holding opposing points of view—can be useful in winning short-term victories. However, this practice may have brought public education into a situation not unlike that with which politicians currently struggle. Voters, having heard at length—from each candidate in a political campaign—that the other candidate is incompetent, and cannot be trusted, still find themselves faced with the prospect that one of the two will represent them in the statehouse or in Congress. In politics, this has apparently resulted in distrust and dissatisfaction. In Western State, one result was term limits.

The national term limit movement got its start in Western State, which has often been looked on as a bellwether state. One can only speculate about how the political impulse to arbitrarily "throw the bums out" after a predetermined number of years might have been related to the appearance on the Western State ballot of a voucher initiative that would have allowed parents to use money the state would have paid the public school their child attended as tuition at a private school. (On average, this amount was equal to half the per-pupil funding available to public schools, with the other half raised through property taxes.) This initiative appeared on the same ballot as the governor's one cent sales tax for education. Like that measure, it failed. But supporters of the voucher initiative argued that voters would soon be frustrated enough with the public schools that they would demand alternatives, giving future voucher initiatives a better chance of passing.

Amidst this turbulent political environment, the thoughtful, collaborative approach to school reform taken in Cottonwood got far less attention than the attention-getting claims made by political partisans. This might partly explain the lack of knowledge many Cottonwood stakeholders showed about their own school district's successes. Yet Cottonwood School District administrators were correct when they pointed out that shared decision-making methods had allowed Cottonwood to weather a series of crises better than neighboring districts. Considering the challenges it had faced, Cottonwood had come through surprisingly well and there was reason to believe that shared decision-making was likely to prove a valuable tool in dealing with future crises.

What was less certain was that the tools the school district had at its disposal would prove to be adequate to cope with outside factors such as the continuing state-level budget crisis or the tensions created by economic and social distress in Old Metroville. Such social contextual factors present a continuing challenge to the district's continued well-being. Shared decision-making has served the district well. However, to consider shared decision-making to be, in some sense, the answer to the challenges the district faced would be a mistake.

CHAPTER 9

DIFFERING PERSPECTIVES ON THE PURPOSE OF SCHOOLING

Whether among groups of teachers writing curriculum materials, staff members on a school's site-based planning team, or community members serving on districtwide shared decision-making groups, similar struggles were played out. Few groups found it easy both to give every member a voice *and* tackle the group's declared goals with sufficient efficiency to satisfy the group's most highly motivated members. Recurring questions surfaced: How much discussion is enough? How do we get beyond the deep-seated differences in priorities that separate group members? How should the group deal with "difficult" or intransigent members so that it neither wastes precious meeting time nor creates hard feelings? In sum, how might shared decision-making groups effectively reconcile the goal-oriented and collaborative aspects of their missions?

Although many participants had received individual training in the shared decision-making process, they still found it difficult to lay aside the roles that they had played under a more hierarchical system of school governance. For example, when a building principal expressed an opinion about a policy, parents and staff members often assumed that the issue had been decided. Principals who were sensitive to the need for collaboration were often made to feel uncertain as to what their role should be. Other principals took advantage of such acquiescence to shut down discussions that made them uncomfortable. Faculty members reacting to long-standing interdepartmental rivalries found it difficult to open-mindedly discuss issues that had proved contentious before. Staff members who cared deeply about specific issues found it difficult to switch from the role of advocate to that of collaboratively deciding what was best for the school community as a whole.

THE ROLE OF MEETING FACILITATORS

Many long-standing shared decision-making groups within the Cottonwood School District found that the most effective way to deal with the tension between maintaining an accepting, collaborative atmosphere and achieving group goals was to appoint an experienced facilitator to guide their deliberations. (The Cottonwood district's staff development office arranged for trained facilitators on request.) By guiding the sharing of ideas into the channels that had been agreed upon, the facilitator kept the discussion moving and legitimized the deliberative role that all participants assumed during shared decision-making sessions. Repetitive discussion was nudged toward more constructive alternatives. Off-task social pleasantries were tactfully cut short. Administrators were allowed to relax and participate as part of the group, without feeling they had to take charge whenever other participants appeared to be ignoring the agenda.

Facilitators had to be constantly alert to the attitudes and perceptions of the decision-making groups they were dealing with, adjusting to very different school cultures. A facilitator might work on Monday with an elementary school planning team in the outer suburbs, encouraging a more open sharing of views between teachers who were just familiarizing themselves with the new math curriculum framework and affluent parents who wanted to know why faster progress had not been made toward implementing a more rigorous math program. The next week the facilitator might be at a middle school where parents were hotly debating whether a new dress code, aimed at regulating gang-related attire, discriminated against minority students. Even within a single shared decision-making team, the viewpoints of various interest groups were often so different that what seemed self-evident to one group apparently escaped the notice of another. The facilitator had continually to refocus discussion in such a way that shared interests were emphasized and discussion did not degenerate into an exercise in choosing sides.

THE POWER OF UNDERLYING ASSUMPTIONS

In the concluding sentences of his *General Theory*, Lord Keynes—widely considered the most influential economist of the twentieth century—made the claim that even those who considered themselves quite exempt from intellectual influences routinely turned out to be, in fact, heavily influenced by theorists whose ideas had gradually come to be regarded as "common sense":

> Practical men, who believe themselves to be quite exempt from any intellectual influences, are usually the slaves of some defunct economist. . . . I am sure that the power of vested interests is vastly exaggerated compared with the gradual encroachment of ideas. Not, indeed, immediately, but after a certain interval; for in the field of economic and political philosophy there are not many who are influenced by new theories after they are twenty-five or thirty years of age, so that the ideas which civil servants and politicians and even agitators apply to current events are not likely to be the newest. But, soon or late, it is ideas, not vested interests, which are dangerous for good or evil.

Keynes pointed out that it is commonly the habit of self-proclaimed "practical men" to downplay the intellectual underpinnings of their accustomed viewpoint, acting as if their perceptions were nothing more than the result of "common sense." The attitude taken by many respondents in the Cottonwood district was similar. Yet, when their remarks were analyzed, broad opinion groupings could easily be recognized.

In a district where shared decision-making was expected to be the norm, special challenges were created for principals whose early experience as administrators had been in a highly structured, hierarchical environment. During the Davis administration, expectations for building principals had been quite different. In the 1970s, every effort had been made to present educational administration as a "science." The underlying assumption was that the procedures of the physical sciences could be transferred in a fairly direct manner to the social sciences.

Since then, the applicability of such "scientific" management techniques to all situations has been called into question. Human beings have proven to be far too diverse for effective educational interventions to be formulated so that they work well with all students at all times. To adequately test an intervention the characteristics of the target population have to be taken into consideration. The social scientist must follow different procedures than the natural scientist. As Earl Babbie has pointed out:

> The chemist who wants to test certain properties of carbon, for example, need not undertake a painstaking enumeration of

all the carbon in the world and then carefully select a proba-
bility sample of carbon molecules for study. (Babbie 1990, 69)

But social scientists had to consider the effect of human vari-
ability. Such changes in the way theories about human behavior
were being discussed at the national level did not have an immediate
effect upon practitioners in the field. Principals who began their
careers as administrators during the Davis years, within an organizational structure which made little allowance for human variation,
tended to find it frustrating to sit through lengthy meetings when
they felt they could have solved the problem quicker and better
alone.

Blind Spots Stemming from Different Points of View

References to the "art" practiced by experienced facilitators
and collaborative administrators surfaced relatively early in the
study. By defining effective administrative practice as an art, rather
than a science, staff members active in the shared decision-making
process expressed the dramatic change in thinking that had taken
place in Cottonwood. Advocates of shared decision-making insisted
that giving each school the same treatment, or each child the same
educational experience, regardless of the individual requirements of
that school or that child, was "the most unfair." They compared
such forced uniformity to making everyone wear the same size
shoes, or use the same eyeglasses. True excellence in education was
seen as meeting individual schools, and children, where they were,
then helping them to maximize their potential. Recognizing and
responding to individual needs was seen as an "art" in the same
sense that the practice of medicine could be seen as an art—in contrast to the sciences of chemistry or physics.

Old-line administrators countered that, although standardized
policies might not meet the needs of all buildings, or children in an
optimum manner, they did make the educator accountable in a politically important sense. An outside observer could at least evaluate
whether all buildings or children in the district had been treated
equally. Within a politically controlled system—such as a U.S. school
district—being able to show that all constituents had been treated in
the same way provided a kind of accountability. It provided an acceptable way to answering parents or community members who might
otherwise demand to know: Why was this building or child treated in
one way, while that building or child was treated differently?

The Importance of
Examining Underlying Assumptions

Whenever we speak of someone's "point of view," we are implicitly referring to the unique angle from which that person views the world. In attempting to understand the complexity of our social environment, all of us tend to focus on what our prior experience has caused us to consider to be most important. A useful analogy is the process a map maker goes through in representing physical space in a way that is easily understood. Over the centuries map makers have developed numerous projections to serve the professional needs of navigators, surveyors, school teachers, and airline pilots. Each projection has its uses. Yet each suffers from certain limitations: a two-dimensional map can represent our three-dimensional planet only by representing its surface as it would appear from specific points in space. Seen from a different vantage point, the earth's surface appears quite different.

Similarly, when we attempt to create a conceptual "snapshot" of the workings of a complex human institution, the manner in which we carry out our observations determines what we see. Any concise explanation—or mental model—of the workings of a social institution tends to focus on certain aspects. Which functions get more attention than others usually depends on the purpose the model is meant to serve. For example, each of the four education outlooks—humanist, social efficiency, developmentalist, and social meliorist—referred to in earlier chapters focuses strongly on some aspects of the educational system, while giving far less attention to others. In this sense, each of these educational outlooks shares some characteristics of a map projection. Alternatively, adherents of each outlook can be said to operate on the basis of their own cognitive map.

Although there were individuals in the Cottonwood district whose views differed in unexpected ways from the four broad opinion groups that have been described, understanding the point of view of these four groups proved important to understanding how tensions and frictions between people with very different outlooks had affected the restructuring effort in Cottonwood. Broadly speaking, the four most common ways of viewing the central purpose of public education, as encountered in the Cottonwood School District, could be summarized as follows:

1. *Humanist:* The purpose of public education is seen as preparing students for citizenship, so that they understand the values

embodied in U.S. institutions, possess the cultural literacy necessary to communicate meaningfully with their fellow citizens, and have sufficient basic knowledge to understand current issues and cast their vote in an intelligent manner

2. *Social Efficiency:* The purpose of public education is seen as preparing students to be self-supporting, useful members of society who can get along well with others, possess the skills to hold down a job, and are able to cope with the challenges of day-to-day existence in contemporary society

3. *Developmentalist:* The purpose of public education is seen as enabling individual students to fulfill their personal potential, so that they are prepared to be creative, self-motivated lifelong learners who are effective problem-solvers, able to communicate and collaborate with others, and to meet the varied challenges they will encounter in their adult lives

4. *Social Meliorist:* The purpose of public education is seen as bringing about a more just society, through using the schools to help those children whose background puts them at risk to get the resources they need to succeed, and through teaching all students about diverse cultures and ethnic heritages, thus helping them to grow into open-minded, tolerant adults

Developmentalists Take a Collaborative, Child-Centered Approach

During the Roberts era, which began in 1982, developmentalists played the leading part in both the movement toward shared decision-making and in the creation of the new curriculum framework. Collaboration and flexibility were emphasized. Developmentalists emphasized helping children to become more inventive, creative, critical thinkers. Rote memorization was seen as meaningless to the child and soon forgotten. The sort of learning developmentalists emphasized enabled the child to connect new concepts with prior understanding. Such an approach to classroom practice fit in well with a site-based decision-making approach to school governance. Yet frictions arose between developmentalists and other groups. Table 9.1 summarizes how developmentalists tended to conceptualize differences between their views and the approaches favored by those who held humanist, social-efficiency, or social-meliorist outlooks.

The sharpest conflicts tended to arise between developmentalists and old-line administrators who held a social-efficiency outlook

TABLE 9.1
Developmentalist View of Competing Curriculums

Humanist = emphasis on teaching academics as understood by analytic
    adult intelligence rather than tying subject matter to the immediate,
    wholistic experience of the child, often leaving students feeling bored,
    uninterested, unconvinced of relevance of school learning to world
    outside

Social efficiency = emphasis on reaching principal's or central administra-
    tor's goals, often resulting in testing for isolated skills or memorized
    facts, often leaving children feeling that what they are learning is
    meaningless and that they are simply "jumping through hoops" on
    the way to graduation

Social meliorist = emphasis on teaching students about social injustices
    rather than teaching them the critical thinking skills that would allow
    them to examine facts in an open-minded manner and reach their
    own conclusions; often end up "turning off" those students who resent
    being preached to

---

and preferred standardized policies and practices aimed at guaran-
teeing that "everyone was singing from the same sheet of music."
However, tensions also arose between developmentalists and those
college-educated parents whose humanist leanings caused them to
press for more emphasis on academic content.

Humanists Worry about Grammar, Spelling, Punctuation

On the national level, humanists have tended to see education
in terms of the effective teaching of the traditional liberal arts (perhaps with computer literacy added on). As the term "liberal arts"
indicates, humanists are not adverse to framing the discussion in
terms of the "art" of the educator. But they differ from developmentalists in that they take a content-centered, rather than a child-
centered approach. The function of the arts within humanist education was aptly described, centuries ago, by William Shakespeare:

> As imagination bodies forth
> The forms of things unknown, the poets pen
> Turns them to shapes, and gives to airy nothing
> A local habitation and a name.

Through art the abstract is brought down to a human level. In
the traditional humanist classroom, for example, Macbeth often

became for students the personification of unbridled ambition—and its results. This is not to say that humanist teachers were unaware that there is more to the character of Macbeth than the quality of ambition, or to Hamlet than indecision, or to Othello than jealousy. Effective teachers made it clear that satisfying interpretations of these plays could be made on many levels. The intriguing mix of complexity and visceral appeal found in these plays makes them an appealing way to introduce discussion of weighty ethical and social issues into the classroom. Shakespeare's success during his own lifetime was in large part due to his ability to present complex ideas to his largely illiterate audience in a powerful and direct manner. Humanist teachers often argue that, although the twentieth-century middle school or high school student may not be illiterate, prolonged exposure to the media has left many with shortened attention spans so that they often need the support of dramatic interest to become fully engaged with complex subject matter. Through the arts, students can be introduced to a broader understanding of how others have wrestled with complex issues and the insights they gained.

In part, the differences between humanists and developmentalists in Cottonwood came down to where they put their emphasis. For example, humanists and developmentalists differed strongly in the emphasis they put on proper form. Developmentalists argued that, in order to improve their writing, children must first come to see it as a pleasurable experience, as a chance to write in their own voices about the concerns and issues closest to them—their feelings, friends, memories, families, communities. Humanists, on the other hand, often felt uneasy about the inventive spelling, run-on sentences, and grammatical errors that developmentalists were willing to overlook in the writing of children in the early grades. Their instinct was to spend more time on direct teaching of spelling, punctuation, and grammar. Developmentalists felt that children could be more effectively encouraged to revise their work, as well as give creative suggestions on revision to their classmates, if emphasis was put *not* on formal correctness, but on making the sort of changes that helped others to understand as they understood. Humanists often saw this as less efficient than teaching grammar rules.

The differing priorities of developmentalist and humanist teachers were highlighted when the first cohort of students to experience a whole language curriculum in elementary school arrived in seventh grade. Junior high teachers complained that these students lacked the knowledge of spelling and grammar that secondary teachers had come to expect. Gradually, as elementary teachers learned how to integrate phonics, spelling, and grammar into the literature-based curriculum at the lower grades, these aspects of student writing improved. However, the more staunchly humanist teachers at the secondary level continued to view whole language with suspicion. Also, many parents continued to express a preference for the more traditional academic emphasis they remembered from their own high school days. Introduction of the International Baccalaureate at Metroville High was a specific attempt to offer an inviting option to families throughout the district who held strong humanist views. The humanist perspective on the other outlooks might be schematically portrayed as shown in table 9.2.

TABLE 9.2
Humanist View of Competing Curriculums

Social efficiency = an accountant's view of education, emphasizing seat time rather than learning and too often underestimating the intelligence of students through setting low standards and providing watered down course work which does not properly prepare students either to become informed citizens or to successfully complete college course work

Developmentalist = too often emphasizes student interests at the expense of presenting underlying theory and breath of subject matter, thus giving students a fragmented, incoherent view of world; may provide insufficient basis for further learning and thus handicap students at college level

Social Meliorist = too often doesn't give children a thorough grounding in their own culture before asking them to critique it or compare it to others, thus creating confusion and frustration rather than enlightenment; by emphasizing group rights rather than individual responsibility may weaken social cohesiveness

Social-Efficiency Concerns Appeal to School Board

The continued influence of the social-efficiency point of view in the Cottonwood district was due in large part to the appeal it held for business-oriented school board members. They tended to approach education through the lens of what it enabled a student to do after graduation: Will this person be employable? Will this student be equipped to handle college? Since they were not educators themselves, school board members had to rely on information supplied by the superintendent in order to determine whether students were learning the skills they would need to function as responsible adults. Results-oriented, board members wanted to be presented with nationally accepted measures, such as standardized test scores, that would give them the assurance they felt it necessary to have that the district was being effectively managed.

Although supportive of Dr. Roberts, school board members also wanted to adhere to the sort of standardized procedures that could be easily explained to parents and community members. Like other community members, some board members tended to feel most comfortable with the sort of schooling they had experienced as children. Board members who harbored such feelings tended to see the influence of veteran principals and department heads who had held the same jobs during Dr. Davis' tenure as beneficial to the overall efficiency of the district. They wanted reform, but they did not want the change process to "get out of hand." That the actions of some staff members acted as a kind of brake on the reform process did not strike them as an entirely bad thing. A political pragmatist, Dr. Roberts thus found it expedient to put up with a certain amount of noncooperation on the part of some veteran Cottonwood administrators. The way social-efficiency advocates perceived other viewpoints could be broadly characterized as shown in table 9.3.

TABLE 9.3
Social Efficiency View of Competing Curriculums

Developmentalist = emphasis on personal growth too subjective, focused on feelings, doesn't teach students to survive in the real world of work outside of school, where they will often have to perform tasks they find boring and where they will get scant sympathy from employers when they fail to perform well

Humanist = many students have neither aptitude for nor interest in the traditional academic subjects; although educators ought to make sure that all students possess basic skills, students who are not planning on attending college should have the option of learning vocational skills they can use in their future jobs

Social meliorist = the business of the schools is to educate children, to give all an equal educational opportunity, not to guarantee equal educational outcomes; to put too much emphasis on society's injustices at expense of teaching needed knowledge and skills effectively guarantees that disadvantaged students will end up as resentful, but culturally aware dishwashers

Social Meliorists Strive to
Have Social Problems Recognized

Although a number of teachers and some community activists within the Cottonwood district expressed social meliorist views, this group lacked a cohesive community power base. Although the superintendent was sympathetic to social meliorist concerns, he put most of his energy into introducing site-based decision-making and a more child-centered curriculum. When big budget cuts (forced by state-level funding shortfalls) became necessary, Dr. Roberts agreed to have his own central administrative office funded at only 65 percent, while the Office of Curriculum and Instruction was funded at 95 percent—a level of funding considered to be necessary if effective implementation of the curriculum framework was to continue. Staff members with strong social-meliorist views took his action as a fairly direct answer to the implicit question: "If Dr. Roberts could only save one thing . . ."

The new elementary social studies curriculum included stories from other cultures and encouraged discussion of human differences. Teachers with social-meliorist sympathies welcomed the increased diversity in the curriculum, but worried that the school board's lack of attention to issues of demographic change, poverty, and social disorganization in the older, heavily urbanized parts of the district might lead to further decisions like the closure of Goose Pond Alternative School.

Although they were appreciative of the multicultural literature included in the new curriculum, some social meliorists also questioned whether a whole language approach was best for all students. Several elementary teachers from Old Metroville voiced doubts about the applicability of the whole language curriculum to children who arrived at school without a strong background in "school English." They felt that such children needed more direct teaching in specific language skills. In a site-based decision-making environment, these teachers were free to act on this perception. However, they received little assistance from the district curriculum specialists, who were already stretched thin. Teachers were left to find their own way to adapt the curriculum framework to the needs of students who spoke a language, or a dialect, other than standard English at home. Social meliorists in Cottonwood tended to characterize the other standpoints as shown in table 9.4.

TABLE 9.4
Social Meliorist View of Competing Curriculums

Humanist = tendency toward narrow and elitist study of the traditional academic subjects, with a focus on the accomplishments of "dead white men" that deprived minority children of appropriate role models, while implicitly validating an unjust status quo; make no adjustment for differing needs of children with differing learning styles and diverse home cultures

Social efficiency = unthinking replication of present social injustices through a sorting system based on standardized testing that prepared children of professionals for college and children of the working class for manual labor, while refusing to spend money on needed special programs which increased the life chances of at-risk students

Developmentalist = single-minded emphasis on individual growth often ignored social context factors and social ills that might determine whether individual students would be able to take advantage of educational opportunities they were offered; emphasis on collaboration and consensus neglected need for confrontation if entrenched privilege and social injustice were to be exposed and rooted out

---

The Difficulty of Getting Participants to Take a Broader View

Reducing these four philosophical groupings to the brief, schematic form used here does not do justice to the complexity of the issues involved. However, it is useful in demonstrating how, having staked out a particular aspect of the educational process as its primary focus, each group went on to evaluate the actions of the other interest groups in terms of its own mental model. Many of the criticisms are insightful, pointing out effects produced by the too-narrow focus of other groups. Yet it was rare for any group to take the criticisms made by its competitors to heart. When criticized, each group had a tendency to emphasize its own good intentions while finding plausible excuses to explain why its plans had not produced the expected results. So, instead of reevaluating the adequacy of their approach, members of each group tended to react to criticism with feelings of resentment that opponents had focused so strongly on negative outcomes and failed to take their initial intentions into account.

Perhaps such reactions were inevitable, given the tendency of parties involved in heated public debates to compare their own best qualities to the opposition's worst. But such debates routinely produced more heat than light. Objectivity became difficult. Voices calling for a balanced approach—which recognized the contributions that each group could make to a better understanding of the challenges the school district faced—were put at a distinct disadvantage. As the debate became more heated, attention too often shifted to focus on who was "siding with" whom. Those participants whose comments were less strident or emotional frequently had trouble making themselves heard.

This tendency to take sides became especially problematic for the Cottonwood district, which had adopted a system of school governance that relied heavily on building consensus. Working toward consensus required participants to listen to the views of others with an open mind. But facilitators who worked with shared decision-making groups often referred, during interviews, to the use of "positioning" by meeting participants who were more interested in getting what they wanted than in hearing from those who might disagree. By "positioning" they meant the tendency of many individuals to enter the decision-making process with an outlook that was better suited to negotiation than consensus building. Facilitators who had the task of guiding the decision-making process were often forced, in such instances, to rely on negotiation techniques in order to avoid deadlock. In such circumstances, experienced facilitators tended to adopt techniques that resembled those outlined by Fisher, Ury, and Patton in *Getting to Yes: Negotiating Agreement without Giving In:*

People: Separate the people from the problem.
Interests: Focus on interests, not positions.
Options: Generate a variety of possibilities before deciding what to do.
Criteria: Insist that the result be based on some objective standard.

In focusing on the problem, rather than on personality conflicts, this approach had clear similarities to the shared decision-making approach outlined in chapter 2. However, it left out the key component of envisioning how schools might provide a more healthy and stimulating learning environment for children.

The initial goal of enthusiastic advocates of shared decision-making had been to go beyond mere compromise to create something new. The assumption had been made that, if all stakeholders were treated fairly and given a voice, all would: (1) willingly entertain a wide range of possibilities for change; (2) establish mutually acceptable criteria for evaluating proposals; and (3) go about reaching consensus in a manner that put the good of the school community above personal advantage. Reformers failed to foresee how difficult it would be to get people who were emotionally invested in an issue to lay aside personal concerns. For example, the display of open hostility that followed the opening of Sagebrush High caught sincere advocates of shared decision-making off guard. The conflicting perceptions—and explosive feelings—present during Sagebrush High's first years are exemplified by the following quotes:

> Originally the thought was that building a new high school would create opportunities. There would be fewer kids in the older schools and that would lessen the burden, give them a chance to innovate. But declining enrollment created fear. Teachers feared losing their jobs, being moved to a junior high. A little of that happened, but not nearly to the extent that had been feared. Still the tensions were there.

> During the first couple of years after Sagebrush was built, just terrible things were being said in the teacher's lounge at Suburban about people at Sagebrush. There has been very little interchange between the schools, other than some people transferring.

> We have limited open enrollment. The result was a loss of population at Metroville High when students went to Sagebrush. Metroville's athletics went down. There was great anger among some people. Later the same thing happened at Suburban. They thought they were losing the better students to Sagebrush. There were rumors of Sagebrush robbing the best teachers from the other schools.

> The joke was that Sagebrush was supposed to be "Happy High." In other words, they were trying to accomplish something that is "pie in the sky . . . impractical."

> Their [Sagebrush High's] advising system has been a point of attack. The feeling in the other high schools was, "What are they trying to do?"

> Our master agreement [between the teacher's union and the Cottonwood district] says that transfers and layoffs of teachers

will be done according to seniority. So there was a lot of tension between older and younger teachers. People would talk in whispers about how many years of service different people had, how many points. . . . Sagebrush took a lot of the blame.

Tremendous emotional energy was expended upon defensive positioning. When this confrontational atmosphere finally cooled to an uneasy truce, the impulse on all sides was to avoid contact, for each high school to concentrate on its own affairs. Valuable opportunities for cross-fertilization were foregone in the interest of preserving the peace.

EVENTS IN COTTONWOOD AS A
REFLECTION OF A LARGER DEBATE

Although the residual effect of the acrimonious debate that followed the opening of Sagebrush High was to create a reluctance to tackle additional reforms, on certain fronts pressure for change continued to increase. Parents who felt uneasy about the peer culture their children entered when they went to junior high and high school had begun to push for larger changes than could easily be brought about through shared decision-making, at either the building or the district level. From the educator's point of view, such pressures had a puzzling aspect. Cottonwood was a school district where many things were going well. According to the measures by which we are accustomed to judging educational organizations—student performance, quality of the teaching staff, morale within the district—Cottonwood was an excellent school district. Yet success in these areas did not, during the period of this study, insulate the district from the effects of a broader sense of disillusionment with the public schools.

In chapter 1 we heard Superintendent Dave Roberts saying: "Those of us who strongly believe in public education must regain the public's support and confidence." He was referring to the recent statewide elections. A one-cent sales tax, which would have been dedicated to education, had been defeated. A stringent tax limitation amendment to the state constitution had instead been passed. In combination, these two measures made it likely that the yearly budget crises which had proved so destructive to morale within the Cottonwood district would continue. Another initiative on the ballot would have allowed parents to receive a state voucher worth approximately half the money used to educate their child at a public school.

This voucher could be used to pay their child's tuition at a private school. This measure was defeated, but was likely to be reintroduced in subsequent statewide elections.

During the months before the election, public criticism of the state's schools had been intense. As Dr. Roberts' words showed educators had taken the outpouring of criticism—along with the failure of voters to address the ongoing school budget crisis—as a de facto vote of no-confidence in the public schools. Indeed, within a year of making these remarks, Dr. Roberts left Cottonwood to become superintendent of a school district in another state. Other key Cottonwood administrators chose to retire or take a leave of absence. Observers were left with the impression that, after ten years, many of those who had been involved in the Cottonwood restructuring effort had concluded that the meaningful restructuring of the public schools could not be brought about without broader public support.

Concerns Expressed by Parents

In the end education is the nurturing and nourishment of the mind and soul within the child. To have it driven by economics or other concerns . . . goes against the very nature of education. (Cottonwood District Accountability Committee Chair)

Over the forty-year history of the Cottonwood School District, attitudes toward the public schools had clearly undergone a sea of change. The relationship between the school and community had changed. Whereas, in the early years, meetings between educators and parents had revolved around deciding how the parents could contribute to the effectiveness of their children's overcrowded schools, more recent meetings between parents and school personnel often centered on decisions about how the school district planned to parcel out scarce resources. Despite school district declarations that parent contributions were highly valued, many parents had come to see themselves as petitioners, rather than partners.

A disgruntled parent expressed her perception of the subtle ways in which she felt outwardly open discussions were controlled:

For most parents the most important thing is to be "in" with the teacher and "in" with the principal, to be well-liked and "in the know." If you questioned things you were considered negative. There is a kind of ostracism that goes on.

Another parent commented that teachers sometimes seemed to be reading from an unseen script: "They've got their lines down real good." Still another parent chimed in: "Too often they're thinking about what they are going to answer, instead of hearing what you're saying." In a sense, educators and community members no longer spoke the same language.

Ironically, the communication problem appeared to be rooted in part in the Cottonwood district's diligent efforts to keep its teachers abreast of current research in their fields. The kind of educational terms that were fashionable in educational journals were often looked upon with distrust, even by parents whose vocabularies included words like *metacognition*. Comments such as "If she talks that way to Johnny, no wonder he doesn't understand," implied both a perception that such language was unnecessarily pretentious and a suspicion that jargon-laden speech was a smoke-screen used to hide inattention to the real needs of children in the classroom.

Uneasiness about the ever-changing jargon which has characterized educational discourse has also been expressed by scholars. For example, Lois A. Bader has described the confusion and lack of continuity caused by continually repackaging old ideas, using new labels. She describes the history of what is now called "whole language":

> Recently the *Christian Science Monitor* and the *New York Times* described a "new" writing program that was being used in a number of schools across the country. In this approach, children write stories that describe what they do in and outside of school. Reading and writing grow out of the experiences of the children; interests and experiences are extended through wide reading; skills are taught—by the teacher or by peers—as the children need them.
>
> The method described above, often called the language-experience method, is not new. It has been researched, endorsed, and packaged by educators countless times. To name just a few: Francis Parker in 1894, Edmund Huey in 1908, Emmett Betts in 1957, Doris Lee and Roach Van Allen in 1963, and Jeanette Veatch in 1966. (Bader 1989)

Shared decision-making also made some parents nervous. These parents tended to see the collaborative, conciliatory attitude taken by many school administrators as too "soft" to deal effectively with increasingly troubled and alienated cohorts of students.

Conservative parents worried that the vacuum created by the failure of schools to immerse students in a meaningful moral tradition had, too often, been filled by disorienting images supplied by popular culture. As these parents saw it, too many children had been allowed to become unthinking consumers of media-created sensation, whereas they should have been helped to become active shapers of their experience. Parents worried aloud that children who were bombarded by an ever-present media perspective that treated resort to drugs or violence as just another lifestyle choice, were being offered too few healthy cultural alternatives. They felt strongly that, in turning away from a strong focus on Western literature and traditions, the schools had taken away from children the opportunity to live imaginatively within the moral vision of a coherent cultural tradition.

A politically powerful local legislator noted that more and more of the parents he talked to were worried that the public schools were not serving their children well. These parents felt uneasy about the attitude and behavior changes they observed in their children as they moved through their middle school and high school years. As this legislator saw it, public schools across the United States had become so fearful of stirring up controversy that they had largely given up trying to address value issues; school districts found it more comfortable to discuss "hard," quantifiable data like test scores or dropout rates. In such a climate, parents who feared that they might be losing their children to the influence of an unhealthy peer culture felt as if they had few allies. They said they were given the impression, by school personnel, that such concerns lay outside the schools' area of authority.

Even those parents who made a point of declaring themselves liberal on social issues frequently expressed anxiety about the risky behavior—such as heavy drinking, taking illicit drugs, and engaging in unprotected premarital sex—that they felt was all too prevalent within the peer culture that their teenage sons and daughters entered when they went to school. Ironically, concerns about the setting of mutually agreed upon standards of behavior were among the matters that shared decision-making had been intended to address. However, for the reasons already discussed, consensus on these and other issues proved elusive. Yet the need remained. Sizer (1992) has posited a fairly direct connection between the overall culture of a school and personal decisions made by students:

> Much of learning depends on a student's disposition. He will try hard if it seems worthwhile to try hard, if the people whom he respects believe that trying hard is a good thing, if the com-

munity supports that kind of effort, and if something inside himself impels him to try hard. It is easy for him not to try hard. The opportunities for procrastination and for diversion are legion. He knows—as do his teachers—that the decision to use his mind is entirely up to him. It is easy to shut out new ideas, or any ideas. (p. 56)

It's ironic that, of all the Cottonwood schools, the most controversial proved to be Sagebrush High, which was set up to closely follow the Sizer model. As has been pointed out, much of the controversy was rooted in resentment toward a new school whose facilities were perceived to be superior to those elsewhere. However, it was also true that the goal of creating a more wholesome and stimulating environment for students was never effectively communicated to parents. This caused a situation to arise in which parents and teachers who privately expressed similar goals and concerns—albeit in very different language—never perceived how much they had in common.

FINDING SOME COMMON GROUND

Localized reforms such as site-based decision-making were found by this study to be powerful tools for faculty self-renewal at individual schools. However, an important school district goal when the policy of shifting decision-making authority to the school site had been set forth was to encourage more active participation by all stakeholders, including parents, in an effort to foster a greater sense of community responsibility for the public schools. With teachers the expectation that a greater sense of ownership would be fostered was, in large part, fulfilled. However, the parent community was far more diffuse. Even where schools put considerable effort into involving parents in decision-making, shared decision-making did not appear to have changed the overall quality of the school's relationship with its parent community. If, as Sarason (1991) has suggested, the level of success of any educational reform is dependent upon the extent to which the affected constituencies are identified and involved, shared decision-making in Cottonwood must be said to have met with only limited success.

There is evidence that the concept of parent participation as "reform" has recurred through the nineteenth and twentieth centuries, but rarely has it resulted in longer term, or substantial, structural or pedagogical change (Bloch and Tabachnick 1994). When public education is being examined and criticized, and when public dissatisfaction is apparent, the notion of sharing decision-making power surfaces (Malen et al. 1990). However, encouraging lay participation in technical areas of educational decision-making has consistently proved problematic (Mann 1974). The documented gap between the knowledge base of the professional educator and that of the general public can easily be used to justify excluding parents from decision-making. If parents do not have the information to meaningfully take part in decision-making, it cannot be surprising that inclusion of parents as decision-makers has been labeled "perfunctory" and "window-dressing" (Henderson, Marburger, and Ooms 1986; McLaughlin and Shields 1987).

We need to find a way to widen the present dialogue about how schools can be improved. For decades, the nation has put its future, in the form of its children, in the hands of public school educators. So central has this bond of trust been to the work of educators that it is difficult to come to terms with the realization that this trust might be withdrawn. This may be why, even as passage of voter initiatives that amount to de facto votes of "no confidence" in the public schools looms as an ever greater possibility, there has been a tendency for many public school educators to turn inward, communicating primarily with each other and discounting the relevance of criticisms voiced by the public at large. However, this head-in-the-sand response to the decline of public confidence in the nation's schools poses grave dangers. If we, as educators, do not become part of a larger coalition—with the goal of addressing parent concerns about the peer culture children encounter in public schools, as well as community concerns about the readiness of high school graduates to deal with the challenges that will await them outside the schoolhouse door—we may find that the general public increasingly perceives us to be part of the problem.

What people in our communities are saying about public schools must be taken into consideration. At the same time, the loudest voices are not the only ones we must listen to. In Cottonwood, for example, the college-educated parents whose voices tended to be heard most distinctly at the district level often had not given careful consideration, either to the social justice issues raised by the policies they favored, or to the special educational needs of children who came from cultural backgrounds quite unlike their own. Striking parallels exist between the outlook of these Cottonwood parents and the outlook John Dewey advocated in *The School and Society*:

That which interests us most is naturally the progress made by the individual child of our acquaintance, his normal physical development, his advance in ability to read, write, and figure, his growth in the knowledge of geography and history, improvement in manners, habits of promptness, order, and industry—it is from such standards as these that we judge the work of the school. And rightly so. Yet the range of the outlook needs to be enlarged. What the best and wisest parent wants for his own child, that must the community want for all of its children. (1981, 455)

Parents enter the educational arena primarily as advocates for their own children. The educator's duty is to speak up on behalf of the best interests of all the children in our communities. To carry this task out effectively, we may have to pay less attention to relatively narrow differences of opinion among professional educators and devote more energy to addressing larger issues of educational policy. No longer can we afford to assume that the only educational discussions of real consequence are those carried on in professional journals. Indeed, there is evidence that the specialized terminology educators have adopted for professional discussions has become a barrier to reaching a larger public. We must relearn the art, which Dewey once exemplified, of expressing important ideas in plain language.

Here, the geological metaphor may be especially apt. Just as the solid outer crust of the earth, which is all we see from day to day, is but a thin, solid skin covering fluid, molten rock, our social institutions—including the public school system—form a thin veneer covering less stable cultural strata characterized by fluidity and ongoing change. At times molten rock escapes from beneath the earth's surface in the form of volcanic eruptions. Similarly, there are moments when social conflicts erupt through the seeming predictability of everyday life. However, from year to year, most alterations happen so gradually that we hardly notice the change. Continents drift inches each year. Attitudes toward schooling slowly change. Yet we only see the cumulative effect when something causes us to step back far enough to gain a sense of perspective.

The demographic changes that accompanied the Cottonwood District's transformation from a sparsely populated rural area to a densely populated series of suburbs were part of a nationwide pattern. Decision-making by local school district personnel was, of necessity, focused on how the Cottonwood district could continue to deliver high-quality programs, given the rapid population growth taking place. Only later did the long-term effects of the strategies administrators used as they reorganized the district become clear. When hierarchical organizational structures cut off the flow of information, resistance and opposition grew. In those years when the organization of the school district was collegial enough to allow a free flow of information between teachers, administrators, and community members, decisions tended to be made in a way that built public confidence, and strengthened educational programs.

Similarly, achieving a working consensus among all who have a stake in the success of our public schools, so that the efforts of all stakeholders reinforce one another and the resources communities dedicate to education are used as effectively as possible, will require the collaboration of individuals with widely varying viewpoints. We need to gain a better understanding of the root causes of our differences. As Dewey pointed out in *The Child and the Curriculum*:

> Profound differences in theory are never gratuitous or invented. They grow out of conflicting elements in a genuine problem— a problem which is genuine just because the elements, taken as they stand, are conflicting. Any significant problem involves conditions that for the moment contradict each other. Solution comes only by getting away from the meaning of terms that is already fixed upon and coming to see the conditions from another point of view, and hence in a fresh light. (1981, 468)

We must not view it as a form of intellectual treason—to any of the viewpoints we may have supported in the past—to turn down the heat of the current debate and listen earnestly to others who care deeply about the state of public education in the United States. Creating a broader dialogue must be seen as the necessary first step toward creating an effective consensus behind constructive change.

BIBLIOGRAPHY

Babbie, E. 1990. *Survey research methods*, 2nd Edition.d Belmont, CA: Wadsworth Publishing Co.

Bader, L. A. 1989. Communicating with teachers—honestly. *Phi Delta Kappan*, 70, 626–629.

Barth, R. S. 1991. Restructuring schools: Some questions for teachers and principals. *Phi Delta Kappan*, October 1991, 73, 123–128.

Bennett, K. P. and LeCompte, M. D. 1990. *The way schools work*. New York: Longman.

Bloch, M. N. and Tabachnick, B. R. 1994. Improving parent involvement as school reform: Rhetoric or reality? In K. M. Borman and N. P. Greenman (Eds.), *Changing American Education* (pp. 261–293). Albany, SUNY Press.

Bloom, B. 1981. *All our children learning*. New York: McGraw-Hill.

Boyd, W. L. and Crowson, R. L. 1981. The changing conception and practice of public school administration. In D. C. Berliner (Ed.), *Review of Research in Education, Vol. 9* (pp. 311–377). Washington, DC: American Educational Research Association.

Butts, R. F. and Cremin, L. A. 1953. *History of education in American culture*. New York: Henry Holt Company.

———. 1978. *Public education in the United States: From revolution to reform*. New York: Holt, Rinehart, and Winston.

Combs, A. W. 1972. Educational accountability—Beyond behavioral objectives. Washington, DC: Association for Supervision and Curriculum Development, pp. 1–40.

Commission on Teaching Standards for School Mathematics. 1991. *Professional standards for teaching mathematics*. Reston, VA: National Council of Teachers of Mathematics.

Cuban, L. 1984. *How teachers taught*. New York: Longman.

———. 1990, April. Reforming, again, again, and again. *Educational Researcher*, 19, 3–13.

Cubberly, E. P. 1919. *Public education in the United States: A study and interpretation of American educational history*. Boston: Houghton Mifflin.

Dewey, J. 1956. *The child and the curriculum* and *The school and society*. Chicago: University of Chicago Press.

Education Commission of the States. 1991. *Restructuring the education system*, volume 1. Denver, CO: Education Commission of the States.

Fisher, R., Ury, W., and Patton, B. 1991. *Getting to yes: Negotiating agreement without giving in*. New York: Penguin Books.

Fullan, M. G. and Miles, M. B. 1992, June. Getting reform right: What works and what doesn't. *Phi Delta Kappan*, 73, 745–752.

Gardner, H. 1987. *The mind's new science: A history of the cognitive revolution*. New York: Basic Books.

Goodlad, J. I. 1984. *A place called school: Prospects for the future*. New York: McGraw-Hill.

Guba, E. G. and Lincoln, Y. S. 1981. *Effective evaluation*. San Francisco: Jossey-Bass.

Henderson, A., Marburger., C., and Ooms, T. 1986. *Beyond the bake sale*. Columbus, MD: National Committee for Citizens in Education.

Johnson, D. 1992, June 14. Leaving the land. *Boulder Daily Camera*, p. 1B.

Katz, M. B. 1971. *Class, bureaucracy, and schools: The illusion of educational change in America*. New York: Praeger.

Kirst, M. W. and Meister, G. 1985. Turbulence in American secondary schools: What reforms last? *Curriculum Inquiry*, 15, 169–186.

Kliebard, H. 1987. *The struggle for the American curriculum 1893–1958*. New York: Routledge.

Kuhn, T. S. 1970. *The structure of scientific revolutions*. Chicago: University of Chicago Press.

Likert, R. 1967. *The Human Organization*. Boston: McGraw-Hill.

Lortie, D. 1969. The balance of control and autonomy in elementary school teaching. In A. Etzioni (Ed.), *The semi-professions and their organization: Teachers, nurses, social workers* (pp. 1–53). New York: Free Press.

Malen, B. and Ogawa, R. T. 1988. Professional-patron influence on site-based governance councils: A confounding case study. *Educational Evaluation and Policy Analysis*, 10, 251–270.

Malen, B., Ogawa, R. T., and Krantz, J. 1990. What do we know about school-based management? A case study of the literature—A call for research. In W. H. Clune and J. F. Witte (Eds.), *Choice and control in American education*, Vol. 2: *The practice of choice, decentralization and school restructuring*, (pp. 289–342). New York: The Falmer Press.

Mann, D. 1974. Public understanding and education decision-making. *Educational Administration Quarterly* 10(2), 1–18.

McLaughlin, M. W. and Shields, P. M. 1987. Involving low-income parents in the schools: A role for policy. *Phi Delta Kappan*, 69, 156–160.

Mechanic, D. 1961. Sources of power of lower participants in complex organizations. *Administrative Science Quarterly*, 349—364.

National Governors' Association. 1986. *A time for results: The governors' 1991 report on education*. Washington, DC: National Governors' Association.

Paulos, J. A. 1991. *Beyond numeracy: Ruminations of a numbers man*. New York: Alfred A. Knopf.

Powell, A. G., Farrar, E., and Cohen, D. K. 1985. *The shopping mall high school: Winners and losers in the educational marketplace*. Boston: Houghton Mifflin.

Raywid, M. A. 1988. Community and schools: A prolegomenon. *Teachers College Record*, 90, 197–210.

Rist, R. C. 1977. On the relations among educational research paradigms. *Anthropology and Education Quarterly*, 8, 42–49.

Samuelson, R. J. 1992, March 2. How our American dream unraveled: After World War II, we believed that prosperity would create the ultimate good society. We were wrong. *Newsweek*, 99(2), 36.

Sarason, S. B. 1971. *The culture of the school and the problem of change*. Boston: Allyn and Bacon.

———. 1991. *The predictable failure of educational reform: Can we change course before it's too late?* San Francisco: Jossey-Bass.

Sichel, B. 1988. *Moral education: Character, community, and ideals*. Philadelphia: Temple University Press.

Sizer, T. R. 1983, June. High school reform: The need for engineering. *Phi Delta Kappan*, 64, 679–683.

————. 1992. *Horace's school: Redesigning the American high school.* Boston: Houghton Mifflin.

Tyack, D. 1974. *The one best system: A history of American urban education.* Cambridge, MA: Harvard University Press.

————. 1990. "Restructuring" in historical perspective. *Teacher's College Record*, 92(2), 170–191.

Zeichner, K. 1991. Contradictions and tensions in the professionalization of teaching and the democratization of schools. *Teacher's College Record*, 92(3).

INDEX